The Politics of Sport in South Asia

Behind the spectacle of entertainment, sport is a subject with political issues at every level. These issues range from the social, with divisions created along gender and class lines, to the use of sport to pursue diplomatic and statecraft goals. In addition, some sports are positioned and promoted as national events both in public opinion and in the media.

This book seeks to explore some aspects of the notion of power in sport in south Asia and among south Asians abroad. The first two chapters deal with the internal societal dimensions of the politics of sport; the next three relate to the politics inside the sporting world in the subcontinent and its bridge with the broader arena of the society through the media, while the last five relate to the use of sports in statecraft, consensus building and international politics.

This book was based on two special issues of the *International Journal of the History of Sport*.

Subhas Ranjan Chakraborty teaches European History at Presidency College, Kolkata. He is the Historical and Archaeological Secretary of The Asiatic Society, Kolkata. He has recently edited The Uprisings of 1857: Perspectives and Peripheries (Kolkata, The Asiatic Society, 2009).

Shantanu Chakraborti is a Reader in the Department of History, Calcutta University. He specialises in Indian Foreign Policy, and is the author of Cooperation in South Asia: the Indian Perspective (Kolkata: KP Bagchi, 2008). He was formerly a fellow at the Institute for Defence Studies and Analyses (IDSA) in New Delhi where he worked on privatisation of security in South Asia.

Kingshuk Chatterjee is a Lecturer in the Department of History, Calcutta University. He specialises in Political Islam, with particular reference to modern Iran. He was formerly Fulbright Scholar-in-Residence at the US Naval Academy, Annapolis.

The Politics of Sport in South Asia

Edited by Subhas Ranjan Chakraborty, Shantanu Chakrabarti and Kingshuk Chatterjee

Routledge
Taylor & Francis Group

LONDON AND NEW YORK

First published 2010 by Routledge
2 Park Square, Milton Park, Abingdon, Oxon, OX14 4RN

Simultaneously published in the USA and Canada
by Routledge
711 Third Avenue, New York, NY 10017

Routledge is an imprint of the Taylor & Francis Group, an informa business

© 2010 Taylor & Francis
First issued in paperback 2013

Typeset in Minion by Value Chain, India

British Library Cataloguing in Publication Data
A catalogue record for this book is available from the British Library

ISBN13: 978-0-415-37168-1 (hbk)
ISBN13: 978-0-415-85005-6 (pbk)

CONTENTS

SERIES EDITORS' FOREWORD

SPORT IN THE GLOBAL SOCIETY was launched in the late nineties. It now has over one hundred volumes. Until recently an odd myopia characterised academia with regard to sport. The global *groves of academe* remained essentially Cartesian in inclination. They favoured a mind/body dichotomy: thus the study of ideas was acceptable; the study of sport was not. All that has now changed. Sport is now incorporated, intelligently, within debate about *inter alia* ideologies, power, stratification, mobility and inequality. The reason is simple. In the modern world sport is everywhere: it is as ubiquitous as war. E.J. Hobsbawm, the Marxist historian, once called it the one of the most significant of the new manifestations of late nineteenth century Europe. Today it is one of the most significant manifestations of the twenty-first century world. Such is its power, politically, culturally, economically, spiritually and aesthetically, that sport beckons the academic more persuasively than ever – to borrow, and refocus, an expression of the radical historian Peter Gay – 'to explore its familiar terrain and to wrest new interpretations from its inexhaustible materials'. As a subject for inquiry, it is replete, as he remarked of history, with profound 'questions unanswered and for that matter questions unasked'.

Sport seduces the teeming 'global village'; it is the new opiate of the masses; it is one of the great modern experiences; its attraction astonishes only the recluse; its appeal spans the globe. Without exaggeration, sport is a mirror in which nations, communities, men and women now see themselves. That reflection is sometimes bright, sometimes dark, sometimes distorted, sometimes magnified. This metaphorical mirror is a source of mass exhilaration and depression, security and insecurity, pride and humiliation, bonding and alienation. Sport, for many, has replaced religion as a source of emotional catharsis and spiritual passion, and for many, since it is among the earliest of memorable childhood experiences, it infiltrates memory, shapes enthusiasms, serves fantasies. To co-opt Gay again: it blends memory and desire.

Sport, in addition, can be a lens through which to scrutinise major themes in the political and social sciences: democracy and despotism and the great associated movements of socialism, fascism, communism and capitalism as well as political cohesion and confrontation, social reform and social stability.

The story of modern sport is the story of the modern world – in microcosm; a modern global tapestry permanently being woven. Furthermore, nationalist and imperialist, philosopher and politician, radical and conservative have all sought in sport a manifestation of national identity, status and superiority.

Finally, for countless millions sport is the personal pursuit of ambition, assertion, well-being and enjoyment.

For all the above reasons, sport demands the attention of the academic. *Sport in the Global Society* is a response.

J.A.Mangan, Boria Majumdar
and Mark Dyreson – Series Editors
Sport in the Global Society

Sport in the Global Society

Series Editors: J.A. Mangan, Boria Majumdar and Mark Dyreson

The Politics of Sport in South Asia

Sport in the Global Society

Series Editors: J.A. Mangan, Boria Majumdar and Mark Dyreson

As Robert Hands in *The Times* recently observed the growth of sports studies in recent years has been considerable. This unique series with over one hundred volumes in the last decade has played its part. Politically, culturally, emotionally and aesthetically, sport is a major force in the modern world. Its impact will grow as the world embraces ever more tightly the contemporary secular trinity: the English language, technology and sport. *Sport in the Global Society* will continue to record sport's phenomenal progress across the world stage.

Other Titles in the Series

Africa, Football and FIFA
Politics, Colonialism and Resistance
Paul Darby

Amateurism in British Sport
'It Matters Not Who Won or Lost'
Edited by Dilwyn Porter and Stephen Wagg

Amateurism in Sport
An Analysis and Defence
Lincoln Allison

America's Game(s)
A Critical Anthropology of Sport
Edited by Benjamin Eastman, Sean Brown and Michael Ralph

American Sports
An Evolutionary Approach
Edited by Alan Klein

A Social History of Indian Football
Striving to Score
Kausik Bandyopadhya and Boria Majumdar

A Social History of Swimming in England, 1800–1918
Splashing in the Serpentine
Christopher Love

A Sport-Loving Society
Victorian and Edwardian Middle-Class
England at Play
Edited by J.A. Mangan

Athleticism in the Victorian and Edwardian Public School
The Emergence and Consolidation of an Educational Ideology, New Edition
J.A. Mangan

Australian Beach Cultures
The History of Sun, Sand and Surf
Douglas Booth

Australian Sport
Antipodean Waves of Change
Edited by Kristine Toohey and Tracy Taylor

Barbarians, Gentlemen and Players
A Sociological Study of the Development of Rugby Football, Second Edition
Eric Dunning and Kenneth Sheard

Beijing 2008: Preparing for Glory
Chinese Challenge in the 'Chinese Century'
Edited by J.A. Mangan and Dong Jinxia

Acknowledgement

This Sport in the Global Society volume comprises the contributions in IJHS South Asia 2007 and 2008 edited in both IJHS and SGS by the Guest Editors Professor Subhas Ranjan Chakraborty, Dr. Shantanu Chakraborti and Dr. Kingshuk Chatterjee.

The Series Editors take the opportunity to thank the Guest Editors for their excellent work.

INTRODUCTION – FIELDS OF POWER

Subhas Ranjan Chakraborty, Shantanu Chakrabarti & Kingshuk Chatterjee

How seriously do you take your sports? For a large number of the people worldwide, sports remains associated with the private sphere of an individual. Most people relate it with childhood, adolescence and youth – representing partly companionship, partly leisure, and full enjoyment. A growing number of people in our modern and/or post-modern times have begun to take sports seriously even past their youth for more utilitarian reasons – to retain the physical fitness that slips with time. Yet, caught off guard with the question we began with, perhaps a large number of people would continue to think of 'sports' merely as pastime for the young and young-at-heart.

Sports has a different dimension as well, where it is organised as a spectacle in the public sphere. Oriented towards providing public entertainment, sports functions as an important ingredient in public sociability, culture and even economy in the modern society as much, if not more, than in the past. The interface with the public sphere of a modern society almost axiomatically entails relationships among the various protagonists in the sporting arena – players, spectators, administrators, die-hard enthusiasts, casual observers, the media, the sports industry and even political establishments – which are neither necessarily equal nor benign. Hence, as with nearly every other arena within the public sphere, the sporting arena also is bound by relations of power.

The relations of power operating within the world of sport, however, are quite distinctive because of the very character of sports. The twin assumptions on which any sporting activity rests are that i) the sporting arena provides the only field of human life where it is possible to obtain a truly level playing field among competitors; and that b) any sporting activity is to be broadly conducted within a set of regulations that are not so much regulatory as emancipatory. And if you look carefully, you see that the first assumption is intricately tied up with the second.

The whole idea of sport is related to honing some basic survival skills that mankind evolved over time – skills such as running, swimming, flinging a missile (such as for hunting), fighting. It is possible to trace almost every sporting activity to a variation or combination of such survival skills – and the list is by no means exhaustive. In the 'state of nature' (bad and archaic choice of words, but perhaps the best), such skills were never equally endowed. Sports originated possibly from an urge to hone such skills in an 'ideal' condition, where two or more competitors with a similar range of skills would be in a friendly confrontation. Sport, thus, is essentially predicated upon the creation of an unreal world where usual structural/human impediments are assumed to be inexistent – relying, as it were, on a temporary suspension of reality which emancipates the protagonists from circumstances mostly beyond their control.

The suspension of reality, this emancipatory character of sports, however, is contingent upon regulatory codes of behaviour/performance associated with every sport that is there. It is precisely because some sorts of conduct or behaviour are *not allowed* that the playing fields become (supposedly) level. That is to say, in order for certain protagonists to perform in a particular manner, it is axiomatic for some others to do, or refrain from doing, certain other things. Accordingly, a certain logic of inclusion and exclusion automatically begins to operate in determining acceptable behaviour with regard to all sporting activities. Evolution of games simply denotes permutations in that very logic of inclusion and exclusion with changing times, circumstances and preferences.

Power relations in the world of sport pertain primarily to the interface between the sporting theatre and the greater societal context within which the logic of inclusion and exclusion has to operate. A range of actors become crucial to the process of defining the parameters of such regulatory logic – the participants, who set limits about what can be done; the spectators, who set limits to what they want to see being done; the administrators, who detail what cannot be done; and other actors (enthusiasts, commentators, the media, power of capital, etc.) who speak of how else to do what can be done.

The regulatory parameters are, of course, set in a manner which suggests that the only consideration behind such regulation is *sports* – in truth, there can be rarely any such insulation. The frequency with which non-sporting considerations intrude upon these parameters that it becomes very interesting to observe the seriousness with which claims to the autonomy of sports are made and taken. Ever since sports began to play a role in public life, it is possible to contextualise various phases of its evolution within a specific historical conjuncture – including perhaps the illusion of autonomy of sports. What would constitute a spectacle in public perception at a particular conjuncture would invariably take its toll on how a logic of inclusion and exclusion would shape the frame of a sport – [see, for instance, the essays by Alter and Chakraborty in this volume]. Such public perception, in its turn, is seldom (shall we say, almost never) spontaneous – it is very elaborately yet deceptively 'manufactured' by the considerations of commerce (i.e. the 'saleability' of a sport as a commodity) and the power of the media. In the modern times, with the nearly all-pervasive character of global commercial capital and a media that is in the process of undergoing a prolonged revolution, such considerations have become more and more powerful. Could you have imagined the Ashes series being played out in Canada in the early 20th century? Sharjah, though, beat the logic of territoriality of Indo-Pak matches being played out in the subcontinent in the 1980s. At the risk of probably exaggerating it a bit, it can be said that in the age of live telecast and advertising revenues spiralling upwards, it probably would not matter much if the next series were played on the moon, so long as it was telecast to the TV in terrestrial living rooms.

It is not, however, that sports simply functions as a passive recipient in its interfaces with the society. Very often, some of the dynamics generated or reinforced by the world of sports leave a lasting impact on the world 'outside' it. It is not perhaps that sports *determines* any of the many major forces that operate in the society ostensibly independently of sports – viz. identity (such as of class, community, nation, etc), movement of capital, popular culture, etc. It is rather that sport has the potential to work its way into these areas, and *condition* their trajectories in various manners, subtle or unsubtle.

Fields of Power means to explore various aspects of the power relationships that impinge upon the world of sport. Some of these relations leave their imprint on the sporting arena, other relations allow sports to have some impact on the societal space around it – still others have a mutually reinforcing or even transmuting effect. This volume was planned primarily as a study of the various 'fields' within which power relations operate in the world of modern (and/or post-modern) sports. We, the editors, intended to cast the net wide both in terms of the contributors as well as themes for the contributions, believing the resultant diversity would indicate the ranges of the 'fields of power' in the sporting arena. We were mildly surprised to see eight out of ten contributions revolving around cricket without any prodding from any quarters – surely there is some sort of 'power game' on in the realm of writing sports history as well?

Of the two essays that seem to have dodged that particular logic, Alter in a way sets the tone for the volume by beginning with the oft-repeated argument (but requiring still further repetition) of 'multiple modernities'. Through his treatment of the *Hanuman Vyayam Prasarak Mandal*, an organisation promoting physical culture of the traditional sort in 19th-20th century North India, Alter contends that the very meaning of 'traditional' underwent a silent transformation in keeping with changing societal context of 'modern' India. He further argues, that such a transmutation fitted perfectly with a worldwide trend of adapting 'traditional' sporting behaviour into a spectacle, while at the same time refraining from being subsumed by the dominant 'modernist' logic of competitive sport. The transmutation of the North Indian tradition of physical culture was a response of a society that, uncomfortable with the pace of rapid change gripping colonial India, was looking for ways stemming the tide (but not for setting the clock back).

Chakraborty takes the argument further with her treatment on the revival of Yoga as a major tradition of physical culture. The process began in the colonial period as part of a 'nationalist' project of winning back the 'body' of the colonial subject after the displacement of traditional therapeutics by its 'modern'/'western' counterpart. Chakraborty then goes on to push the argument that in the post-colonial times, what used to be a 'nationalist' agenda became the part of a 'post-modern' one where solutions to various problems spawned by 'modern' society were sought beyond the bounds of 'modernity'. Hence, the virtual rebirth of the Hindu ascetic – the *yogi* – as a physical instructor on the global map (as opposed to the previous local theatre of operations), concerned not with personal ends, but willing to relieve suffering in the world around.

While Alter and Chakraborty highlight the role of dissatisfaction of certain aspects of modern life as a propellant behind reworking of certain 'traditional' forms of sport, Stoddart, Bandopadhyay, Majumdar, Ray and Mukharji delve into the manner in which sports can work its way into the cultural life of 'modern' societies, and end up by occasionally reworking it. It is said wherever the Germans went to colonise, first they built roads; the French set up a restaurant and the British laid out a cricket pitch. Stoddart contends that, beginning from the premise of cricket as an ingredient of imagining the

Indian and Australian identity against the 'other' of the colonial ruler, India's fascination with the game evolved along a completely different trajectory from that of Australia. Divergence of the two trajectories gets reflected in terms of the differences that characterise cricket as cultural practice in these two countries. Stoddart argues that for Australia cricket denoted something like an ethereal tie between the two arms of the British people on two sides of the globe, where it was nonetheless important to beat the representatives of metropolitan culture. That is to say, Australian imagination of cricket was firmly located within the matrix of British colonialism. For India by contrast, cricket begun as an assertion of parity within the colonial context, and then – because of the dialectical relationship with colonialism – graduated into an assertion of the national identity. This, Stoddart would contend, is the reason why Australians take to cricket as simply another game, while for Indians it is simply one of the markers of national identity.

Bandopadhyay takes on the same Indo-Pak relationship from a different [aggregated?] perspective. He looks at the manner in which the Indo-Pakistan cricket series of 2004, billed as the 'Goodwill Series' was used to flag off the process of thaw in the frigidity that characterised Indo-Pak diplomatic relations after the Kargil war of 1999. He details the usage of the metaphor of war by the media and politicians alike to evoke the mood of a friendly contest structured upon a relationship that has been anything but friendly. Bandopadhyay also underscores the potential diplomatic mileage that the Indian government tried to garner from this series – not in order to show simply what was done, but rather how the benign world of sport can develop, or be made to develop, a set of interfaces with the state and society around it.

Majumdar moves away from cricket to bring to life once again India's glory years in international hockey. His vivid narrative makes the personalities, the victories and the impact of India's domination of international hockey in the first half of the twentieth century come to life once again. As cricket looms ever larger over India's sporting horizon, Majumdar's piece is a well-conceived re-visitation of the sport that brought India its first laurels in the international sporting arena. In line with the other pieces in this section Majumdar also interrogates the cultural and social role and position of hockey. In his concluding section entitled 'what was special about hockey', he presents a nuanced and complex analysis of hockey's place in Indian society and the reasons for its enormous success. This analysis is sharpened by his ability to draw upon his own past work to contrast the developments in Indian hockey with those in Indian cricket and football at the time.

Ray chooses to narrate the gradual process of the emergence of cricket as the premier sport in Indian subcontinent. Identifying a set of landmarks in the history of Indian cricket in the 20th century, he contends that easy replicability of the game by ordinary people coupled with the incremental successes on the cricket pitch were not the only reasons behind the emergence of the game as the most popular sporting spectacle. The corresponding decline in the rate of success of other forms of sport – at a time when achievements in the friendly contests would have done the psyche of the anti-colonial movement and later of the fledgling republic a world of good by way of imbuing these with a sense of confidence – virtually ensured that cricket would enjoy such easy ascendancy over other sports in independent India. In other words, the ascendancy of cricket in the subcontinent is not simply a sporting achievement, but also a socio-cultural phenomenon located within a specific matrix of time. (Which probably means, if another volume like this was planned thirty years on, the same contributors might choose a different game as their point of entry, if it replaces cricket in public imagination.)

In the last piece in this section, Mukharji seeks to explore the cultural role and description of the 'local sporting hero'. Using a micro-historical account of a single life— that of a talented student sportsman, Santimoy Pati—Mukharji explores what attracted young, politically sensitive men to sport and how their on-field exploits then affected their political lives. Instead of focussing on a single sport, by looking at a single sportsman, Mukharji succeeds in highlighting how the same individual often participated—with success—in many different sports and how this interest in sport was part of a larger set of practices associated with radical student politics. His account therefore serves to de-mystify individual motivations for taking up sports by suggesting that in given historical contexts, structural readings of what attracts a certain kind of people to sport might be possible.

In the last set of essays Datta, Mehta, Mannathukkaren and Joshi handle the more complicated set of issues arising out of the differential impact the media and the world of sport have on each other. Datta's contribution, although the briefest piece, probably makes the most incisive set of comments encapsulated in this volume by handling one of the most important components of the media revolution of the 20th century - advertisements. Engaging in a feminist and postcolonial deconstruction of a popular face cream advertisement, she unpacks a set of values that were disseminated using the highly influential media-cricket interface. She contends, that this advertisement appealed to a set of dominant gender (viz. cricket-is-for-men) and aesthetic (you-need-to-be-fair-to-have-a-career-on-television) prejudices by seducing the careerist and consumerist desires of educated young Indian women. Although every reader may choose to deconstruct even Dutta's contribution, it is difficult to escape a fairly intelligible deduction from her piece – that the corporate interests of commercial capital and media in modern societies can be a bastion of social conservatism, and such conservatism can be upholstered fairly benignly through the most popular game in the conservative heart of the Indian subcontinent.

Mehta's piece analyses the relationship between sport and the other crucial component of media in the public space of 20th century– the news programme. In India, a veritable revolution began in the realm of TV news programmes in the late 1980s, beginning with electoral and budget analyses which soon went on to spawn a crop of 24-hour news channels in the late-1990s. Mehta concentrates on the second phase of this revolution when, partly in order to cope up with the 24-hour sports channels, the 24-hour news channels began to inject a sizeable dose of sports-specific news programmes or capsules. He contends, this reworking of at least a part of the media's *raison d'etre* was to do with the economy of television and the logic of popularity ratings, which have their fall outs in either leaving channels awash with advertisement revenue, or else high and dry.

Manathukkaren's piece is considerably different from any other piece in this volume. Engaging with what is fast developing into an orthodox position on interpretations of the tremendously popular cricket-centric Bollywood period-piece *Lagaan*, he reminds us that every period-piece depicts not so much the period which is being looked at, rather the period *from* which it is being looked at. Vehemently opposed to the idea that *Lagaan* tries to capture the inter-class, -caste and -community solidarity that is supposed to have characterised the national movement (despite all its internal tensions that ran along the lines of caste, class and community), Manathukkaren contends that *Lagaan* is more symptomatic of the tensions in the nation building project of India of the 1990s, rather than of the 1890s, and should be understood as such. Hence, the choice for the instrument of resistance was taken to be cricket – and not for instance, hockey – so that the film could be loaded with a spectacle within a spectacle, and could also be woven around arguably around the only phenomenon that can bind the whole country in an extended moment of feeling of being a 'national community'.

Joshi's piece is the true marker of our supposedly post-modern times, when the 'virtual' and 'real' can interchange places without much confusion. He maps the emergence of a 'virtual' community of (mostly Indian) cricket enthusiasts on the cyberspace, connecting cyber-really people in the subcontinent with their diasporas around the world. In an age of ever-increasing spatial mobility, where the boundaries of nation state are reduced simply to barriers that exist only in being crossed, the virtual community of cricket enthusiasts that Joshi observes – and belongs to – is an interesting comment on our times. It denotes an interface between commerce (for the virtual community has a material foundation which it was initially not meant to have) and the world of sport, in a phase of globalisation where labour as much capital has increasingly gone beyond the confines of territoriality. It also, however, shows the resilience of the 'modern' vis-à-vis the 'post-modern', in the sense that the community runs principally along the lines of the 'imagined community' of the nation.

The contributions in this volume, between themselves, revolve around two central issues pertaining to power relations in the sporting arena – namely the manufacture of sports as a spectacle, and the marketing of the spectacle as something *more than* a spectacle – that lays down a part of the logic of inclusion and exclusion that we began with. If you probe deeper, you see that both of these issues are a comment on how illusory the autonomous character of the sporting world really is. This is because manufacture of a spectacle and its marketing are concerns driven, or at least conditioned, by commercial capital and the media.

This is not to suggest that these are the only determining/conditioning factors. This volume has (unconsciously) steered clear of the manner in which the spectators and sports enthusiasts play a pro-active role in the evolution of sports. The emphasis on this volume, by contrast, has tended to be on the reactive role played by them – as in the essays of Ray, Joshi and Chakraborty. While the omission is noted, we the editors would nonetheless like to believe that the volume 'hangs together' precisely because of this omission. Given the growing sway of global capital over an ever-burgeoning sports industry – with firms manufacturing sports and non-sports utilities assuming the role of sponsors of individual teams and tournaments – the leverage supporters and enthusiasts used to enjoy has become a thing of the past.

This leverage has tended to recede even further with the 'mediatisation of sports': with the growing opportunities for prolific dissemination of information in print and electronic media, sport has emerged as the biggest spectacle that can be repeatedly made use of without generating monotony. The consequent opening up the advertisement opportunities in the media has brought about a major conjoining of forces between the media and capital. Enlargement of the constituency of spectators from the local/regional/national to global levels has not only poured in millions of dollars, but also reduced actual physical presence of the spectators into simply an emotive factor for the players and fans alike – the fans are needed only to cheer or jeer at a game, financially they are virtually irrelevant for matches that are telecast on TV. Cricket in India, soccer in Europe and basketball in USA are good examples of this phenomenon. Indeed, this is yet to be true for all sorts of sports – and maybe it will never be true for many. Either way, the outcomes would be conditioned by the interplay of the various relations of power that operate within each sport – and would conform, we hope, to the basic postulates of this volume.

Physical Education, Sport and the Intersection and Articulation of 'Modernities': The *Hanuman Vyayam Prasarak Mandal*

Joseph S. Alter

This paper focuses on the problem of delimiting and contextualizing 'alternative modernities,' and the way in which sport factors into the logic of delimitation. After postulating six ideal type alternative sportive modernities in India, the Hanuman Vyayam Prasarak Mandal *is analyzed as the articulation of a type of modernity that is linked to liberal secular nationalism. By looking at both the development of the HVPM through time as well as the performance of yoga and* mallakhamba *in various international sporting and gymnastic events, a specific relationship between nationalist and transnational social imaginaries is examined. Finally, the HVPM is compared and contrasted with the sportive activities of the Rashtriya Swayamsevak Sangh, a militant Hindu nationalist organization. Through this comparison it is possible to see how similar configurations of sport and gymnastics articulate different modernities, and how these alternative modernities both intersect and diverge from one another.*

Introduction: Multiple Modernities and their Articulation

As Bruce Knauft has noted, it is ironic that modernity has emerged – or rather re-emerged – as a problematic issue in the wake of postmodernism. [1] The irony of chronological rupture notwithstanding, a postmodern critique of the master narratives of reason, progress and development – among other things – has, in fact, enabled a critical re-evaluation of modernity.

Following on from this, recent scholarship in anthropology and cultural studies has focused on the emergence of different kinds of modernity and on the articulation of 'alternative modernities' in the context of globalization. Among the central problems in the study of these articulations are two questions: In what way do modernities intersect and what is the reference point for the construction of

Joseph S. Alter, University of Pittsburgh.

modernity in a given context? Related to this is the larger question: what counts as a context for a given modernity? The reflex answer to this last question is, most often, a state, since modernity and nationalism are intimately connected. But 'the local' is not necessarily coterminous with the nation, and context is not synonymous with bounded, encompassing coherence.

Defining the context for modernities – or anything else – is a knotty problem, since contextualization is ultimately an analytical procedure rather than a descriptive one. It is partly for this reason that it is rather imprecise and problematic to speak of Western modernity. Why is Euro-American modernity both left unmarked – since it is most commonly referred to as just 'modernity' – and coded as a cardinal direction? Clearly the answer has to do with the perspectivity, with the key points of reference being the Enlightenment – and the notion of progress – in one eye and colonialism in the other. Contexts are constructed, and the process of construction is intimately linked to the question of relativism and the contingency of relativism in the light of history – the emergence of modernity in one context as different from, but dependent on, the emergence of modernity in another.

The question of where modernities intersect and articulate is particularly problematic given that by definition modernities are the product of what Charles Taylor refers to as 'social imaginaries'. These imaginaries necessarily operate on a large scale where those involved do not always occupy the same space or even the same time. It is partly for this reason that many scholars have tended to use state boundaries as somewhat arbitrary markers for the contextualization of modernities, without too much concern for the fact that states are not created equal or encompass directly comparable social formations. Even if one does not refer to, say, Japanese modernity, it has become quite common to talk about modernity in Japan, China and India without to much concern for the dynamic of various possible 'social imaginaries' within and across the boundaries of these states. The dynamic of globalization of course blurs boundaries, produces fractured identities and structures what might be called transnational social imaginaries. But to move from a concern with the rupture and disarticulation of globalization to an analysis of the plurality of modernity begs the relativist question of boundedness and delineated comparability.

With this in mind my concern here is to explore the dynamics of various tangents of development that are linked to a range of different possible modernities in India, and to work through the problem of contextualization. The case I wish to examine is that of sports and physical education, two closely intertwined institutions that are unambiguously modern. Sport and physical education are also directly relevant to a consideration of modernity since they exemplify the relationship among social theory, the social imaginary of everyday life and the formation of moral order. [2]

Working through the educational matrix of the British Empire and the missionary networks extending around the globe from the North Atlantic, muscular Christianity has had a profound impact on the globalization of sports and regimens of fitness. Given the way in which it links the development of ethics, morality and character to the development of muscles and athletic ability, muscular Christianity is the articulation of a particularly powerful – although by no means seamless – disciplinary regime. In many respects, therefore, sports and physical education exemplify modernity. Significantly, however, they are at once highly structured, rule-bound entities linked to transnational institutions and also activities that are easily assigned local meaning and significance. [3] Sports in particular exemplify an important paradox in the articulations of modernity since regional differences in meaning and significance are coextensive with international competition. Thus it is possible to see, quite easily, how cricket – the sine qua non of postcolonial globalization – is linked to North Atlantic modernity as well as modernities in Southern Asia, Southern Africa, Australia and elsewhere. Competition, preparation for competition and the institutionalization of physical education can highlight subtle dynamics and differences in the articulation of regional modernities, just as they can clearly highlight geopolitics and nationalism.

Although sports became an integral part of elite education in Southern Asia during the late nineteenth century, there was a surge of interest in physical fitness and sport in British India around the turn of the century, particularly in the 1920s. As M.L. Kamlesh notes, Macaulay's reform minute of 1835 makes no mention of the integration of sports and physical education into education, and it was not until 1882 that the Indian Education Commission recommended 'physical training to be promoted in the interest of the youth by encouragement of native games, gymnastics and other exercises suited to each class of school'. [4]

Although Macaulay's oversight can be explained by the fact that his minute predates the era of Muscular Christianity and the formalization of most modern sports, it is noteworthy that there did not seem to be overarching governmental concern with the institutionalization of compulsory physical education and sport until 1895. As Kamlesh points out, this did not mean that there was no development, just that it was the project of what he refers to as voluntary organizations and done within the purview of various princely states. Until 1920 and the founding of the YMCA College of Physical Education in Madras – and to a considerable extent up through 1947 – there was significant diversity in how individuals engaged with modernity through the medium of sport and physical education. In order to construct an analysis of this diversity it is possible to delineate – along the modernist lines outlined by Weber – six ideal types: (1) the elite public school; (2) the populist missionary; (3) the militant nationalist; (4) the extreme traditionalist; (5) princely patronage; and (6) the liberal secular nationalist.

Ideal Types – Sports, Physical Education and Modernity

Space does not allow more than a cryptic, nominal survey of specific examples that fit into these ideal types.

1. There are numerous elite public schools in India such as the Mayo College, Ajmer, Doon School in Dehra Dun, St George's in Mussoorie, St Joseph's in

Darjeeling, St Xavier's in Bombay and Calcutta and many others in large metropolitan centres. In most cases the sports programme in these schools was consciously modelled on that of English public schools, as these programmes took shape in the later half of the nineteenth century.

2. Although missionaries founded a number of these schools, other missionaries were also active in promoting sports outside the framework of elite education. Regional schools in villages and small towns founded by Presbyterian, Methodist, Baptist and United Church of Canada missionaries often used sports and physical education to effect the goals of muscular Christianity among the poor and outcaste groups with whom they worked. Other missionaries were active in establishing teacher-training programmes and formalizing the rules for state and national competition. Most prominent among these was Harry Buck of the YMCA, but Win Mumby of the United Presbyterian Church also played an important role through his involvement with Lucknow Christian College.

3. In the early part of the twentieth century various militant, nationalist organizations established programmes that incorporated physical fitness training and paramilitary drill routines. The best example of this type of organization is the *Rashtriya Swayamsevak Sangh*, which used mass physical training drill and choreographed stave training, as well as modernized indigenous games and sports such as *kabaddi*, to inculcate its ideology of disciplined Hindu masculinity. [5]

4. What I am referring to as the extreme traditionalist ideal type is not, by any means, traditional in the unreflexive modern sense of the term. Rather these organizations seek to construct programmes that are self-consciously traditional, and therefore can more accurately be described as radical alternatives to what they perceive of as global modernity. As such they articulate a kind of modernity. Guru Hanuman's *akhara* (gymnasium) in Delhi fits into this category, as do the *akharas* in Banaras. [6]

5. Many rajas and maharajas of the princely states funded and promoted both indigenous and non-indigenous sports. Most prominent among these was Prince Bhupendra Singh of Patiala who supported Gama, the world champion wrestler, in the first half of the twentieth century. [7] He also was president of both the Board of Control of the Cricket Club of India and the Indian Olympic Association. There are many other examples as well, such as the Raja of Aundh, who promoted the practice of *Surya Namaskar* drill [8] and the Raja of Mysore, under whose auspices Krishnamacharya developed a programme of hybrid yoga gymnastics. [9]

6. The last ideal type is characterized by a sensibility of liberal secular nationalism reflected in the Indian National Congress and embodied by men such as Swami Kuvalayananda and his mentor Rajratan Manikrao, among others. Kuvalayananda in particular sought to modernize indigenous sports and turn postural yoga into a modern form of traditional Indian physical culture. In doing so he advocated the use and development of scientific methods and procedures. Another organization that fits this ideal type is the *Maharashtra Sharirik Shiksha*

Mandal, under whose auspices the game of *kabbadi* was transformed into a standardized sport. [10]

Before looking in detail at one specific liberal nationalist institution in relation to pertinent contrasting examples of other types, it is necessary to make three points. The first is quite obvious with regard to ideal types: as analytical constructs they make sharp distinctions, whereas in fact there are ambiguities. In some cases these ambiguities are significant, as when militant organizations support and to some degree are involved in extreme traditionalist gymnasiums and when rulers of princely states lend their support to projects, such as the Indian Olympic Committee, that are part of the liberal nationalist agenda. Nevertheless, thinking in terms of ideal types is a very useful way to reflect on the articulation of various modernities in India.

The second point is that these ideal types are analytical constructs and not descriptive ones. As such it would be misleading to assume that the types in question engaged with each other as types during the course of the development of a range of different institutions, organizations and societies that can be fit into these types. Moreover, historically an institution that fits into one type may overtime develop and change to fit into another, as we will see below. Nevertheless it is possible to infer the nature of the articulation between types and to conceptualize a discursive field in which multiple modernities are configured relative to the specific activities of sport and physical education that are common to them all.

Third, in order to facilitate comparison between types and to highlight the dynamic of modernities, I will focus primarily on postural yoga as an example of a so-called ancient tradition that organizations and groups have integrated into their conceptualization and performance of modernity. For reasons that will become clear, yoga is an interesting case since its conceptualization as physical fitness is directly linked to North Atlantic modernity, as well as a range of modernities in Southern Asia. Up until the turn of the nineteenth century it was more closely linked to philosophy than to athletics.

The *Hanuman Vyayam Prasarak Mandal*

In 1914 Shri Ambadaspant Vaidya and his brother Anant Krishna, two middle-class Brahmins from the small town of Amravati in central western Maharashtra, established an *akhara* under the auspices of a group they called the Hanuman Club. Inspired by Shri Veer Wamanrao Joshi, a militant freedom fighter, as well as by the nationalist principle of *swadeshi* (nationalistic self reliance) the Vaidya brothers turned their gymnasium into a voluntary organization dedicated to the secular and non-sectarian propagation of Indian physical culture and to the development of 'the Indian system of physical culture' along modern scientific lines. In 1922 the club, which had grown considerably in size and scope, was renamed the *Hanuman Vyayam Prasarak Mandal* (HVPM – the Hanuman Association for the Propagation of Physical Exercise).

Although himself an activist who led a boycott against the local government school in 1921, along with 350 members of the gymnasium, in 1922 Ambadas Vaidya defined the HVPM as an apolitical, inclusive, non-violent organization dedicated to the cause of physical fitness to the end of national reconstruction. K.G. Jodh provides the following perspective on the HVPM mission:

> Shri Vaidya dedicated his entire life to the cause of physical betterment of the younger generation of which he has become a great pioneer and a source of infinite strength. He brought to bear upon Hanuman Vyayam Prasarak Mandal his vast experience and superb skill...in physical exercises but much more invaluable was...his contribution in imparting a scientific and modern aspect to the national system of physical culture. He realized...that if the Indian System were to hold [a] candle to other systems prevalent in the world, it was absolutely necessary to approach it from a scientific angle and to reshape it in the context of...present day advances in different fields of life. [11]

In a fascinating book called *We Go to the Lingiad*, which details the story of a gymnastics team from the HVPM participating in the 1949 *Lingiad* festival in Sweden, and its subsequent tour of Europe – about which more will be said below – the team leader D.D. Ganorkar provides a clear perspective on the larger project of the HVPM. In a chapter entitled 'Indian Physical Culture Through the Ages' Ganorkar points out that in the Vedic age physical culture was a spiritual activity most clearly apparent in the disciplines of yoga and *surya namaskar*. During the epic age there was a shift towards the martial arts, which lasted up through the Mughals and the Marathas. It was not until the eighteenth century that sport and physical exercise was engaged in for purely recreational purposes and simply for the sake of body-building and strength development. He then makes the following remarkable statement: 'Under these circumstances, most of the physical culture activities could not help becoming the property of illiterate and uneducated persons who could not possibly conceive anything in the nature of the development of the community – not to speak of the whole nation.' [12]

Significantly, he associates this shift with the emergence of regional *akhara*s that were linked to strong individual personalities and which were exclusively concerned with individual achievement – the notion of regionalism and individuality being clearly pejorative. Although Ganorkar blames the British for promoting their own forms of physical education and sport, and for characterizing Indian sports as 'uncouth', he comes across as a somewhat ambivalent apologist for their crackdown on so-called subversive *akhara*s. As one might expect, he credits the Indian physical culture renaissance to the nationalist movement when 'a few educated persons began taking interest in physical education [and] realized that its real function was not to bring out a few "stars" but to build up a nation of men and women with well-adjusted and balanced personality'. [13] The practice of yoga is identified as the single most important system of physical education in the indigenous repertoire. It is conceptualized as an ancient form of 'medical gymnastics' that is uniquely suited to 'modern life'. It is also distinctly 'Indian' in the sense that the performance of *asana* (posture) and *pranayam* (breathing exercises) can be interpreted as athletic and can be compared to gymnastics but is nevertheless different: And the comparability-based-on-difference is of critical importance. Gonarkar's discussion of yoga is framed by the larger question of which form of physical culture is the best. As one might guess, he refers to yoga as 'unbeaten,' 'at the top' and 'supreme' in the realm of gymnastics. However, he qualifies this with reference to the need to 'find out if our system was based on sound scientific principles'. With reference to the laboratory and clinical work of Swami Kuvalayananda, he points out that 'it had to be organized and shaped into such form that millions could profit by it' and this sometimes entailed 'amplifi[cation] through the inclusion of new techniques'. [14] Beginning in 1924 the HVPM started offering summer courses and certification for physical education instructors. This was probably done, at least in part, as an alternative to certification and training – primarily in basketball, track and field and other modern sports of the North Atlantic – provided by the YMCA in Madras. [15] In conjunction with this, the HVPM sent out trained organizers to establish gymnasiums throughout the country. Ganorkar claims that as many as 500 gymnasiums were established and that over 50,000 boys and girls 'are daily receiving training'. [16] Clearly these were modern gymnasiums linked to a distinct social imaginary and not traditionalist *akharas*.

More than anything else, however, the HVPM gained national recognition through athletic and gymnastic performances, starting with a demonstration given in Pune in 1928. A team performed regularly at the annual meeting of the Indian National Congress and toured north, west, central and eastern India between 1935 and 1950, but mostly in what was then called the Bombay Presidency. Soon after 1928 Vaidya decided that it was necessary to send advanced students to various parts of the world to learn about different systems of physical education. Dr L.J. Kokardekar was sent to Germany and D.S. Deshpande to Japan. The idea was to allow for the development of a scientific system of Indian physical education based on cross-cultural comparison and hybridization.

Then, in the year that India was to win the Olympic gold medal in field hockey – defeating Germany 8–1 in the process (a historic fact that tends to be eclipsed by Jesse Owens's accomplishments against the Aryan pretenders) – a team of 25 gymnasts from the HVPM was invited to the World Sports Pedagogic Congress held in conjunction with the Olympiad. In addition to taking part in the congress, the team put on choreographed demonstrations of Indian gymnastics and sports, specifically *kabaddi*, *kho-kho*, *mallakhamba* and yoga. Following the success of the tour, Ambadas Vaidya and the general secretary of the HVPM, H.V. Deshpande, intensified their efforts to make the *mandal* a national centre for training physical education instructors. In 1946 they organized the first All India Physical Education Conference, attended by 3,000 delegates from around the country. [17] After independence Deshpande was nominated to serve on the Central Advisory Board for Physical Education and Recreation.

In 1949 the HVPM was invited to send a team to participate in the *Lingiad* festival first organized by the Swedish government in 1939 to commemorate the death centenary of Per Henrik Ling, the creator of Swedish Gymnastic and Swedish massage therapy. Although Ling himself was a fencing instructor, his brand of gymnastics was more medical and aesthetic than competitive. He was heavily influenced by the German *Turnen* system of gymnastics as well as by the ideology of *Turnen* – vehemently articulated by its founder Fredrich Ludwig Jahn – that was anti-competitive and anti-modern sports. *Turnen* advocated group-oriented collective physical fitness drill that would transform practitioners into a strong-bodied collective. In Jahn's view, the strong-bodied collective embodied German nationalism. Ling was scornful of the *Turnen*'s use of rings, ropes, bars and vaulting equipment and claimed that his system of floor exercises was more scientific and more effective as therapy. It is unclear if Ambadas Vaidya was familiar with Ling's method prior to the team's European tour, but in any case mass drill gymnastic exercise performance was very popular throughout much of the nineteenth century in Europe. German and Scandinavian immigrants popularized it in the United States, but, as Allen Guttman points out, 'stripped of the emotional prop of nationalistic fervour, [*Turnen*] was never a match for modern sports'. [18] It was, however, a perfect match – in the non-competitive sense – with yoga and another form of Indian gymnastics known as *mallakhamba*.

The 1949 *Lingiad* was, in many ways, a remarkable event explicitly designed to bring nations together in a spirit of cooperation rather than competition. Over 100 teams from 46 different nations amounting to 15,000 gymnasts – including a team of 5,000 'Swedish housewives' who performed a mass drill of domestic chore gymnastics – came together in the Olympic Stadium near Stockholm. As P.M Ganorkar recounts, he, Vaidya, D.D. Ganorkar and Deshpande were watching from the stands: 'As the tiny brown skinned Indian contingent – the only group to relieve the monotony of fair skin – was marching around the track to take up its position in the arena before the Royal Box and was being cheered, it must be admitted that we were visibly moved.' [19] In selecting gymnasts to participate, Vaidya and his colleagues had made an explicit point in having the team reflect India's ethnic and religious diversity, including Hindus, Parsees, Sikhs, Muslims and Christians. Although there were enough applicants to field a women's team, finances did not allow and so two women were included to reflect gender equality. The team's dress uniform consisted of white caps, black *sherwani* (long tunics) and tight *churidar* pyjamas for the men and black saris for the women. Thus what Vaidya was doing at the *Lingiad* was, in a sense, performing the modernity of the Indian National Congress on an international stage. It is with intense pride that Ganorkar quotes the following from a correspondent for the German paper *Schwabisches Tageblatt*:

> The Indian Amanda was fully justified in saying on the final day of the International Gymnastic Congress, which was held within the frame-work of the second Lingiad in Stockholm, that Kipling's words 'East is East and West is West' are meaningless so far as the Lingiad is concerned. If 66 nations in the world can show their gymnastics, their own interpretation of gymnastics, it is an event that proves the nation-uniting character of this World Gymnastic Festival. This show of

pure body-aesthetics, without rivalry or prizes, without ranks or medals, without first or second place, without winner or loser – yes! – this was something beautiful; because real sport aims at the performance itself. [20]

In this context we can turn our attention to the 'performance itself' of yoga as a form of gymnastic exercise uniquely suited to the modern condition. In a published speech given at the World Physical Culture Congress of 1949, H.V. Deshpande goes into considerable detail to characterize yoga as, in effect, the most perfect form of gymnastic exercise and also the antithesis of vigorous sport and competitive athleticism. Although he makes passing reference to yoga's ancient history – and speaks at length about the emphasis placed on strength in the Upanishads and in the Ayurvedic literature – he draws direct attention to the way in which Swami Kuvalayanada's scientific research proves yoga's efficacy with reference to modern physiology:

> The most outstanding contribution of Yoga to the science of physical culture is the invention of certain physical poses, known as *yogasanas*.... [I]t is [Swami Kuvalayananda] who has carried out intensive scientific research into the Yogic system and has tried to prove that Yogic Physical Culture is most helpful in maintaining the health of the endocrine glands which govern the entire organic system of the body. Yoga has indeed tried to carry the science of life to perfection....
>
> In the practice of the yogic poses the element of muscle fatigue and artificially accelerated circulation of blood are minimized. 'Perfect ease and comfort' – is the caution administered to the disciples of the Yoga. No violent or strenuous muscular activity! No deliberate acceleration of the circulation!...The principal factor due to which attention of the scientists has been attracted toward Yogasanas is their capacity to ensure control of the nerves and maintain adequate and continuous blood supply to particular parts of the body....
>
> [Describing the rationale of the Yogic poses Swami Kuvalayananda says:] 'The present day life requires far more nerve activity than the life we had a score of years ago. Hence an ideal system of physical culture must make special provision for nerve building.' [21]

Yoga is, thus, distinctly modern and particularly suited to the modern condition. It is constructed by Deshpande as an expression of Indian modernity.

The kind of yoga performed by the HVPM team in Stockholm was predominantly postural and most likely conformed to the standardized techniques described by Kuvalayananda in his book *Asana*. In conjunction with choreographed *asana* performances, the team also put on a number of *mallakhamba* demonstrations, both during the festival and after when they toured a number of European countries.

Mallakhamba is an interesting case for a number of reasons. Technically it can be translated as 'wrestler's pillar' and is most often described in the literature as an apparatus on which wrestlers perform exercises. These are referred to in the medieval *Mallapurana* text as *stambhashrama*. Although the details are unclear, in its modern form the *mallakhamba* was first popularized by Shri Balambhatta Dada Deodhar, the guru-cum-physical instructor in charge of Baji Rao Peshwa II's gymnasium around the turn of the eighteenth century. Since then, *mallakhamba* has developed as a gymnastic sport unto itself, performed on a range of free-standing, hanging and flexible 'pillars', most recently incorporating yoga postures. The HVPM was one of the first institutions to develop gymnastic *mallakhamba*, where teams of performers assume different yoga and yoga-inspired postures on a single apparatus. Thus it gives the impression of being 'traditional' but is in fact an expression of modernity that articulates directly with the aesthetic dimension of Swedish gymnastics, just as yoga articulates with the medical dimension.

After the *Lingiad* team's return to India, the HVPM sought to start a 'full fledged college of Physical Education teaching both western and eastern system'. [22] Soon it established a one-year course providing certification referred to as a 'Diploma in Physical Culture and Recreation', offered under the auspices of the Indian Institute that was established as an independent body closely linked to the HVPM. In 1959 the institute was renamed *Bharatiya Sharirik Shikshan Mahavidyalya*, which was soon recognized by the central government. Between 1964 and 1973 the Mandal started BPEd, MPEd and DPEd degree courses. Through affiliation with Nagpur University, it now offers PhD courses.

Since 1950 the HVPM's articulation with various modernities has changed significantly. Although indigenous sports and physical education remain important, the *mandal* has consciously embraced 'western' sports and physical education. As Jodh puts it, '[I]n order to be in line with the time and changed circumstances Mandal had changed its constitution by making necessary amendments in 1971 and opened new departments to meet exigencies of time'. [23] Since 1950, but especially since the early 1970s, the HVPM has increased dramatically in size and scope. It boasts a multipurpose sports pavilion which can accommodate 3,000 spectators and is used for gymnastics, table tennis, badminton, judo, wrestling, weightlifting and roller skating, among other activities; an Olympic standard swimming pool with a gallery capacity of 4,000; an outdoor sports stadium that can accommodate 30,000; two 400-metre cinder tracks; two football (soccer) fields; two handball courts; six volleyball courts; four basketball courts; two hockey fields; six *kabaddi* courts; six *kho-kho* courts; a cricket pitch; an archery range; a tennis court; and a *mallakhamba* area. One of the most recent construction projects was the Netaji Subhash Chandra Bose Indoor Badminton Stadium, with a capacity of 3,000. There is a 'Modern Health Centre' with aerobic training equipment, a physiotherapy centre, a nature cure centre with 50 beds for in-patient treatment and a yoga centre. In the nearby hill station of Chikhaldara, the *mandal* has built a centre for yoga.

The campus accommodates 13 different educational institutions: a Department of Computer Science and Technology; College of Engineering and Technology; Degree College of Physical Education (established 1964); Bharatiya Sharirik Shikshan Mahavidyalaya (established 1948); Girijan Sharirik Shikshan Mahavidyalaya (established 1996); Ramkrishan Krida Vidyalaya and Junior College (established 1937); Vidarbha Ayurveda Mahavidyalaya (established 1934); Yoga and Naturopathy Institute, Chikhaldara (established 1990); Computer Institute (established 1991); Adhyapak Mahavidyalaya (established 1970); Veer Vamanrao Joshi Primary and

Pre-Primary School (established 1970); Ashram Shala (established 1986); and four Ashram Shalas for tribal children in Chikhaldara, Hatru, Harisal and Achalpur (established 1992). Altogether these institutions accommodate several thousand students: 2,000 boys and 600 girls from all over India enrol in the regular summer physical education courses and 1,500 take specialized courses. [24] As these details make obvious, the HVPM has not only grown rapidly but has expanded its activities beyond sport into areas such as general education, engineering, computer science, Ayurvedic medicine and naturopathy. It has also become actively involved in social work and public health outreach, particularly with the regional tribal population. It would be very easy to see these developments as simply a dramatic example of modernization in action and the ultimate triumph of hegemonic Western modernity. But from its very inception, the HVPM has engaged with a range of different modernities and has defined itself as unique. The fact that it now boasts an enormous modern sports complex that includes facilities for yoga, *kabbadi*, *kho kho* and *mallakhamba* reflects the global scope of its local vision, as this vision of modernity – with its emphasis on non-sectarian equality and justice – is a sharp alternative to other possible configurations.

Contrasting Modernities: The HVPM in Comparative Perspective

The HVPM considers itself to be a pre-eminently modern institution that has both national and international standards and recognition. Its vision of modernity seamlessly accommodates ultra-modern technology – computers, saunas, physiotherapy equipment – and so-called traditional sports – yoga, *kabbadi*, *kho-kho* and *mallakhamba*. The fact that *kabbadi* and *kho-kho* have been standardized and that *mallakhamba* and yoga competitions are judged along lines established for international gymnastic competition does not present any problems since, in the view of the HVPM, scientifically based modifications are what make tradition relevant and useful in the context of modernity.

Stepping back from the specific programmes the HVPM offers, its overarching programmatic concern is to improve the health and well-being of youth. It is on this level that one may speak of a modern social imaginary that is only nominally bounded by the nation state and clearly extends to Japan, Germany and Sweden as well as to many other countries beyond those visited by the *Lingiad* teams of 1936 and 1949. On a more regional level, a number of students from Nepal and Bhutan have taken degrees from the HVPM. Obviously, therefore, on both a national and international level there are numerous organizations and bodies – the YMCA for example – that explicitly seek to articulate with the specific moral component of this global social imaginary. Within India alone there are groups that engage with it in terms of some formal and structural similarities, but which have significantly different visions of modernity. While it would be possible to compare and contrast the HVPM with institutions that fall into any one of the other five ideal types outlined above, I would like to conclude with a stark contrast, while continuing to focus on yoga.

The *Rashtriya Swayamsevak Sangh*: The Modernity of Tradition

The *Rashtriya Swayamsevak Sangh* (RSS) was founded in 1925 as an organization dedicated to the reconstruction of Hindu masculinity. Since then it has developed into a multi-faceted militant nationalist organization. Although it is not, by any means, an organization devoted to the promotion and development of sports, an ideal of physical education was central to Dr Hedgewar's original goal, and sports and mass drill training continue to be an important feature of recruitment and training, particularly on the level of neighbourhood *shakhas*. In Dr Hedgewar's vision the elite, urban middle-class *shakhas* were modelled on popular peasant wrestling *akharas*, with several significant modifications. The physical exercises practiced in the *shakha* were oriented towards mass-drill regimentation and the development of choreographic coordination rather than wrestling or the distinctive exercises associated with wrestling. As Thomas Bloom Hansen points out, the *shakha* also took on the formal structure of a religious sect, [25] with the object of spiritual authority and devotion being the quasi-divine Hindu nation in the feminized form of Bharat Mata. To a large extent the masculinity inculcated through *shakha* training – both physical and ideological – was designed to protect the feminized nation from the imagined assault of hyper-masculine Muslims.

In general terms the RSS has a conflicted, ambivalent and somewhat paradoxical orientation towards what it perceives to be Western modernity. This is clearly reflected in its orientation towards sport and physical education. As I have pointed out elsewhere, [26] *shakha* drill involves a number of different kinds of regimented mass drill and organized team games, primarily stave training and *kabaddi*. The rationale for practising these physical activities is that they are thought to be intrinsically 'Hindu' in so far as they are rooted in pre-colonial and pre-Mogul history. In other words, they invoke the purity of tradition and a kind of masculinity associated with that tradition. In fact, however, *kabaddi* is played following rules established first in the 1920s by the YMCA. These rules were revised in the 1930s by the *Maharashtra Sharirik Shiksha Mandal*, an organization closely linked to the Vaidya brothers and the HVPM. [27] Although *kabbadi* is 'traditional', it is the rule-bound structure of the game that renders it useful as a mechanism for the development of discipline and organized teamwork. In other words, its modern form makes it particularly useful on the level of nationalistic *shakha* training. Wrestling – the athletic activity directly linked to the 'traditional' institution on which the *shakha* is modelled – is not very often included in the *shakha* regimen, in part because it is 'too traditional' and in part because it promotes individual prowess and success rather than regimented discipline and teamwork. [28]

Similarly, the RSS does not place very much emphasis on yoga, even though – as the case of the HVPM clearly indicates – *asanas* have been choreographed for mass drill performance since at least the late 1920s. Although yoga would seem to fit perfectly into the traditionalist ideology of Hindu nationalism, it is highly problematic largely because its practice invokes non-violence and non-sectarian inclusiveness as well as a very problematic form of ascetic self-discipline that is difficult to reconcile with athleticism and muscular masculinity:

> Hedgewar wished to create a 'new man' – patriotic selfless individuals, loyal to the Hindu nation and the RSS – physically well trained, 'manly,' courageous, self-disciplined, and capable of organization. The RSS swayamsevak was to be the kshatriyaized antithesis to Gandhi's non-violent, 'effeminate' bhakti-inspired Hindu. The ideal swayamsevak was supposed to be a selfless activist dedicated to lifelong service of the nation, but not only preoccupied with a search for truth and perfection of the soul, as were the traditional yogis. [29]

Although reflecting a degree of confusion between signified and signifier, the blurring of *hatha yoga, bhakti yoga* and spirituality – which produces RSS angst – is itself a function of modernity, since the medieval practitioners of *asana* and *pranayama* were interested in the acquisition of supernatural power in the context of material, worldly existence. It was not until the early nineteenth century that a discourse of spirituality was employed to replace magic and esoteric sexuality in the practice of *asana* and *pranayama*. In any case, it is significant that when yoga is included in the *shakha* regimen it most often involves hybrid *asana* that have been modified through the incorporation of various muscle-toning movements. These movements derive from Euro-American physical training regimens.

Shakha drill must be understood within the framework of RSS ideology, as this ideology involves an explicit articulation of modernity and an engagement with various other forms of modernity and their articulation with one another. As Hansen points out, both Savarkar and Golwalkar – the two most prominent ideologues of the Sangh – were inspired by Italian and German nationalism. However, their nationalist rhetoric was not simply a derivative of Mazzini's, Herder's or Fichte's. Rather they infused this rhetoric with a kind of indigenous Orientalism that was pervasive in the first half of the twentieth century and characterized the rhetoric of the Hindu Mahasabha and the Indian National Congress among other institutions. In Savarkar and Golwalkar's interpretation, German and Italian modernist ideals of racial, linguistic and cultural purity, as well as what might be called visceral territorial emotionalism, were informed by a notion of essential Hindu spirituality. This spirituality counteracted the materialist decadence of the West, while allowing for the emergence of an alternative nationalist modernity grounded in the legacy of Hindu civilization.

In most general terms – and obvious differences in priorities, methods and goals notwithstanding – the difference between RSS nationalist modernity and the nationalist modernity of the HVPM, at their point of articulation, is that the former looks outward and backward in time to look inward, and constructs a regimen of physical fitness that is designed to produce a new, modern Hindu man, whereas the latter looks inward to express itself outward with a future orientation toward the health and well-being of modern youth based on the practice of 'indigenous' physical fitness that is unique but on par with other forms. In both cases what counts as indigenous or traditional in the context of modernity is open to a significant range of rather open-ended interpretations, given the fact that almost everything that is known about *mallakhamba* is based on Balambhatt Dada Deodar's early-nineteenth-century development of both the technology of the pillar and the gymnastic routines performed on it; that almost everything that is known – and considered relevant – about *asana* and *pranayama* is based on early-twentieth-century forms of practice; and that until 1920 *kabaddi* was not a sport, much less a national sport – or even a single entity at all – but rather a variety of different games played in different ways in different parts of the country by children and teenage boys who called it by different names.

Even though the RSS and the HVPM are different kinds of institutions, what makes them comparable is the way in which key features of their respective modernities intersect and articulate and the way in which formal correspondence – mass drill yoga in Berlin and mass *shakha* drill in Pune or Nagpur, circa 1936 – can have completely different meanings and reflect quite different realities that cannot be resolved into a single framework with clearly demarcated national boundaries.

What might legitimately be called – with reference to the legacy of the Indian National Congress – 'Indian modernity' in fact incorporates a range of different visions. On one level this is obvious. However a shift in focus away from state-bounded nationalism raises the important question of how local modernities articulate, and problematizes the question of contextualization. Although the difference between the RSS and the HVPM is stark and clear, I would like to suggest that a careful comparison of subtle differences in range of comparable institutions based on the delineation of ideal types would demonstrate that something as seemingly straightforward as the practice of yoga is complicated by the fact that it is located – either as a consequence of an *asana* being performed on the top of a *mallakhamba* or in mass drill format – at the point of articulation between a number of different localized modernities.

Contextualizing local modernities is, in effect, an exercise in understanding how something that is apparently simple and straightforward can become something that manifests radical difference. The scope, scale and extent of difference itself – as against the cultural logic of congruence and affinity – defines context as the logical discord of history manifest in the present, rather than as the continuity of cultural meaning across space and time. The same could also be said for the practice of a range of other modern, globalized things that are beyond the purview of sport and physical education – democracy, for example. But the history of localized democracy – and the modernities that articulate therein – is truly a twisted tale of visionary idealism and contorted practice that involves the breathless fabrication of state boundaries. In any case to disconnect modernities from state nationalism provides a clearer – although not by any means neater – perspective on the dynamics of local and global in the history of the present.

Notes

[1] Knauft, *Critically Modern*, 11–13.
[2] Taylor, *Modern Social Imaginaries*, 23–30.
[3] MacAloon, 'Interval Training', 32–53.
[4] Kamlesh, *Physical Education*, 371.
[5] Alter, 'Somatic Nationalism'; *Yoga in Modern India*, 142–77.
[6] See Alter, *The Wrestler's Body*; 'The Body of One Color'.
[7] Alter, 'Subaltern Bodies'.
[8] Alter, *Gandhi's Body*, 83–112.
[9] See Sjoman, *The Yoga Tradition of the Mysore Palace*.
[10] Alter, 'Kabaddi.'
[11] Jodh, *Amravati Cradles the Nationalist Movement*, 131.
[12] Ganorkar, *We Go to The Lingiad*, 28.
[13] Ibid., 29.
[14] Ibid.
[15] Jodh, *Amravati Cradles the 16. Nationalist Movement*, 123.
[16] Ganorkar, *We Go to The Lingiad*, 32.
[17] Jodh, *Amravati Cradles the Nationalist Movement*, 125.
[18] Guttman, *Games and Empires*, 156.
[19] Ganorkar, *We Go to The Lingiad*, 60.
[20] Ibid., 64
[21] Deshpande, 'Some Concepts and Aspects of Indian Physical Culture', 5–7.
[22] Jodh, *Amravati Cradles the Nationalist Movement*, 126.
[23] Ibid., 126.
[24] See www.hvpm.org, accessed 12 Aug. 2005.
[25] Hansen, *The Saffron Wave*, 93.
[26] Alter, 'Kabaddi'; *Yoga in Modern India*, 142–3, 145–9, 171–5.
[27] Ibid.
[28] Alter, *The Wrestler's Body*.
[29] Hansen, *The Saffron Wave*, 93.

References

Alter, J. *The Wrestler's Body*. Berkeley, CA: University of California Press, 1992.
——. 'The Body of One Color'. *Cultural Anthropology* 8 (1993): 49–72.
——. 'Somatic Nationalism: Indian Wrestling and Militant Hinduism'. *Modern Asian Studies* 28 (1994): 557–88.
——. 'Subaltern Bodies and Nationalist Physiques'. *Body and Society* 6 (2000): 45–72.
——. 'Kabaddi, a National Sport of India'. In *Getting Into the Game*, edited by Noel Dyke. Oxford and New York: Berg, 2000: 81–116.
——. *Gandhi's Body*. Philadelphia, PA: University of Pennsylvania Press, 2000.
——. *Yoga in Modern India*. Princeton, NJ: Princeton University Press, 2004.
Deshpande, H.V. 'Some Concepts and Aspects of Indian Physical Culture'. In The 2nd Lingiad Festival – 1949: The World Physical Congress, 1 – 6 August, 1949. Pamphlet insert in Ganorkar's *We Go to the Lingiad*. Amravati: HVPM, 1951.
Ganorkar, D.D. *We Go to the Lingiad*. Amravati: HVPM, 1951.
Guttman, A. *Games and Empires*. New York: Columbia University Press, 1994.

Hansen, T.B. *The Saffron Wave*. Princeton, NJ: Princeton University Press, 1999.

Jodh, K.G. *Amravati Cradles the Nationalist Movement*. Amravati: All Indian Languages Literary Conference, 1983.

Kamlesh, M.L. *Physical Education: Facts and Foundation*. Faridabad: P.B. Publications, 1988.

Knauft, B. *Critically Modern*. Bloomington, IN: Indiana University Press, 2002.

MacAloon, J. 'Interval Training'. In *Choreographing History*, edited by Susan L. Foster. Bloomington, IN: Indiana University Press, 1995.

Sjoman, N.E. *The Yoga Tradition of the Mysore Palace*. New Delhi: Abhinav Publications, 1996.

Taylor, C. *Modern Social Imaginaries*. Durham, NC, and London: Duke University Press, 2004.

The Hindu Ascetic As Fitness Instructor: Reviving Faith in Yoga

Chandrima Chakraborty

Indian ascetics have recognized both the boom in the fitness industry in India and the global market potential for yoga and ayurveda. *Swami Ramdev's yoga programme on Aastha channel broadcast daily on Indian television and available to diasporic and Western viewers is dipping in to this new era of the fitness consumer. Drawing from available nationalist and cultural repertoires, this new-age fitness guru imagines a new India embodied in the discipline associated with the practice of yoga and offers yoga as the effective 'Indian' antidote to both modern lifestyles and modern pharmaceuticals. His cures for consumerism denote a longing to transform discourses of health into commoditized regimens of medicalized self-help. He prescribes yoga not only as a personal self-care and spiritual development regimen, but as a way to create a nation of fit/healthy citizens. Such television-mediated religiosity variously aids the ideological work of Hindutva both within and outside India.*

The debates on health and medicine in colonial India point to the political and cultural problematics of the body in a colonized society. In spite of multiple histories of dialectical interaction between European and Indian practitioners of medicine, by the mid-nineteenth century, 'Western medicine assumed a position of clear authority over Indian medicine and Indian bodies'. [1] 'Western' medicine (or biomedicine or allopathy) as the normative category came to be seen as dynamic, progressive and scientifically superior to the allegedly static and degraded state of 'Indian' systems of medicine, i.e. 'other' or 'alternative' medicine. [2] Cecilia Van Hollen argues that '[t]his othering of medical practice tends to reflect nineteenth-century racialized categories in which an emerging "Western" white societies' system of medicine was viewed as the "norm" and non-Western, non-white peoples' systems of medicine was "other"'. [3] The crystallization of this binary legitimized the British impetus in colonial India to develop and expand biomedical educational institutions, hospitals and clinics, while 'calling for the regulation, even the outlawing of its Indian rivals'.

Chandrima Chakraborty, McMaster University, Canada.

[4] Vociferous debates between Indian nationalist leaders on the place of the body in the state followed. [5] Subsequently, the body emerged as a site of contestation between the colonized and the colonizer and not simply of colonial appropriation. Practitioners of 'Indian' medicine confronted their marginalization in the face of global ascendance of 'Western' medicine by reinterpreting and rejuvenating their practice, partly through emulation of 'Western' medicine and partly in conscious rivalry with it.

Yoga and *ayurveda* in this context variously articulated concerns with fitness, health and nationalism. Reinvented as cure for the cultural malaise of the colonized, they emerged as powerful symbols of Indian nationalist identity and of resistance to Westernization. [6] Ironically, yoga and *ayurveda* in contemporary times seemingly offer cures for the ex-colonists and for the late capitalist illness of modernity. Yoga and *ayurveda* now comprise an influential segment of the modern wellness industry. Statistical data reveal that a large section of adults in the Western world (United States, Canada, France and the United Kingdom) seek treatment from outside the conventional biomedical system. [7] Further, an increasing number of physicians in the West are integrating 'Eastern' therapies and complementary and alternative medicine into conventional medicine. [8]

In the United States and Canada obesity is often cited as a national crisis and television programmes incessantly promote diets, health gadgets and fitness clubs. Obesity is also becoming a health hazard in India as the Indian middle and upper classes are using their increase in discretionary incomes to reduce activities that involve physical exertion and to frequently eat out, often consuming foods with greater proportion of fats and calories. The rising spending and purchasing power, the increasing exposure to international markets and growing consciousness of urban consumers have resulted in spending on fitness goods and services as never before. There is an increased desire to look and feel good, and therefore invest on the body. The expanding middle class forms a lucrative market and cable television programmes are increasingly geared to their social and lifestyle aspirations. Thus advertisements for fitness clubs and products along with programmes promoting yoga, aerobics, pilates and tai chi are increasing on Indian television. Hindu ascetics, too, seem to have recognized both the recent boom in the fitness industry in India and the global market potential for yoga. They are increasingly dipping in to this new era of the fitness consumer by self-representing themselves as fitness instructors. A proliferation of spiritual channels and programmes with various ascetics giving religious, moral and fitness lessons has resulted in the new phenomenon of television-mediated religiosity.

Swami Ramdev's psycho-somatic fitness programme, broadcast daily on the Aastha (faith) channel, is exceptionally popular in India. [9] An influential proponent of alternative medicine, Ramdev primarily teaches *pranayamas*, the art of deeply inhaling and exhaling in several postures. His fitness programme promises 'amazing' health benefits. He has become a household name in north and east India and is slowly penetrating south India with yoga-training camps in Karnataka, Tamil

Nadu and Kerala. He is commended as the spearhead behind the Rajasthan government's recent decision to make yoga a compulsory subject in schools; Madhya Pradesh, Uttaranchal, and Chhattisgarh could soon follow suit. Each month, his week-long yoga camps attract about 75,000 people. An additional 60,000 Indians visit his permanent camp at Haridwar, north of Delhi. The television broadcast of his yoga camps began in 2002, and now boasts one million viewers. His Divya Yog Trust receives about 1,000 phone calls and 1,400 letters and emails every day. [10]

This essay analyses Ramdev's fitness discourse as a strategic sign for political and cultural manoeuvres. His popularity demonstrates the power of yoga to satisfy a national and transnational nostalgia for 'tradition'. His distinctiveness as a new-age fitness guru lies in his linking of civic bodies to the national body politic. His daily fitness lessons, comprising *pranayamas* (breathing exercises), *asanas* (postures) and acupressure techniques mixed with social and spiritual instructions, seek to create new and improved national subjects. He promotes yoga as alternative and effective medicine as opposed to biomedicine and as a national programme for the improvement of the nation's health and for a redefinition of the 'self'. His yoga *shivirs* (training camps) aim to attain a collective, national perfection. They are reminiscent of early twentieth-century *akhara*s (gymnasiums), which were key sites of both bodily reform and political instruction. His fitness programme echoes views of popular ascetic nationalists such as Swami Vivekananda, who started an ascetic order to bring together dedicated ascetics to work for national regeneration, and Mahatma Gandhi, who questioned the assumptions of the superiority of biomedicine and conducted experiments on himself and his followers in order to develop an indigenous system of health care for the public.

Drawing upon Michel Foucault, I examine Ramdev's articulation of various 'technologies of the self' to analyse the power of embodied nationalism in contemporary India. Ramdev's television-mediated religiosity and advocacy for physical culture, I argue, promote a somaticized religio-nationalism as an alternative lifestyle. The ascetic as fitness instructor enables religious symbols and tropes to enter the collective consciousness, thus aiding the ideological work of *Hindutva* (put simply, the notion that 'India' is synonymous with 'Hindu'). Yoga, Ramdev claims, can eradicate undesirable traits, control desires and cultivate a new nationalist subject in this era of globalization. Yet his anti-globalization rhetoric coupled with his assertion of 'Indianness' is in tension with his aspirations for counter-hegemony.

Body and Nation: Resonances of Colonial and Anti-colonial Discourse

Discourses on the body were an important element in the ideological apparatus of empire, and, later, in the emergence of anti-colonial discourse. R.W. Connell, Paul Hoch and Revathi Krishnaswamy among others argue that imperial masculinity was formalized through the 'unmanning' of colonial others. [11] The body of the colonized functioned as a site for the construction of colonial authority and legitimacy. The British, for instance, characterized India as a land of enervated and emasculated 'Hindu' men. [12] They constructed 'Indians' as children or emasculated adults to legitimize their advanced superior manhood and dismiss Indian claims for self-rule as inappropriate and premature. James Mill, in his 'authoritative' *History of British India*, writes that the Hindus 'possess a feminine softness both in their persons and in their address' that distinguishes them from the manlier races of Europe. Their physical constitution is 'slender and delicate', and their 'muscular strength' is 'even less... than the appearance of their bodies'. [13] Mill's *History* exemplifies how the 'effeminate' Indian/Bengali/Hindu was constructed in Foucauldian terms through practices or technologies of power/knowledge. Mill had never been to India. His version of 'Hindoo nature' was selectively culled from the translations of orientalists – William Jones, Horace Hayman Wilson, Nathaniel Brassey Halhed, Henry Thomas Colebrook and others. Yet his three-volume work on Indian life and society functioned as a valuable resource for scholars, administrators and missionaries working in India.

Irrespective of its derisive or fictitious nature, the Hindus/Bengalis/Indians accepted their physical and moral 'weakness' and thereby their inferior or subordinate masculinity. It resulted in a frenzy of self-creation and self-transformation. Bodily reform, both personal and collective, was seen as the key to the building of national character. Thus the nineteenth century saw an increased Indian interest in physical culture as the body assumed a new centrality in the redefining of Indian men and their masculinities. Reformers held that a collective reform of the male body could rejuvenate the national body politic. Sports were encouraged to make men healthy and instil the required moral virtues. In 1866 the Nationality Promotion Society began its campaign for the revival of 'national gymnastic exercises' and tried to reform the Hindu diet. [14] Founded in 1867, the Hindu *Mela* (fair) was devoted to cultural and sporting events, particularly wrestling, gymnastics and traditional sports. The *Anusilan Samiti*, begun in 1901, was one of the first in a series of such societies that were set up all over Bengal. They soon became the locus for secret terrorist groups that violently challenged colonial rule. [15] Thus *akhara*s were sites of both bodily reform and political instruction.

In response to the colonial encounter with Britain, Indian nationalist ideologues such as Swami Vivekananda (1863–1902) and Mohandas Karamchand Gandhi, a.k.a. Mahatma Gandhi (1869–1948) made responsibility to the nation an aspect of asceticism. The notion of an 'ideal' Hindu male translated into the reconstruction of an indigenous masculinity formulated in terms of ascetic principles and the nationalist requirements of the present. V. Subramaniam notes that the notion of *karmayoga* (selfless action) in the *Bhagavad Gita* gained in significance only during the nineteenth century. *Karma* shifted from its orientalist meaning of fatalism and disengagement with the material world to mean active service (*seva*) for the improvement of the society and the nation. [16] Vivekananda was the most important proponent of *karmayoga* and *seva*. To revitalize the Hindu nation, in 1897 he 'founded an ascetic order, the Ramakrishna Mission, to make ascetics available for the nationalist task. National self-determination, social reform and spiritual awakening were all linked in his perception'. [17] He transformed Hindu discourse on asceticism into the nationalist call for service to the nation by combining Hindu spirituality with ascetic traditions, or what he called 'practical Vedanta'. Vivekananda held that renunciation is not a superior ethical discipline if it means escape. He asked: 'What will you do with individual salvation? That is sheer selfishness....Does renunciation demand that we all become ascetics? Who then is to help the other? Renunciation is not asceticism.' [18] When the *karmayogi* is asked to be a renunciate it means, according to Vivekananda, that he should work or do his duty without thinking of the fruits of his actions. He argues that the *Gita* portrays *karmayoga* as superior to the renunciation of action. Mahatma Gandhi, too, considered renunciation worthless unless it manifested itself in selfless service and social reform. Therefore he urged ascetics to participate in the nationalist movement:

> In this age, only political *sannyasis* can fulfil and adorn the ideal of *sannyasa*, others will more than likely disgrace the *sannyasi*'s saffron garb. No Indian who aspires to follow the way of true religion can afford to remain aloof from politics. In other words, one who aspires to a truly religious life cannot fail to undertake public service as his mission. [19]

Echoing Vivekananda's and Gandhi's views on the duty of the *karmayogi*, Ramdev urges fellow ascetics to recognize their primary affiliation to the nation and to perform their filial duty to the motherland. He asserts: 'I am an Indian before being a *sannyasi*. India's *sannyasis* need to think of their national good before thinking of their personal good'. Bubbling with national pride, he claims to have dedicated his life to the cause of the sacred motherland, Mother India.

Both Vivekananda and Gandhi posited the body as a site to contest imperial ideologies. Vivekananda advocated a 'man-making religion' that could aid Hindu men to reclaim their lost or forgotten masculinity. He advocated the need for a masculinized Hindu/Indian identity that could restore the nation to health and build up its strength. He urged: 'My child, what I want is muscles of iron and nerves of steel, inside which dwells a mind of the same material as that of which the thunderbolt is made. Strength, manhood, Kshatra-Virya + Brahma-Teja'. [20] Wanting to initiate a masculine culture, he remarked: 'You will be nearer to God through football than through the *Bhagawad Gita*'. [21] Thus, while reiterating the colonialist allegation of the effeminacy of the Hindus, Vivekananda believed that they were educable to some degree through careful 'technologies of the self', which 'implies certain modes of training and modification of individuals'. [22] Foucault argues that 'technologies of the self' are codes of self-cultivation, a set of guidelines for a relation to the self that could define the self. In his lecture, 'Technologies of the Self', he explains that technologies of the self 'permit individuals to effect by their own means, or with the help of others, a certain number of operations on their own bodies and souls, thoughts, conduct, and way of being, so as to transform themselves in order to attain a certain state of happiness, purity, wisdom, perfection or immortality'. [23] They are 'applied to oneself as a means of enhancing one's own life, vigour and progeny'. [24]

Foucault's *The History of Sexuality* (1978–86) suggests that the body is the site on which discourses are enacted and where they are contested. Rather than seeing individuals as stable identities, he analyses the discursive processes through which bodies are constituted. Vivekananda's careful selection of robes and postures for photographs, seen through the Foucauldian lens, was clearly an effort to render the ascetic as distinctly and visibly Indian. [25] Vivekananda also authorized a new ascetic masculinity by suggesting that celibacy translated directly into his spiritual, intellectual and virile prowess. He considered 'concentrated masculinity' made possible through meditation and daily practice of yoga as a central aspect of the energized male body.

In a similar vein, Ramdev, a new-age proponent of spirituality, presents his yoga-practising body as a built body – an achievement made possible through the control of the mind and bodily practices. He claims to sleep only for five hours (from 10 p.m. to 3 a.m.), eat only fruits and vegetables, and says he has never had sexual relations: 'I sublimate my libido to positive energy through yoga'. [26] He tells listeners that Krishna was a *brahmacharya* for 12 years and advises men to emulate Krishna by being celibate for at least 12 days, and thereby experience first-hand the power of 'concentrated masculinity'. Ramdev, as fitness instructor, teaches yoga to his disciples/trainees as the precondition for the possession and nurturing of desirable masculine qualities such as health, physical strength and youthfulness.

Vivekananda responded to Western material prowess and science with India's superior spirituality. He presented spiritual health and purity as transcending material and medical competencies and found the West wanting when matched against 'traditional' Indian 'values'. Ramdev, too, wants Indians to believe in their personal worth and abilities and cherish past 'traditions' and 'values'. The recovery of health and 'traditional' Indian values is interlinked in his drive for national self-improvement and for a redefinition of 'self'. He views the health of the nation as organically tied to individual bodies and souls and presents fitness as psycho-spiritual well-being rather than as merely physical well-being. He conflates the crisis of physical disease with the crisis of cultural disease. For him, the malaise of the human body is a reflection of the malaise of the national body in a globalizing era. In his view, the construction of the yoga-practising citizen will enable a reconstruction of the true 'Indian' self that has been lost in modernity. Therefore, he posits the bodies of Indians as *the* primary site for transforming India through discipline and education.

Gandhi, more than Vivekananda, posited the body as a site on which to resist colonialism and stage the nation, creating a community of healthy, self-governing citizens. He urged Indians to rejuvenate and restore the health of the nation first by healing themselves. His intentional change of dress from English suits and bowler hats to homespun *khadi* is emblematic of an attempt to decolonize the body (similar to Vivekananda's careful selection of saffron robes). This informs his rejection of Western medicine as well. He saw Western medicine as an instrument that made colonized Indians dependent on and subject to colonial policy. Therefore, he advocated self-cure (diet, exercise, herbal medicines) as the basis of a public health policy, which could return agency to the colonized Indians.

In *Hind Swaraj* Gandhi constructs an opposition between biomedicine as a quick fix to alleviate symptoms but with only temporary effects versus Indian medicine's more holistic and spiritual approach which views illness and health as caused by a mind-body connection. Modern doctors, in his view, encourage people to indulge, deprive them of self-control and make them 'unfit to serve the country'. [27] Indian 'traditional' medicine, on the other hand, requires much greater effort and self-control on the part of the patient to heal, but it ultimately gets to the root cause of the problem and rids the body of the disease. He writes:

> Let us consider: the business of a doctor is to take care of the body, or, properly speaking, not even that. Their business is really to rid the body of diseases that may afflict it. How do these diseases arise? Surely by our negligence or indulgence. I overeat, I have indigestion, I go to a doctor, he gives me medicine, I am cured. I overeat again, I take his pills again. Had I not taken the pills in the first instance, I would have suffered the punishment deserved by me and I would not have overeaten again. The doctor intervened and helped me to indulge myself. My body thereby felt more at ease; but my mind became more weakened. A continuance of a course of medicine must, therefore, result in loss of control over mind. [28]

Gandhi's contention that the psychic and somatic components of health are isolated from one another in biomedical systems is integrated in Ramdev's fitness practice as he conflates person, self, and cosmic soul. He asserts that his fitness programme enables individuals to control bodily desires, which prevents disease and nurtures one's spiritual well being. He also invokes the Gandhian binary of biomedicine versus Indian systems of medicine: his herbal medicines as more holistic with the promise to rejuvenate and heal versus biomedicine, a temporary fix that depletes the body and soul. He also recounts his own miraculous recovery from childhood paralysis to visibly embody the benefits of yoga. [29] Yoga, Ramdev argues, is an easily available, low-cost, alternative and effective medicine that can bring about permanent cure. He promotes yoga for both wellness and specific health issues and calls for increased medical self-competence. His discourse on national health echoes Gandhi's advocacy for the practice of *pranayama*, the importance of breathing fresh air and doing regular moderate exercise to build a nation of healthy citizens. [30] The ineffectuality of biomedicine, coupled with increasing incidence of modern diseases, justifies the self-proclaimed ascetic nationalist's assumption of the 'duty' to prescribe yoga, acupressure and herbal remedies to the ill and the 'enlightened' (devotee/viewer/fitness trainee).

Ramdev sees the nation as sapped of its strength by globalization (= Westernization) and in need of rejuvenation and disciplining. His mission is to replace feeble physiques and modern diseases reflecting modern forms of indulgence with the fit and beautiful body. He suggests an investment-oriented attitude towards the body and continually reminds his viewers that yoga can help them to look youthful. Youthfulness is no more natural but self-produced through bodily practices. He claims that the daily practice of yoga can stop and, in many cases, reverse the ageing process (natural glow of the skin will be retained; grey hair will turn black; in some cases the elderly will grow new teeth). Thus Ramdev harnesses fitness industry discourse to popularize his yoga-in-30-minutes programme. However, he de-emphasizes the looks of the body in favour of the functional benefits of fitness. He articulates yoga not merely as a personal self-care and spiritual-development regimen, but as a way to create a nation of fit/healthy citizens. He holds Indians responsible for the nation's present condition and its future recovery. He imagines a new India embodied in the discipline associated with the practice of yoga. If every individual embraces his programme of daily practice of *pranayama*s along with a disciplined diet, the nation as the sum total of these individuals, he believes, will become strong and healthy. Thus his life's mission to bring forth a *nirjara* (disease free) and *swasth* (healthy) nation will be accomplished.

He upholds the Foucauldian notion that 'discipline "makes" individuals'. [31] Wanting to decolonize Indian bodies and minds and restore the nation to its past glory, Ramdev, reminiscent of Vivekananda and Gandhi, urges for the sustained production of docile and productive bodies through participation in his disciplinary activities. Discipline through his fitness regimen seeks to produce Indians who will embody the essence of national strength. He sees the health and the wealth of the nation as complementary. [32] He often concludes his daily psychosomatic lessons by stating his desire to create 'a healthy India, a spiritual India, a prosperous India, and a nationalist India'. Undertaken through vigilant monitoring and continual body work, the success of self-improvement and self-care falls upon the shoulders of the individual. Foucault's discussion of practices of the self as *askēsis*, in its Greek sense of self-discipline rather than a Christian sense of self-denial, is pertinent here. Ramdev's fitness programme echoes the work of Foucault on the role of confession, fear and role models in the prescriptive texts of the ancient Greeks and Greco-Romans. [33] Foucault discerns ways in which people participate in their own 'subjectivation' by exercising power over themselves, according to scientific or moral definitions of who they are. In Ramdev's yoga camps, like the monasteries that Foucault discusses, 'obedience is complete control of behaviour by the master, not a final autonomous state. It is the sacrifice of the self, of the subject's own will. This is the new technology of the self'. [34] Confession to the spiritual/fitness instructor, submission to his advice, and permanent obedience to him are prerequisites to participation in Ramdev's fitness regimen. He endorses self-reflection and confession as motivational strategies and invites participants to confess about their lifestyle excesses. He routinely asks participants to raise their hands if they have lost weight or solved stomach ailments, thyroid problems and so on. He regularly displays star achievers and broadcasts their testimonies. He offers lessons in social issues, scriptures and mythology without any possibility for disagreement or questioning. The emphasis is unequivocally placed on following instructions. A complete submission of the self to the fitness (and spiritual) instructor, Ramdev suggests, can bring forth a healthy and fit nationalist subject.

The Fitness Consumer: Recontextualizing the Local, the National and the Global

Given television's crucial role in circulating narratives and symbols of collective belonging, Ramdev's significance needs to be located not only in the domain of health but also in a wider reading of cultural and political hegemony. Ramdev promises to give Indians the power to control not only the microcosm of the body but also the macrocosm – the nation. He believes that the daily performance of yoga would result in the transformation of both distorted individual bodies and minds and the modern nation. In order to compete with biomedicine, he self-consciously frames his fitness/health discourse as a national programme that is spiritual and secular. He urges Indians across age, gender, religion and class boundaries to practise yoga. 'Illness crosses all sectarian boundaries, so does yoga. But if you do *pranayama* for half an hour daily, you will never fall sick', he asserts. He broadcasts interviews with Muslim physical education teachers and Muslim participants in his yoga camps, who have embraced yoga for both wellness and fitness. Despite such strategies, Ramdev's promotion of a somaticized religio-nationalism as an alternative lifestyle contributes to the articulation of the Hinduness of 'national' culture. His spiritual/secular manoeuvres carry with them implicit communal connotations.

His fitness consumers are primarily Hindus from west and north India, who speak Hindi and share the religious mythologies and belief systems that he draws upon to popularize yoga. Since celibate ascetics have a special claim to respect and authority in the Hindu world view, Ramdev's saffron attire immediately makes him a moral authority figure. He sits on a raised open stage on the background of a saffron screen that prominently displays the 'Om' symbol and, often, images of Vivekananda, Krishna and Rana Pratap, which serve as visual reminders of Hindu masculine and martial prowess of the past. [35] He reminds viewers that he has 'neither revived nor established' yoga; 'it already existed. I just take it to the people. These are traditional sciences practised by our great hermits. I learnt these in gurukuls'. [36] Thus he evokes the seemingly unchanging figure of the sacred as he draws upon the 'traditional' authority of 'great hermits' and echoes views of popular nationalist ideologues of the past. At the same time, he underlines yoga's status as science (discussed in detail later). In evoking eternal knowledge belonging to a golden age of hermits and heroes, Ramdev's historiography tacitly makes yoga available to the Hindu fundamentalist imagery of *Ram Rajya* (kingdom of Ram) as a Hindu golden age. He usually concludes the fitness lessons with patriotic or devotional songs and urges participants/viewers to clap to the rhythms in order to benefit from acupressure. Interestingly, these songs are either taken from old Hindi films or patriotic and devotional lyrics are set to new, popular Hindi film music. This not only ensures their mass appeal but also facilitates north Indian (Hindi) devotional songs mostly devoted to Ram and Krishna to pass as 'national'. Ramdev's spiritual and anti-globalization rhetoric continually invokes the divine heroes Krishna and Ram, and idioms from the Hindu epics, the *Ramayana* and *Mahabharata*, to underline the need to develop masculine strength. This enables religious symbols and tropes to enter the collective consciousness, thus aiding the ideological work of *Hindutva*. The *Hindutva* allegory of the mother as nation is also invoked and naturalized through his body lessons. He describes 'Mother India' thus: 'The head is the Himalayas, the hands are Rajasthan and Bengal, the legs are Kanyakumari'. He establishes a reverential, hierarchichal equation between *ma-matribhumi-matribhasha-rashtrabhakti* (mother-motherland-mother-tongue-nationalism): 'Awake! Find your lost values and national traditions', he urges. The recurring refrain is to become masculine and create one's own destiny rather than wait for divine or governmental intervention to solve the nation's problems. The value attached to traditional masculine attributes – strength, endurance and self-control – provides the vision of the body as shaped through regular exercise, diet control and self-discipline as superior to those who do not submit themselves to Ramdev's bodily practices. Further, with his television programme now being broadcast in Canada and in the United States, he is contributing to the construction of a Hinduized-Indian diasporic imaginary.

His yoga *shivir*s present the image of bodies set to work in the service of the nation. Fitness activities are not performed in a private or institutional space in the presence of a personal trainer. Ramdev recognizes the power of embodied nationalism and gives his yoga lessons every morning and evening in open public spaces. Thus disciplining the body becomes a public display of obedience and discipline, breaking bad habits and self-care/self-cure. Even when one does the *pranayama*s in the confines of one's living room, the members of the yoga *shivir* visible on the television screen help to motivate the viewer to perform along with them. Ramdev also urges viewers to collectively practise in parks. Unlike the secret *akhara*s of the anti-colonial era, the use of open spaces such as public fields and school grounds for yoga *shivir*s reflects a civic legitimization strategy. [37] Further, the yoga *shivir*s, similar to the nineteenth-century *akhara*s and the Rashtriya Swayamsevak Sangh (RSS) *shakha*s, provide the foundation for the construction of a somatic nationalist bond through shared bodily performances. Interaction within the yoga *shivir*s creates an awareness of belonging to the larger national community. For the television viewer, too, the daily vision of a community of sufferers and initiated actively engaged in body practices in different parts of India creates an imagined, somatic community.

According to Jennifer Smith Maguire,

> fitness has been promoted as a widespread mode of empowerment, through which people – men and women, young and (especially) old – can take control of their bodies and health. The interest of individuals in (re)claiming control over their health care has also been reinforced at the level of health economics, which have been characterized since the 1970s by a discourse of personal responsibility for risk reduction and the 'duty to be well'. [38]

Thus the notion that exercise and fitness define a total way of life is not new. But Ramdev problematically equates exercise with control over health. He continually affirms that if people have patience, they can be entirely disease free; it will take time to heal from serious or long illnesses (polio, paralysis, asthma, diabetes, depression, AIDS et al.). This discourse effectively assigns individuals the responsibility for societal problems regarding ill health. As Pirkko Markula notes in the context of 'mindful fitness', such 'a justification can easily turn into a disciplinary practice where participation in fitness becomes an individual's responsibility for reducing such mental-health problems as stress, depression, and anxiety, but leaves the underlying social origins for these problems untouched'. [39] Ramdev's advocacy for a simple, healthy lifestyle and his vision of public health in India as a low-cost, easily available, self-treatment rings hollow for the majority of Indians, who live below the poverty line and whose basic needs are not fulfilled by the state. For the starving masses tormented by hunger, the prescription to regularly drink milk and eat fresh fruit and vegetables or fast once a week is both ludicrous and undeniably cruel.

Evidently, the poor have no place in Ramdev's health programme. His attempt to situate his body practices in the discourse of the wellness industry and routinize institutional practices that are elements of the modern research system indicates his preferred consumer profile. He claims ignorance of the English language, yet his psychosomatic discourse is filled with English words. His self-help books and CDs on herbal medicine and yoga, first published in Hindi, are now available in English and in various other Indian languages. Through a combination of the 'ancient' science of yoga with 'modern' medical science, Ramdev seeks to convince literate, scientific-minded and Westernized Indians to shift their allegiance from biomedicine to herbal medicine and yoga. He proudly asserts India's position as a front runner in the information technology sector. He holds that after the completion of *Patanjali Yogapith*, a Rs100-crore health-care project at Bhadarabad, 20 km from Haridwar, India will be at the centre of the health field. The architectural design for the *Yogapith* is shown daily at the beginning of his programme along with a voice-over that announces that the hospital's laboratory will be equipped with modern medical technologies (X-Rays, CAT-scan, MRI etc.). That is, his choice of consumers determines the content of his discourse of fitness/health.

Ramdev also seems to be engaged in an active dialogue with the 'West' or, at least, with Western representations of 'India'. The transformation of yoga on modernist lines interrogates orientalist perceptions that 'traditional' medicine is static and has remained unchanged since ancient times, whereas biomedicine is progressive and modern. His evocation of traditional knowledge, values and norms is more or less shaped by the idea of the modern. He makes yoga and self-cure remedies available to the public through modern technologies: cassettes, CDs, books, television and the internet. He consistently uses English names for diseases and organs of the body, while prescribing medicines in Hindi. Thus the modern seeps into a discourse of the traditional, transforming it in various ways. He invites health professionals and members of the Indian Medical Association to confirm the benefits of yoga and publicize the failure of biomedicine to cure numerous common diseases. To motivate individuals to adopt fitness as a regular lifestyle activity, he presents testimonies and biographical vignettes of patients (laymen, dignitaries and professionals). For his yoga *shivirs*, he puts patients suffering from various diseases through pathological tests done by allopathic doctors before and after the camp. The clinical trials, patient-recovery data and interviews seek to establish the merits of his (Indian) medicine, and thereby successfully redirect consumption practices.

To answer challenges from biomedicine, Ramdev accepts the terms that give legitimacy to biomedicine. He presents yoga as a traditional health-care system and as a scientific health-care system that has been modernized. However, he supports the modernization of 'tradition' in terms of science as long as the essential Indianness of tradition is clearly preserved. This informs his attempts to mediate between conventions of the domestic and the public domain, between traditional values and a beckoning global lifestyle. This is evident from his repeated reminders to his fitness trainees/viewers that the *Patanjali Yogapith* will be run at a minimal cost-recovery, no-profit basis. He consistently lashes out at biomedicine, echoing Gandhi's contention that biomedicine is expensive and biomedical doctors charge exorbitant fees. In contrast, he presents himself as rendering his services free of cost for the national cause. That is, he nationalistically theorizes the practice of medicine and manipulates the politics of culture to establish himself as medical doctor and fitness trainer for the nation.

The discursive opposition between a materialist 'West' and a spiritual 'India', while resonant of orientalist and anti-colonial discourses of the past, is invoked to mask Ramdev's globalizing aspirations. His articulation of Indianness in national terms to local, regional and international audiences is simultaneously modern and in tension with the modern. He employs a discourse of authenticity and antiquity as he links the reinstating of yoga and herbal medicine to a recovery of 'Indian' culture. At the same time, he is actively involved in the modernization of yoga as a modern, international fitness regimen. Further, with yoga and *ayurveda* becoming a transnational phenomenon, Ramdev's defence of his practice on moral, anti-imperialist, anti-capitalist grounds, reminiscent of Gandhian discourse, is now joining with claims to legitimacy based on the degree of penetration into the global market. He is aware that traditional medicine has a lucrative transnational market and wants to capitalize on the profits. His cures for consumerism denote a longing to transform discourses of health into commoditized regimens of medicalized self-help. He provides statistical data on yearly consumption of allopathic medicines to urge Indians (and others) to try out the cost-free 'Indian' treatment of *pranayama*-for-30-minutes every day. Yet the high membership rates for his week-long yoga camps and the *Yogapith*-under-construction suggest that very few Indians will be able to partake of his fitness and medical services.

He wants Indians to stop buying foreign goods and vociferously critiques globalization. To counter the negative effects of globalization on Indian bodies and souls and the body politic, he develops a model of bodily practices so that the bodies of Indian citizens can function as a site to enact and resist power. He utilizes Western typologies of yoga as Indian tradition and orientalist idioms of Indian medicine as spiritually attuned, anti-materialist and non-violent in contrast to biomedicine to enhance the transnational appeal of yoga, but subverts such modes of knowledge by framing yoga as a competitor to biomedicine. [40] His vision of the future includes foreigners coming to his *Yogapith* for treatment, the entire world embracing yoga and herbal remedies and cow urine being exported to the United States. Thus, yoga emerges as the effective 'native'/'Indian' antidote for both modern lifestyles and modern pharmaceuticals; the only global alternative to resist degeneration of mind, body and soul. [41] As Ramdev creates new desires for the purchase of his products beyond national borders, his health/fitness programme extends from recuperating individual health and curing illness to healing modernity itself. Driven by capitalist profit motives, his health/fitness discourse takes on the form of the modern while simultaneously retaining the promise of redemption from the modern.

Notes

[1] Arnold, *Colonizing the Body*, 59. Also see Harrison, 'Medicine and Orientalism', 37–87; Alter, *Yoga in Modern India*.
[2] 'Western' and 'Indian' medicine are not totally independent, nor are they internally homogenous systems of thought and practice.
[3] Van Hollen, 'Nationalism, Transnationalism', 90.
[4] Arnold, *Colonizing the Body*, 59.
[5] Ibid., 76–85, discusses how Indian nationalists variously engaged with science (including biomedicine).
[6] See Alter, *Yoga in Modern India*, 73–108.
[7] Van Hollen, 'Nationalism, Transnationalism', 79–106.
[8] Riley, 'Hatha Yoga and the Treatment of Illness', 20–1, notes that alternative medicine is the fastest-growing sector of American health care. He cites *The Yoga Journal*, which estimates that in 2003 more than 15 million people attended a yoga class in the United States, and the 2 Dec. 2002 cover story in *Newsweek* magazine, which stated that almost half of American adults seek treatment from outside the traditional medical system.
[9] All Ramdev's quotes in this paper are from his television programme in Aastha Channel broadcasts from May–August 2005, unless otherwise indicated. The translations from Hindi to English are my own.
[10] Hari Kumar, 'Busy Indians Embrace Swami's "Easy Yoga"', *New York Times*, 1 Feb. 2005, available online at http://www.iht.com/articles/2005/01/31/news/journal.html, accessed 20 Sept. 2005; Ajay Uprety, 'Zooming Guru', *The Week*, 28 Aug. 2005, available online at http://www.the-week.com/25aug28/currentevents_article10.htm, accessed 20 Sept. 2005.
[11] Connell, *Masculinities*; Hoch, *White Hero Black Beast*; Krishnaswamy, *Effeminism*.
[12] Colonial historiography on India maintained the cultural identity of 'ancient' India as Hindu. Sinha, in *Colonial Masculinity*, 16, argues that the term 'effeminacy' first denoted the entire Bengali Hindu community and sometimes by extension all Indians. But in the second half of the nineteenth century, it referred to *only* Western-educated Indians, a large majority of who were Bengali Hindus. The labouring classes, low-caste groups and the Muslims in Bengal were not included under the category of effeminate groups. Further, the British constructed an elaborate codification of 'martial' (Maratha, Gurkha, Rajput etc.) and non-martial (Bengali) races.
[13] Mill, *The History of British India*, vol. 2, 323, 331.
[14] Rosselli, 'The Self-image of Effeteness,' 127.
[15] Ibid., 130–1.
[16] Subramaniam, 'Karmayoga and the Rise of the Indian Middle Class'.

[17] Van der Veer, *Imperial Encounters*, 47.

[18] Vivekananda, *The Complete Works*, vol. 5, 383; vol. 8, 226.

[19] Iyer, *The Moral and Political Writings of Mahatma Gandhi*, vol. 1, 138.

[20] Vivekananda, *The Complete Works*, vol. 5, 117.

[21] Cited in Sinha, *Colonial Masculinity*, 21.

[22] Foucault, 'Technologies of the Self', 225.

[23] Ibid., 225.

[24] Foucault, *The History of Sexuality*, vol. 1, 120–31.

[25] Dhar, *A Comprehensive Biography of Swami Vivekananda*, analyses the significance of Vivekananda's robes in anchoring the *sannyasi* icon; Parama Roy, *Indian Traffic*, views Vivekananda's photographs as modes of masculinization and eroticization of the male ascetic nationalist icon.

[26] Kumar, 'Busy Indians Embrace Swami's "Easy Yoga"'.

[27] Gandhi later detracted from the ferocity with which he condemned biomedical practice. See, for example, his letter published in *Young India*, January 1921 and printed in *Hind Swaraj*.

[28] Ibid., 58.

[29] According to his own account, in his childhood he suffered paralysis on the left side of his body. The only visible sign of the illness today is his slightly shrunken left eye. The Aastha-USA programme website introduces Ramdev thus: 'The leading Yoga Master attracting millions of practitioners. He was a paralytic till he took to Yoga. Now he teaches it as a complete Medical Science guaranteeing major if not total relief from various ailments eg: Obesity, Diabetes, Migraine, Stress, Depression, Asthma, Hypertension, etc.' See http://www.aasthatv.com/fpc-aasthausa.htm.

[30] Gandhi, *Collected Works*, vol. 11, 449; vol. 30, 551; vol. 31, 188 and 353.

[31] Foucault, *Discipline and Punish*, 170.

[32] According to Ramdev, yoga will create productive citizens and workers who will contribute to the nation's economy. 'If you are well, the nation's businesses and factories will be well', he declares.

[33] Foucault, 'Technologies of the Self'; *History of Sexuality*, vol. 1.

[34] Foucault, 'Technologies of the Self', 246.

[35] He usually does not explain who helps in the organization of his yoga *shivirs*. Each of his yoga camps is well-equipped with stages, loudspeakers, LCD screens, flute and other musical accompaniment and thousands of participants are seen neatly seated in rows. Sometimes at the conclusion of a particular *shivir*, Bajrang Dal and *Vishwa Hindu Parishad* (VHP) cadres are thanked for their help and support along with numerous local and government patrons.

[36] Uprety, 'Zooming Guru'. Ramdev says that at the age of 14, he ran away from home to a nearby *gurukul*. He studied there for ten years before spending many years wandering the Himalayas learning yoga and meditation. He has been teaching yoga for the last 15 years.

[37] During the *swadeshi* era (1903–8), revolutionary action was mostly conceived in secrecy in the *akharas* and took the form of isolated subversive actions; it was not conceived as a mass movement.

[38] Maguire, 'Body Lessons', 453.

[39] Markula, 'Tuning into One's Self,' 319.

[40] Zimmerman, 'Gentle Purge', 209–23, notes that consumers of Indian alternative medicine in Europe and North America associate it with the value of non-violence.

[41] Fitness is portrayed as a way to protect oneself from diseases, dependency on medicines and doctors, an unhealthy lifestyle (overeating, lack of exercise), degeneration of morals, consumerism et al. Ramdev often claims that in one day he can change the food habits of children (such as the desire for Coca-cola, pizzas and burgers) and teach them 'traditional' values (primarily, respect for parents and elders).

References

Alter, Joseph S. *Yoga in Modern India*. Princeton, NJ: Princeton University Press, 2004.

Arnold, David. *Colonizing the Body*. Berkeley and Los Angeles, CA: University of California Press, 1993.

Connell, R.W. *Masculinities*. London: Polity, 1995.

Dhar, S.N. *A Comprehensive Biography of Swami Vivekananda*. Madras: Vivekananda Prakashan Kendra, 1975.

Foucault, Michel. *The History of Sexuality*, translated by Robert Hurley. 3 vols. New York: Random, 1980–90.

——. *Discipline and Punish*. London: Penguin, 1991.

——. 'Technologies of the Self'. In *Ethics: Subjectivity and Truth*, edited and translated by Paul Rainbow, Robert Hurley and others. New York: The New Press, 1997.

Gandhi, Mohandas Karamchand. *Collected Works of Mahatma Gandhi*. 100 vols. New Delhi: The Publications Division, Ministry of Information and Broadcasting, Government of India, 1951–95.

——. *Hind Swaraj*. Ahmedabad: Navajivan Press, 1938.

Harrison, Mark. 'Medicine and Orientalism'. In *Health, Medicine and Empire*, edited by Biswamoy Pati and Mark Harrison. London: Sangam Books, 2001: 37–87.

Hoch, Paul. *White Hero Black Beast*. London: Pluto Press, 1979.

Iyer, Ragahavan, ed. *The Moral and Political Writings of Mahatma Gandhi*. 3 vols. Oxford: Clarendon, 1986–87.

Krishnaswamy, Revathi. *Effeminism: The Economy of Colonial Desire*. Ann Arbor, MI: University of Michigan Press, 1998.

Maguire, Jennifer Smith. 'Body Lessons'. *International Review for the Sociology of Sport* 37 (3–4) (2002).

Markula, Pirkko. 'Tuning into One's Self'. *Sociology of Sport Journal* 21 (2004).

Mill, James. *The History of British India*. 6 vols. New York: Chelsea House Publishers, 1968 [orig. pub. 1817–18].

Riley, David. 'Hatha Yoga and the Treatment of Illness'. *Alternative Therapies in Health and Medicine* 10 (2) (Mar/Apr 2004).

Rosselli, John. 'The Self-image of Effeteness'. *Past and Present* 86 (1980).

Roy, Parama. *Indian Traffic: Identities in Question in Colonial and Postcolonial India*. Berkeley, CA: University of California Press, 1998.

Sinha, Mrinalini. *Colonial Masculinity*. Manchester: Manchester University Press, 1995.

Subramaniam, V. 'Karmayoga and the Rise of the Indian Middle Class'. *Journal of Arts and Ideas* 14–15 (1987): 133–42.

Van der Veer, Peter. *Imperial Encounters*. Princeton, NJ: Princeton University Press, 2001.

Van Hollen, Cecilia. 'Nationalism, Transnationalism, and the Politics of "Traditional" Indian Medicine for HIV/AIDS'. In *Asian Medicine and Globalization*, edited by Joseph S. Alter. Philadelphia, PA: University of Pennsylvania Press, 2005.

Vivekananda, Swami. *The Complete Works of Swami Vivekananda*. 9 vols. Calcutta: Advaita Ashrama, 1967–97.

Zimmerman, Francis. 'Gentle Purge'. In *Paths to Asian Medical Knowledge*, edited by Charles Leslie and Allan Young. Berkeley, CA: University of California Press, 1992: 209–23.

The Centrality of Cricket in Indo-Australian Relations: India, Australia and the 'Cricket Imaginary'

Brian Stoddart

Cricket has become central to Indo-Australian relations in recent years. Not only in diplomatic rhetoric, but in the broader imaginations of each the other too, cricket has provided the template upon which to base mutual understanding. The two countries have often referred to and used cricket as both a metaphor and an idiom by which to mutually relate to each other.

However the approaches to cricket as social practice are distinct in each of the countries and this has sometimes led ironically to a lack of comprehension. This has particularly been brought to light in the wake of recent scandals, which have often precipitated a crisis in the insistent refrain of the 'shared love of cricket'.

The irony of the situation lies in the belief that since cricket started out from the same source in England before travelling to either country it would provide a handy and common theme to base contemporary relationships on. What such an idea ignores is that cricket was crucially transformed in each of its adopted homes and came to signify very distinct social praxes in each of these. Moreover these distinct social praxes often do not readily reconcile with each other making the insistence of a shared common cricketing culture problematic.

During the decade spanning the millennium's turn, Australia enacted another of its periodic South Asia rediscoveries, the cricket motif figuring prominently in attempts to construct shared meanings between the two nations. The reasons are transparent: if cricket can be seen as a substantiating bond then, by extension, interactions in other fields should be straightforward. [1] That might seem (and is) superficial but it has been posited widely, a postmodern spin on the earlier language of sport (especially cricket) as a training for life. [2] Several examples illustrate the point. When the Australian federal government launched its 'New Horizons' project in

Brian Stoddart.

India during 1996, one repeated refrain was of 'a shared love of cricket', coming frequently from people with little interest in or knowledge of the game. [3] To affirm the claim, former Australian cricket captain Alan Border was appointed to the Australia-India Council, a government-funded body designed to enhance Australia-India relations. That same body supported the creation of the Border-Gavaskar Trophy for Test series competition between the two countries; as well as a programme whereby promising young Indian players train at the Australian Cricket Academy. [4] During 1998, an Australian vice-chancellors' mission to boost relations with their Indian counterparts rehearsed the same mantras: we proceed to other things from a shared love of cricket. [5] In 2004, the Australian state of Queensland constructed a marketing campaign to attract fee-paying Indian students around a series of cricket matches in India at which Allan Border was present. [6] In 2005 Alexander Downer, Australian Minister for Foreign Affairs, opened a major speech to the Confederation of Indian Industries by invoking the memory of Sir Donald Bradman, Australia's greatest ever player. [7] The thoughts are shared on the Indian side, too – sportswriter M.K. Dharma Raja wrote in 1999, as part of the Government of India's official media unit, that cricket was among the most important of Indo-Australia links. [8]

Paradoxically, this 'shared cricket culture' protestation is little mirrored elsewhere in the general Indo-Australian relationship. Before and after the formaliization of British rule in India, and eventual political independence, India and Australia shared and continue to share little in common apart from a shared, if different, tutelage within the British Empire. [9] Well into the twentieth century, Australia saw itself politically, culturally and economically as part of the Euro-American world. When relatively popular recognition of Asia confronted Australia from the 1980s, north and south-east rather than south Asia attracted most attention. And that recognition, it should be said, was substantially more in financial and trade realms than in cultural and political ones. Australian horses might have gone to India from the later nineteenth century onwards. [10] An Australian, Lord Casey, might have become Governor of Bengal and the odd Australian might have joined the Indian Civil Service. Australian missionaries might have joined the Indian cause and an Australian (Sir Harold Bailey) become a leading Sanskrit scholar. Australians might have traversed India on the overland route to Europe from the 1960s onwards. Even so, India remained perhaps the quintessential 'foreign' country for most of collective Australia. [11]

That absent long-term and/or deep relationship explains the emphasis placed upon cricket any time cultural bridging is required. That is not unusual in cricket's 'British world'. [12] In the Australian sense, for example, there is virtually no other contact with the inaccurately named 'West Indies' apart from cricket. While cricket specifically and sport more generally forced Australian authorities into an apartheid oppositionist position they might not have adopted otherwise on South Africa, by and large intercultural relations between 'North' and 'South' developed through cricket have been artificial at best, non-existent at worst. [13] Outside the 'white dominions', cricket links have always been thus: an excuse to play another Test or one-day series in a contest sense, but not sufficient reason to build more cultural connections, least of all among the players themselves. [14]

In the India-Australia case the further complexity, however, is that the elaborated 'link', in fact, masks a wide cultural chasm. What cricket becomes, under that recognition, is a touchstone to the whole of the relationship. Interestingly enough, Australian cricket writer Greg Baum remarked similarly on the relationship with Pakistan: 'the longer they spend together, the more apart they grow.' [15]

Two episodes are worth detailing here, because they provide avenues to a fuller understanding of the point being made.

The Great Bookie Scandal

Late in 1998, newspaper reports revealed that Shane Warne and Mark Waugh were fined by the Australian Cricket Board for accepting a bookmaker's money in return for providing him, allegedly, with 'innocent' information concerning pitch and weather conditions about matches in which they were involved. Soon after these revelations, Warne was announced as captain for a one-day series against England and, a little later, as vice-captain to Steve Waugh in the Test series.

There was some telling complexity here. First, it emerged that the incident had occurred during a tour of Sri Lanka almost four years earlier. Second, the Australian Cricket Board had fined the pair then suppressed the story. Third, the story emerged at precisely the time when both players were central witnesses in match-fixing allegations levelled at Pakistan's Salim Malik – that is, the two Australian players had been found guilty by their own governing body but were now appearing in a 'moral high ground' campaign against the Pakistani player, a campaign that was regarded widely as a full-scale accusation of corruption in South Asian cricket.

The Warne-Waugh version of the bookie story went like this. [16] One night after a match in Colombo, Waugh was approached by someone identified only as 'John from Delhi', a bewitchingly Saidian 'Orientalist' invocation, [17] who told the Australian later he was a bookmaker. Waugh took $US4,000 from 'John' and agreed to convey to the Indian pitch and weather information for matches in which the Australians were playing. The next day, Waugh introduced Warne to 'John' – in a casino, ironically enough. Warne was given $US5,000, converted it to gambling chips and lost all of them. Over the following few months, 'John' spoke with Waugh at least ten times and Warne several. Australian philosopher Tony Coady provided an interesting view, [18] arguing that Warne and Waugh were unprepared intellectually for the problems occasioned by the bookmaker's offer. At a time when ethical concerns were sweeping Australian corporate and political life following a series of scandals, cricket, once again, was left behind or, more precisely, indemnified against those wider social movements.

This was ironic, of course, because while several sections of the public saw cricket as an important social artefact and bulwark of propriety they still believed, paradoxically, that the game should not necessarily be subjected to the same performance scrutiny as those other areas of life. While in many ways that paradox was not new, it was certainly highlighted by the bookie scandal. In the weeks immediately following the revelations both Australian players, hitherto popular icons, met vocal disapproval every time they turned out to play. Australian Prime Minister John Howard and Leader of the Opposition Kim Beazley (cricket lovers both) found rare public accord in condemning both the players and the board. Former players such as Neil Harvey called for both players to be banned, and it seemed like the Australian cricket world was turned upside down.

Yet this public discontent was not met by official action; far from it, as the elevation of Warne showed only too clearly. If the public discourse was confused, the cricket board's was not. This is an important point, because it is a guide to the strength of the board's own culture, derived from almost a century of evolution, and far removed from some of the changes sought by the public.

That Australian approach stands in stark contrast to what happened in India. When it became clear that match-fixing was indeed happening, and that the problem was serious, initial investigative reporting was transformed quickly into police inquiries and a formal commission. [19] It emerged, clearly, that the rise of the mobile phone had helped accelerate the spread of betting into cricket, that coincidence fuelled further by the rapid expansion of cricket telecasting. By the late 1990s the betting was rife, with extremely large amounts of money at stake. The bookmakers sought inside information, of the very kind sought from Warne and Waugh. The fate for the players involved was to be very different from that accorded the Australians, however. Former captain and star batsman Mohammed Azharuddin was considered to be at the heart of matters, and shown to have received what in Indian terms were substantial amounts of money (but many of them in the same dimensions as those received by Warne and Waugh). Azharuddin was dismissed from cricket, with the repercussions still occurring in 2005. Other players such as Manoj Prabhakar and Ajay Jadeja received similar treatment.

While it can certainly be argued that the scale and the circumstances of the matters were different between Australia and India, the fact remains that Warne and Waugh were involved in some way in illegal gambling activities on the subcontinent. Waugh retired honourably from the game, and there were many who argued that had Shane Warne been captain of Australia for the 2005 Ashes series the results would have been different. By then, of course, he was Test cricket's leading wicket-taker and famed for his off-field indiscretions. He was still playing, however, while 'Azhar' had not only disappeared from cricket but was still facing criminal accusations and appeared to be the target of underworld attention.

These different response patterns must be seen, at least in part, as the result of very different attitudes prevailing towards cricket as cultural practice in Australia and India. If that is the case, then the 'cricket as cultural bridge' metaphors come under some pressure.

Stop Cricket in the Name of Culture

Late one night in early January 1999, shovel-carrying activists broke into the Ferozeshah Kotla cricket ground in Delhi, dug up the pitch and resisted all attempts to stop them. While such actions had occurred elsewhere in the world (most notably during campaigns to halt South African tours throughout the apartheid era), the background to this particular event was potentially explosive. Months earlier, when it was announced that there would be a Test series, staged in India, between the home nation and Pakistan, the first such series in 12 years, the tension was immediate. In the subcontinental context, inevitably, the tour took on a political hue rarely seen and even less rarely understood elsewhere in the cricket world. An indication of the possibilities had come earlier from Mulayam Singh Yadav, the Indian defence minister and *dalit* leader who argued that cricket was a 'servitude' game imposed by the British and so should be rejected. [20]

By late 1998 the proposed Pakistani tour was a major political issue. Shiv Sena chief Bal Thackeray announced that the government of which he was part in Maharashtra would not host the Pakistanis – how could they, he asked, when Hindus were being slaughtered in Kashmir? Moreover, the Sena promised to disrupt matches wherever possible and, ideally, halt the Pakistani tour. The struggling Union government led by Prime Minister Atal Behari Vajpayee renounced the claim quickly, but the sides were drawn. [21] Delhi Sena chief Jai Bhagwan Goel argued that 'games are played between friends, not enemies'. [22] Political leaders of all persuasions were drawn into the affair. West Bengal Chief Minister Jyoti Basu deplored the Sena actions. Jaswant Singh, Indian External Affairs Minister, said the series would proceed. [23]

A few days after the Delhi incident, a Shiv Sena group entered the Board of Cricket Control in India (BCCI) offices in Mumbai, caused considerable damage, and attacked an official. [24] At that point, Indian Home Minister L.K. Advani went to Mumbai, met Thackeray and brokered a deal to save the series that began soon after, but in Chennai and not in Delhi. [25]

This drama was played out on several levels. An obvious one was the 'international relations through sports' theme. It was 14 years since India and Pakistan had met in a Test series (a 1991 series was aborted following Shiv Sena intervention). Throughout that time Indo-Pakistan relations had been fragile at best, dangerous at worst - the ongoing and still topical nuclear race being a prime example, along with the abiding dispute in Kashmir. Few mediation attempts at official level had any impact. A *Times of India* editorial caught the atmosphere: 'Sport, in many cases, is precisely politics extended by other means. This is particularly true of the embattled no-man's land of Indo-Pak relations which, despite the repeated incantation of people-to-people contact, continue to be hostage to the compromised political establishments of New Delhi and Islamabad.' [26]

The domestic political scene was full of irony. The Shiv Sena held power in Maharashtra in coalition with the BJP, whose Manoj Joshi occupied the chief minister's post. Joshi was also a vice-president of the BCCI, and pledged to provide protection to the Pakistani tourists. The ruling alliance was fragile, and not long after the Test series began Joshi stood down as chief minister. Many commentators argued that the Thackeray ploy was not so much about cricket or, even, about Pakistan, so much as leveraging his national support in order to win a concession from the BJP-dominated Union government. [27]

But the most complex layer was, and remains at the community level, for it is there that people make social choices about what is most important to them. [28] Harsha Bhogle has captured something of this, albeit obliquely. In a charming little essay, he described a club final in Jamshedpur: each team had ten players, only five could come from the club, two had to be the children of members but be under 18 years of age, one had to be over 50 years of age, and two had to be women. It was, he said, through this composition and the modified rules of play, a wonderful community bonding agency:

> There is a lot more to cricket than the daily prime-time soap-opera it sometimes resembles. That can be ... exciting, addictive, frustrating, depressing, it can go through a range of emotions. But it can never match the joy of actually playing it.
>
> The essential point, of course, is that cricket is a man-made construct that can take many forms and be put to many uses. It is also essential that cricket be recognised as often meaning many different things to the same person. [29]

Many Australian cricket enthusiasts were bemused, to the point of being appalled, that the early 1999 India-Pakistan Test series was reported as a political and diplomatic event as much as a cricket one. Rahul Bedi, [30] for example, made an explicit connection between the 'cricket diplomacy' and more mainstream Indo-Pakistani diplomatic efforts, but at least one Australian newspaper ran it as a quirky rather than insightful analysis. In general, Shiv Sena attempts to disrupt matches by digging up pitches in order to assert Hindu solidarity and anti-Pakistani political sentiments were reported in Australia with an air of incredulity. How could this be cricket?

Nowhere did the Australian press carry insights such as those demonstrated by a *Times of India* leader writer:

> Once seen as a symbol of the acquisition of empire by stealth, cricket today has far transcended its imperial origins and been vernacularised into various cultural idioms, from Calcutta to the Caribbean. And when it comes to India playing Pakistan, the game acquires a particularly resonant emotional timbre. It becomes almost an enactment of a morality play, a form of cathartic release. In the clash of absolutes, will Sachin's bat withstand Wasim Akram's bowling; will light – depending on your point of view - triumph over dark? [31]

It was this general gulf in cross-cultural appreciation, incidentally, that helped escalate the 1999 Muralitharan throwing incident into one of cricket's ugliest moments. While the public explanations have been many in Australia (stressed umpire, International Cricket Conference inaction, Sri Lankan intransigence, Australian righteousness), the central factor is inescapable: Australian authority had little if any appreciation of the cultural centrality of cricket as symbol in the Sri Lankan environment. [31]

This has carried into the early twenty-first century. In 2004 India travelled to Pakistan to play a further series, and the interaction between sport and politics was palpable with the issues of Kashmir and other cross-border matters inevitably being read into 'play'. There were suggestions that the Indian government wanted to delay the tour until after the national elections; cricket authorities had to scramble to keep sporting arrangements 'proofed' against intervention, and the tour went ahead only after consideration by the Indian Prime Minister and his senior colleagues. [32] National identities were clearly caught up in all this. [33] The patterns were very similar throughout 2005 and in anticipation of the 2006 series: [34] *Outlook* devoted over 20 pages to a preview of the 2005 series amidst stories on Kashmir, the tsunami, a review of the Kargil War tragedies and Prime Minister A.B. Vajpayee's apparent connections with the Ayodhya site outrages. Cricket, that is, was seen as being just as important as some of the most serious political issues of the day. These immense media and public scrutinies [35] inevitably invest cricket with wider meaning.

Again, little of this has resonated in Australia, where such overt political interaction has been rare. Even at the height of the Bodyline controversy the political dimensions were masked in public, and in the main the 'political' inferences have been contained at the 'creating cordial relations' and 'measuring state progress' levels. For the most part, then, the cricket/politics nexus in Australia remains at the mundane level of public debate over the propriety of the Prime Minster timing his London visits with Test matches, with speculation that one party or another tried to recruit some player or other, or with predictions of results. Even major issues such as engagement with Zimbabwe have been dealt with by invoking the 'sport and politics do not mix' approach, a far cry from India. In part, of course, this draws from the Anglo cricket heritage, in which the game was thought to be just a game even though all the enthusiasts invested it with far greater importance. In part, too, it has stemmed from the increased professionalism of the Australian game, where tours have become as much an industry as a form of cultural interaction.

As a result, the perceptions in India and Australia, if anything, have become further apart than ever. While India's news magazines and television channels were choked with information, opinions and suggestions about the 2005 Indo-Pakistan series, there was little or no coverage in Australia. While that may be attributed to the general Australian media principle that South Asia 'does not count', it must also be seen to derive from a gulf of (mis)understanding about how the two cricket cultures 'work' – Ashis Nandy's depiction of cricket as a game invented by Indians and appropriated by the English [36] has bypassed Australia.

Reflections

The starting point is obvious. It is the idea that because cricket started from a central source – England – it must, necessarily, have created a shared culture globally. Because superficial evidence supports the supposition, it has stuck. Inevitably, confusion has broken out when that apparently shared culture has not been evident. Moreover, where deeper analysis has been attempted, the idea has arisen of cricket (and games in general) as an avenue simultaneously for escape from coloniality and the expression of identity. While there is some weight to these analyses, they have also attained a universality that does not stand close scrutiny.

We begin, then, with the 'home' model of cricket as a starting-point for analysing the game's later radiated varieties. For it may be argued that there arose very early in Australia and India (as for other contemporary cricket powers and non-powers alike), some quite different views about what cricket represented socially: a model for colonial behaviour and cultural aspiration, counterbalanced by one as a model for physical play. This is a very different interpretation from the one that normally considers the social model version as the universal starting point, but it helps explain some of the current and apparent ambiguities. Interestingly, it is an analytical view supported in part by at least one Indian cricket writer. Following a recent trip to Australia, [37] Bhogle wrote that he had long considered that cricket reflects the culture of the country in which it is played. What he has missed, however, is the role played by cricket in creating as opposed to reflecting those cultures, and India and Australia are paramount examples.

Given the game's organization in England by the later nineteenth century, the idea of cricket as a reification of status categories was inevitable. The practice of superior-class amateur captains leading teams of professionals drawn from the more inferior social categories was, in itself, symbolic representation enough of the link between game and life. [38] Given that, the greater public-school ethos of 'learning for life through games' had a powerful impact. [39]

The extension to the colonies was clear. In India Lords Harris, Wenlock and Willingdon respectively all carried the philosophy of cricket into their work as colonial administrators. So, too, did countless others in their roles as civil servants, merchants or military people. M.R. Jardine was a marvellous case in point. One of the greatest university players of his generation, he played county cricket briefly, then went to Bombay for a life in legal circles (his son, Douglas, would achieve far greater notoriety). Jardine was revered in Bombay cricket circles, maintaining a high standard of play despite restricted appearances.

In Australia, the message was more about the role of cricket keeping the English 'race' in philosophical touch over vast distances. This was tied up most in the concept of 'the tour' as a latter-day crusade, albeit of a healing rather than aggressive intent. From the first official Test match encounters in 1877 onwards, the tour rhetoric was always about the role of cricket in strengthening Empire, and in playing a central role in the building of the white dominions, as they became popularized. It was for that very reason, of course, that ruptures in the rapture of the rhetoric (as in 1921 in England and 1932–3, 1946–7 and 1970–1 in Australia) took on far more serious tones than might otherwise have been anticipated.

The point was that those eruptions pointed to the real nature of the contests between England and Australia. From the Australian end, from a very early stage, the message was about winning, about beating the English. At a very early point, English tourists began commenting on the 'hard' nature of the Australian game, on what some came to see as a far too concentrated effort on winning at the expense of the social messages in the game. [40] This was to persist, and the only real difference came in 1932–3 when Jardine was thought to have behaved more like an Australian than an Englishman with his obsession about winning – all the other disruptions were when the Australians were thought to have overreached even their standards of aggression.

In India, on the other hand, things were considered to have been more satisfactory in a social sense. There were, for example, the very well known remarks made by Lord Harris, the later nineteenth-century Governor of Bombay, who would later become a major power in the MCC (the Marylebone Cricket Club) that was (and, in many senses, remains) the scat of world governance for cricket. He was convinced that until Indians could play the game with great skill, they would not be fit to exercise any sort of political authority in the manner to which the British had become accustomed. Nearly 50 years later another old cricketer and India hand, E.H.D. Sewell, repeated the sentiment:

> Chaos would prevail in India if we were ever so foolish as to depart and leave the natives to run their own show. Ye Gods! What a salad of confusion, of bungle, of mismanagement, and far worse, would be the instant result. These grand people will go anywhere and do anything if led by us.
> And the key to much of what happened later lay in the fact that people like Harris could influence elements of local communities into the same psychological state. [41]

J.M. Framjee Patel, for example, was among the earliest of Bombay citizens to take up the cricket cause. Just after the turn of the century he wrote: 'There is something magical about sport, which makes the Englishman forget his racial and habitual reserve.' [42] From there it was a short step to the idea of success in cricket suggesting success in social 'progress' under imperial tutelage. Patel noted, for example, that cricket had been a great influence in the reformation of Parsi dress, manners and literature, and that the Parsi victory over Vernon's English Eleven in 1890 was a compelling moment in the evolution of Indian political pride and confidence.

As Bill Mandle [43] pointed out powerfully, the Australian story was similar in one respect. The colonial mentality there measured the progress of a nation and culture, newer than India, by the growth of a game that had come to symbolize English achievement. Such was the cultural power invested in games throughout the British world by the turn of the century, no matter how illusory those transformations might have been. [44] Perhaps the best example of this was seen during the 1932–3 Bodyline tour, when the Australian captain was depicted widely in Australia as having behaved in a more English-like manner than the English captain himself, who seemed to have forgotten the behavioural principles of cricket. [45]

At this point some of the nuances in all this may be detected, because amidst the high-flown rhetoric about game, empire and character lay trends that would become much more interesting. Take the later nineteenth-century Bombay case, for example. Framjee Patel believed that cricket helped bring the variant social groups 'together', but Harris had a quite different view. While he saw the potential for cohesion, whatever that meant, he also saw that the game was about social separation as much as unity. The game was riven by caste and, realistically, by class with the two categories intermixed. As Ramachandra Guha [46] has sketched out recently, the contest between Parsis, Hindus and Muslims was evident from the beginning in Bombay cricket.

Two general theoretical considerations may be inserted here. The first is the idea of community. It is very clear that throughout cricket history there has been a strong undercurrent of the 'imagined community' as outlined so helpfully by Benedict Anderson. [47] That is, there was throughout the British imperial world the idea that a game of bat and ball united in outlook, attitude, political and social belief like-minded men (and this was a gendered game, of course) who held a common outlook. That was the reason cricket success was seen to imply social 'progress'. That was why players such as Ranji and Woodfull, to take two different examples (and Worrell and Martin Donnelly to take two others from elsewhere in the cricket empire), were given so much emphasis – they showed that colonials could become 'Englishmen' via cricket. The strand was long-lived. Throughout his time as Australian Prime Minister through the 1950s and 1960s, Sir Robert Menzies in his papers always referred to Lords as 'the cathedral of cricket'.

The second, paradoxically, is of separation. In Australia, for example, it may be argued that the parity of the field has been accorded to India only very recently. That is, it was not enough just to play cricket in order to gain esteem; it was necessary to win or, at very least, to appear competitive. As outlined nicely by Mike Coward, early interactions were dominated by an Australian sense of superiority, driven by a potent mixture of racial and playing arrogance. [48] In 1936, for example, when an Australian touring side was hosted privately in India, it was against a background of extreme reluctance on the part of the Australian Board of Control. While the board capitulated, it restricted severely the players who could go with the result that 'names' such as Woodfull, Ponsford, Mailey and Kippax were all missing. The great Vijay Hazare played against the Australians at Indore, and considered the board's approach to have been 'dog in the manger'. [49]

In 1948 Hazare toured Australia as part of the first visiting team to leave the 'new' India after independence. Of his teammates selected initially, the creation of Pakistan saw Fazal Mahmood drop out and move to the new state while Mushtaq Ali stayed behind in view of the political circumstances. Nonetheless, the team to visit Australia was the first to represent independent India. When Gandhi was assassinated the team debated about whether or not to return home, but decided to play on because it thought it 'had a duty to do', and two minutes' silence were observed at the Melbourne test. Despite some outstanding play, including Hazare himself making two centuries in one Test, the tourists lost the series 4–0. Significantly, though, Hazare depicted the tourists as having come to play, learn and enjoy. That was in significant contrast to the approach adopted by the Australians under the leadership of Bradman near the end of his career.

This was a tour, then, redolent with political and emotional drama, yet the Australian public had only the vaguest sense of what it all meant. That is, while the game was being won by Australia, the emotion was supplied by India. From then on, a steady stream of contests ensued. The memories from the Australian side tended to be of riots, mysterious spin bowling, incompetent organization and an unbridled enthusiasm for cricket. One of the best examples of that involved the Australian women's team that toured India in 1975. [50] There were poor hotels, complex travel arrangements, bad organization and enormous crowds along with media coverage. The Australian men's tour in 1979 was a watershed, [51] and after that much more care was taken to prepare Australian sides for what they might encounter – but in 2005 an under-19 team went off with no cultural awareness training whatsoever. On the Indian side there was enormous reverence for the history of success enjoyed by Australia, for Bradman (who never visited the subcontinent despite several invitations to do so) and for players such as Dean Jones whose double century in Chennai in 1986–7 was instrumental in Test cricket's second only tie.

Throughout this, of course, lies the grain of Orientalism and cultural disjunction. The stereotypes of either side are not the norm, but their impact is significant. Much of this is endemic in players and commentators. During India's 1999–2000 tour, for example, Harsha Bhogle consistently broadcast in an even-handed, the-game-is-the-thing way. Australian-based commentators, notably Tony Greig, took a partisan approach, and as India slid into a playing slump produced the old adages about spirit, cohesion and will. This was highlighted in a Melbourne one-day match when a section of Indian supporters rather half-heartedly threw plastic bottles onto the field in exasperation at the dismissal of Saurav Ganguly. It was not a serious incident by any means, but for days Australian commentators pontificated about how serious a blot this was upon the game of cricket in Australia.

That was symbolic of a wider set of geopolitical confusions. In recent years there has been a small explosion of works aiming to understand or even improve Indo-Australian relations. There is a history to this, of course, with Bertram Stevens (premier of New South Wales from 1932 to 1939) foreseeing a major trade interaction between the two countries as early as 1946. [52] A parliamentary inquiry in 1998 [53] noted an absence of cultural and commercial awareness – the subtitle of the report, 'Commonwealth, Common Language, Cricket and Beyond' almost summed up the underlying problem perfectly. A 2003 collection [54] rehearsed a litany of missed opportunities and problems, with A.N. Ram [55] referring to cricket as the symbol of a predominantly dormant and passive relationship. A 2004 collection [56] was similar in tone. Most if not all these sorts of collections reference cricket in some way, as does Foreign Minister Downer and many of his colleagues, yet the references remain at the largely superficial level. The interesting thing is that Australian cricket authorities have clearly now taken the Indian game much more seriously than before, not simply because of the playing competitiveness but also because understanding the commercial aspects of the Indian game holds the future for Australia. This was very clearly the case in 2004, given the interest in and attention paid to Australia's tour of India. If that does not reverberate in those wider reflections, then it should, because understanding the cricket conundrum might well be a cultural key to far more significant understanding.

For the present, though, two teams engage in a game while the two cultures do not. While that remains, the two countries will never be 'joined in cricket'. Rather, they will play at cricket and maintain one of the few public arenas where the two cultures can measure each other off.

Acknowledgement

An earlier version of this article appeared as 'Identity Spin: Imagined Cultures In Australian and Indian Cricket', in a special issue of *South Asia* (XXIII, 2000).

Notes

[1] Tim Harcourt, 'An Indian Summer...Without The Great Steve Waugh', Austrade media release, 2004. Available online at http://www.austrade.gov.au/corporate/layout/0.
[2] Mangan, *Athleticism in the Victorian and Edwardian Public School.*
[3] Personal observations by author, 1996.
[4] Australia India Council, *Annual Report*, 1999–2000.
[5] Personal observations by author of the Australian Vice-Chancellors' Committee (AVCC) delegation to India, 1998.
[6] Australian High Commission, 'Australia Promotes Excellence In Cricket and Education', news release, 26 March 2004.
[7] Alexander Downer, 'Australia And India – Not Just Cricket', speech at the Indian Confederation of India, 9 June 2005, available online at http://www.foreignminister.gov.au/speeches/2005/05050609_australia_and_india_not_j....
[8] M.K. Dharma Raja, 'India-Australia Cricket Links', Government of India Press Information Bureau, 1 Dec. 1999, available online at http://pib.nic.in/feature/fe1299/f0112991.html.
[9] Gurry, *India: Australia's Neglected Neighbour?*
[10] Yarwood, *Walers.*
[11] Lowenthal, *The Past Is A Foreign Country.*
[12] Personal observations by author of the AVCC delegation to India, 1998.

[13] Stoddart, 'Caribbean Cricket'.

[14] Fishman, *Calypso Cricket*.

[15] Greg Baum, 'Caught In Two Lands, Minds', *The Age & Sydney Morning Herald Cricket* (online), 9 Jan. 1999.

[16] Greg Baum and Martin Blake, 'The Seamy Side Of Cricket', *The Age & Sydney Morning Herald Cricket* (online), 9 Jan. 1999.

[17] Said, *Orientalism*.

[18] Tony Coady, 'Sport Brought To Book', *The Age* (online), 16 Dec. 1998.

[19] Majumdar, *Twenty Two Yards To Freedom*.

[20] *New Straits Times*, 1997.

[21] Swami, 'On A Sticky Wicket'.

[22] 'Government Firm On Holding Match In Capital', *Times of India*, 8 Jan. 1999.

[23] 'Pak Team Will Not Be Allowed To Play In India: Thackeray', India Current Affairs (online), 21 Jan. 1999.

[24] 'Triumphant Tiger', *Deccan Herald*, 23 Jan. 1999.

[25] Swami, 'On A Sticky Wicket'.

[26] 'Field Of Dreams', *Times of India*, 29 Jan. 1999.

[27] Uday Khandeparkar, 'India Party Drops Threat To Pakistan Tour', *Sportsweb*, 22 Jan. 1999, available online at http://www.sportsweb.com/1999/01/21/cricket-pakistan3.htm.

[28] Bhogle.

[29] Stoddart, 'Dennis Lillee'.

[30] Rahul Bedi, 'Border Conflict Bowled Over', *The Australian*, 1999.

[31] Roberts and James, *Crosscurrents*.

[32] Kuldip Lal, 'Once More, With Feeling', *Newsline*, March 2004, available online at http://www.newsline.com.pk/NewsMar2004/sportsMar2004.htm.

[33] A. Haseeb Drabu, 'Cricket and Politics: India Should Lose for Diplomatic Gains on Kashmir', *South Asia Tribune* 82 (7–13 March 2004), available online at http://www.satribune.com/archives/mar7_13_04/P1_cricket.htm.

[34] 'Cricket Special', *Outlook*, 7 March 2005.

[35] Lalita Ramdas, 'The Politics of Cricket & Some Reflections' (2003), avilable online at http://www.sacw.net/2002/lramdasMarch03.html.

[36] Nandy, *The Tao of Cricket*.

[37] Bhogle, 'A Question of Culture'.

[38] Sissons, *The Players*.

[39] Mangan, *Athleticism in the Victorian and Edwardian Public School*; Sandiford, *Cricket and the Victorians*; Brookes, *English Cricket*

[40] Sissons and Stoddart, *Cricket and Empire*.

[41] Sewell, *An Outdoor Wallah*.

[42] Patel, *Stray Thoughts On Indian Cricket*.

[43] Mandle, 'Cricket and Australian Nationalism'.

[44] Stoddart, 'Caribbean Cricket'.

[45] Sissons and Stoddart, *Cricket and Empire*.

[46] Guha, 'Cricket and Politics in Colonial India'.

[47] Benedict Anderson, *Imagined Communities*.

[48] Coward, *Cricket Beyond The Bazaar*.

[49] Hazare, *Long Innings*.

[50] Butcher, *Ice-Cream With Chilli Powder*.

[51] Merriman.

[52] Stevens, *New Horizon*.

[53] Commonwealth of Australia, *Australia's Trade Relationship With India*.
[54] Rao, *India and Australia*.
[55] Ram, 'India-Australia Relations'.
[56] Gopal and Rumley, *India and Australia*.

References

Anderson, Benedict. *Imagined Communities: Reflections On the Origin and Spread of Nationalism*. London: Verso, 1991.

Australia India Council. *Annual Report*. Canberra: Commonwealth of Australia, 1999–2000.

Bhogle, Harsha. 'A Question Of Culture', *Sportstar* 22 (4): (23–29 Jan. 1999).

——. 'The Charm Of Community Cricket'. *Sportstar* 22 (15): (10–16 April 1999).

Brookes, Christopher. *English Cricket*. London: Weidenfeld & Nicolson, 1978.

Butcher, Betty. *Ice-Cream With Chilli Powder*. Melbourne: Butcher, 1996.

Commonwealth of Australia. *Australia's Trade Relationship With India*. report from the Joint Standing Committee on Foreign Affairs, Defence and Trade. Canberra: Commonwealth of Australia, 1998.

Coward, Mike. *Cricket Beyond The Bazaar*. Sydney: Allen & Unwin. 1990.

Fishman, Roland. *Calypso Cricket: The Inside Story of the 1991 Windies Tour*. Sydney: Gee, 1991.

Gopal, D. and Dennis Rumley. *India and Australia: Issues and Opportunities*. Delhi: Authors Press, 2004.

Guha, Ramachandra. 'Cricket and Politics in Colonial India'. *Past & Present* 161 (Nov. 1998).

Gurry, Meg. *India: Australia's Neglected Neighbour? 1947–1996*. Brisbane: Griffith University, 1996.

Hazare, Vijay. *Long Innings*. Delhi: Rupa, 1981.

Lowenthal, David. *The Past Is A Foreign Country*. Cambridge: Cambridge University Press, 1988.

Majumdar, Boria. *Twenty Two Yards To Freedom: a Social History of Indian Cricket*. New Delhi: Penguin, 2004.

Mandle, W.F. 'Cricket and Australian Nationalism in the Nineteenth Century'. *Journal of the Royal Australian Historical Society* 59 (Dec. 1973).

Mangan, J.A. *Athleticism in the Victorian and Edwardian Public School*. Cambridge: Cambridge University Press, 1981.

Nandy, Ashis. *The Tao of Cricket: On Games of Destiny and the Destiny of Games*. New Delhi: Penguin, 1989.

Patel, J.M. Framjee. *Stray Thoughts On Indian Cricket*. Bombay: Times Press, 1905.

Ram, A.N. 'India-Australia Relations – a Saga of Missed Opportunities: The Road Ahead' In *India and Australia (New Horizons)*, edited by P.V. Rao. New Delhi: Mittal.2003.

Rao, P.V., ed. *India and Australia (New Horizons)*. New Delhi: Mittal, 2003.

Roberts, Michael and Alf, James. *Crosscurrents*. Walal Walla Press, 1998.

Said, Edward. *Orientalism*. Harmondsworth: Penguin, 1979.

Sandiford, Keith A.P. *Cricket and the Victorians*. London: Scolar Press, 1994.

Sewell, E.H.D. *An Outdoor Wallah*. London: Stanley Paul, 1945.

Sissons, Ric. *The Players*. London: Pluto, 1988.

Sissons, Ric and Brian, Stoddart. *Cricket and Empire*. Sydney: Allen & Unwin, 1984.

Stevens, Bertram. *New Horizon*. Sydney: Huston, 1946.

Stoddart, Brian. 'Dennis Lillee: The Sportsman' In *Westralian Portraits*, edited by Lyall Hunt. Perth: University of Western Australia Press, 1979.

——. 'Caribbean Cricket: The Role of Sport in Emerging Small-Nation Politics'. *International Journal*, 43 (4): (1988).

——. 'Sport, Cultural Imperialism and Colonial Response in the British Empire'. *Comparative Studies in Society and History* 30 (4): (Oct. 1988).

—— 'Sticky Wickets: Cricket In The British World', paper delivered to the 'British World, 1880–1980' conference at the Institute of Commonwealth Studies, London.

Swami, Praveen. 'On A Sticky Wicket'. *Frontline*, 18 Dec. 1998: 31–4.

Yarwood, A.T. *Walers*. Melbourne: Melbourne University Press, 1989.

Feel Good, Goodwill and India's Friendship Tour of Pakistan, 2004: Cricket, Politics and Diplomacy in Twenty-First-Century India

Kausik Bandyopadhyay

India's cricket tour of Pakistan in early 2004 evoked a plethora of responses in Indian public life. From learned to laity people began to consider cricket as a means to various ends: a political instrument to generate electoral confidence, a diplomatic ploy to accelerate peace process, an economic means to ameliorate the neighbour's pecuniary distress, a cultural arena to assert cricketing muscle, an emotional tool to soothe traditional enmity, and so on. More importantly, when it comes to India's cricketing relations with Pakistan, the apparent popular perception of an ever-rising enmity stands in striking contrast to the friendly ties between the two cricket boards at international level while the game still remains one major and viable confidence-building arena in the long-term process of normalization of diplomatic relations between the two neighbouring states. This essay seeks to explore, understand and analyze such varied representations of the tour as evident in popular media in the wider context of domestic political debates, sub-continental diplomatic relations and purely cricketing arch-rivalry.

We are going there to better the relations between the two countries, and I hope the Indian Government will not allow a handful of people to deprive cricket lovers of some action and tension packed cricket.

– Wasim Akram [1]

There's no place for sentiment when India meets Pakistan in cricket. My very first experience in Pakistan makes it amply clear that the political differences between these two countries get translated into this game. If you are batting, you feel that even the fielders are hostile. I wish they played more with a spirit of competition than hostility. I must have played about 20 matches against them. It's the spectators who make it so electrifying because people are so tense. No politician can

Kausik Bandyopadhyay, North Bengal University.

understand the level of this hostility until and unless they go and play on the ground.

– Kapil Dev [2]

I don't really agree with this *goodwill* issue – it's a cricket match and both teams are competing to win.

– Sourav Ganguly [3]

India's Pak tour will surely go down in history as a googly that stumped the jingoists, albeit the debate will go on about how much the tour was about keeping 'India shining'. But then, politics and sports have always had a love-hate relation.

– Boria Majumdar [4]

Introduction

Cricket is the de facto *national* game in India, if not its only secular religion of late. Indians, it is often suggested, likes talking, reading and writing on cricket. Indians love to watch their national cricket team play. They worship their cricketing icons. They also invest safely in the 'cricket industry'. Cricket's pre-eminence in Indian life has also led to its construction and interpretation in terms of political transition, social tension, economic transformation, diplomatic relations or cultural development. And when it comes to India's cricketing relations with Pakistan, it begins to signify different meanings and convey different messages to different people in India: nationalism, communalism, war, infiltration, insurgency, terrorism, diplomacy, peace, election, cultural exchange, commercial boom, cricketing conflict and so on. The Indian cricket team's tour of Pakistan in March–April 2004 is an excellent case in point here. The tour evoked a plethora of responses in Indian public life. From learned to laity, people began to consider cricket as a means to various ends: a political instrument to generate electoral confidence, a diplomatic ploy to accelerate a peace process, an economic means to ameliorate the neighbour's pecuniary distress, a cultural arena to assert cricketing muscle, an emotional tool to soothe traditional enmity and so on. For example, the apparent popular perception of an ever-rising enmity between the two nations stands in striking contrast to the friendly ties between the two cricket boards at international level while the game still remains one major and viable confidence-building arena in the long-term process of normalization of diplomatic relations between the two neighbouring states. This essay seeks to explore, understand and analyse such varied representations of the tour as evidenced in popular media in the wider context of domestic political debates, subcontinental diplomatic relations and purely cricketing arch-rivalry.

Indo-Pak Cricket and Nationalism: the 2003 World Cup Experience

The partition of 1947 and the resultant turmoil triggered off hatred, distrust and prejudice in almost every sphere of activity in the sub-continent. [5]

Interestingly, it was cricket that formed the first bilateral exchange in 1952 when Pakistan, led by Abdul Hafeez Kardar, toured India, evoking a spontaneous, albeit tense, response. It was reciprocated two years later when India paid the first official visit under Vinoo Mankad, generating an equally sensitive response. Yet since 1947 a 'cricket conflict' brewed simultaneously between the two countries, based on the nationalist antagonism between the two teams and backed by passionate fans on both sides. This nationalist fervour perpetuated by the history of hostility cuts across class, caste, ethnicity and gender and leads to unanimous support for the national team. For the millions of India and Pakistan, cricket has become the ultimate test of patriotic zeal and loyalty. On and off the pitches, cricket fans vent their passions against the enemy country – the *other* – in forms that range from the funny to the grotesque. Those among 'us' who may happen to support 'them' for their sportsmanship usually get rebuked for their suspect sense of nationalism, citizenship and loyalty. As one sports writer has recently commented:

> Today Indo-Pak cricket offers a striking case study to see how a political conflict between two states has trickled down to the mass level and saturated the mass psyche to such an extent, that political hostilities are not only played on the Line of Control but also on the cricket field. This mass psyche of a purported nationalist conflict has been also revved by years of state propaganda against the enemy country, which permeated in all forms of interaction and exchange with the enemy – be it sports or war. [6]

The last World Cup may be said to have triggered off and given full fruition to, this new brand of *cricketing nationalism* in India. A brief analysis of the importance of the India–Pakistan match in the cup and its impact on the psyche of the Indian public at that time may serve as a useful exemplar in this context.

Although it has recently been argued quite rightly by a young sports historian that the communal character of cricket sometimes enhances its commercial prospects, [7] in the light of the past 16 years' experience of turbulence and instability in Indian politics, the desirability of such a development is a questionable proposition. In the context of the present political equation, where the lines between nationalism and communalism sometimes seem to be extremely blurred and ambiguous in the post-Godhra age, [8] as well as the rising heat of Indo-Pak foreign relations over the Kashmir issue after Pokhran [9] and Kargil, [10] an India–Pakistan cricket match in a World Cup, especially in its public appeal, cannot be isolated from its overtly political/communal overtones. [11] Victory or defeat in such a match is now looked on as a test of national superiority. Let me give a few instances that would hopefully substantiate my point.

Immediately after India's victory over Pakistan in the World Cup group league match on 1 March 2003, the streets and lanes of Kolkata reverberated with the sound of blowing conches, bursting crackers and the chanting of slogans. At Kalighat, [12] many were seen waving national flags with pictures of Sachin Tendulkar struck in the middle of the *Asoke Chakra*. Cries of 'Sachin! Sachin!' rent the night, alternating with shouts of 'Pakistan hai hai!'. [13] Gujarat, on the other hand, witnessed incidents of

Muslims being stopped from celebrating the occasion. [14] Celebrations led to rioting, injuries and one death in Ahmedabad. [15] Violence followed also in Bangalore during the post-victory celebrations. [16] In all these places, prohibitory orders were to be imposed and security to be tightened in the face of such incidents. More importantly, the reaction of Indian politicians to the victory requires careful notice. Prime Minister Atal Bihari Vajpayee and his deputy, L.K. Advani, also watched the game on television back home. Advani promptly called up the team in the hotel to congratulate the players. [17] Next morning, Finance Minister Jaswant Singh sent a congratulatory message to the team and consequently announced tax concessions on World Cup prize money. [18] Army chief N.C. Vij congratulated the boys over the telephone, too, for their thumping win. [19] Considering all this, it seems, it did not matter to them if India could not make it to the super six, semis or final. Many sensible Indians became critical of this irresponsible behaviour of Indian politicians and even the general public do not seem to have agreed to Jaswant Singh's offer of tax sops to India's extraordinarily well-off cricketers. Here is one voice that furnishes a logical touch to this sentiment:

> While the entire nation salutes Sachin and his men for their epoch-making win against Pakistan, likening it to a victory in war or raising high-voltage jingoistic cries – as our politicians and military brass did – does not augur well for the rapprochement we seek so eagerly with our neighbour. And then to have Jaswant Singh declaring that it did not matter if we won the World Cup or not, and offering tax sops! No wonder our country is in the financial ness it is in. If our cricketers have any sense, they should refuse the Finance Minister's offer in the interest of the nation. [20]

However, amidst the general trend of escalating belligerence over the victory, the best antidote came from the man who creatively and aggressively marshalled this new-look Indian team, Saurav Ganguly. 'Beating Pakistan does not mean we have won the World Cup,' said the Indian captain. 'A lot of work remains to be done and we don't want to be caught napping.' [21]

The question that really surfaces as a result of this incidental communalization and politicization of cricket (which is, of course, neither a universal phenomenon in India nor universally endorsed by the learned or the laity) is whether it is possible to resolve or dissolve these relational complexities between sport and politics in this era of 'hyper-nationalism' where an Indo-Pak match becomes a war by other means. Cricket historian Ramachandra Guha addresses the question more succinctly: 'As society and politics became more polarized, cricket was drawn into the vortex.' [22] In this specific context of communal polarization on the rise, the successes of India's two young guns, Zaheer Khan and Muhammad Kaif, have become an emblem of both solace and hope for the Indian Muslims. Ashis Nandy makes the point more clear:

> For Muslim youth, the presence of Zaheer and Kaif represents an area open to them. If these two can make it, so can they…nationalism is getting to be a headache in India. …Muslims all over are as paranoid as those living in the

riot-prone states of western India. They know India is their country and they will fight it out here, which is why the achievements of Muslim players make them feel good. [23]

The subsequent sections of this essay will try to show how such imagining or imaging of cricket performances could be appropriated by the state as well as its representatives to better effect in order to serve the presumed cause of the nation.

Diplomacy, Nationalism and the 'Goodwill' Series

The two countries did not play any cricket series for two long periods – between 1961 and 1978; and between 1990 and 1999 – due to political bad blood. Then, should we make the point that cricket has the capacity to break the political jinx? Rohit Brijnath thinks otherwise: 'Cricket will not heal wounds. But perhaps it can play a minor role. Perhaps this experiment can only work if we remember it is just cricket, that no nation is a lesser one for losing or a superior one for winning.' [24] Yet, in most circles, the resumption of cricket ties was seen as a political breakthrough, elevating (!) cricket to one of the confidence-building measures that the two countries have gingerly embarked upon. The most glaring example of this attitude is Shaharyar M. Khan, the chairman of the Pakistan Cricket Board. Khan, while writing his classic *Cricket: A Bridge of Peace*, which throws light on his experiences as manager of the Pakistan cricket team's tour of India (January to April 1999) and of South Africa (January to March 2003) acknowledged at the outset:

> I had not intended to publish my impressions until the unexpectedly warm welcome by the people of India to the 'enemy' team. Their enthusiastic response planted the seed in my mind that cricket's vast untapped energy could be harnessed for understanding and tolerance. ... After a lifetime in diplomacy, attempting, most unsuccessfully, to overcome tension, hostility and conflict, I realized that cricket could act as bridge of peace. [25]

And reflecting on overall impressions of the tour, he felt that 'its primary success had been at the political and public relations level'. [26] His continuous attempt to directly relate cricket to issues of politics and diplomacy was quite obvious:

> As the tour progressed, the groundswell of public acclaim provided the ideal stage in both countries for Mr Vajpayee's bus journey to Lahore. The 40,000 strong crowd in Chennai giving a standing ovation to the victorious Pakistan team, ordinary people lined deep in Gwalior to wave the team good bye, the remarkable warmth shown to Pakistani visitors in Mohali where Sikh girls painted both Indian and Pakistani flags on their cheeks, the spontaneous chants of 'Pakistan-Hindustan *dosti Zindabad*' by the Pakistani element of the crowd, were images that seemed unbelievable when seen against the backdrop of the Shiv Sena threat to the team before the tour began and the daily vitriol exchanged between the two governments. The Indian public's response seemed to carry a clear message. It was, that though the two countries had been to war three times in fifty years, faced off, eyeball to eyeball, across the Line of Control in Kashmir and had exploded

nuclear devices to intimidate each other, the time had come for peace and mutual respect, so that poverty, violence and despair could be turned back. This message was as clear as the minarets of the Taj Mahal on a sunny day. [27]

In 2004, when people on both sides yarned for peace, the cricket tour, it was argued, after all the hype of uncertainty and security concerns, 'should pave a new road to constructive friendship and understanding'. [28] While the tour provided a great opportunity to the Pakistan government to demonstrate to the rest of the world its willingness to shake off its bad image that had grown up since the demolition of World Trade Center Towers on 9/11, it could also help re-educate the minds of India and Pakistan conditioned to think in traditional ways about each other. As Asif Iqbal rightly put it:

> It is good to see politicians of India and Pakistan finally batting together for the cause of peace and cricket in the sub-continent. I mention both peace and cricket in the same sentence advisedly, for here is a situation in which both can feed off each other, each enhancing and enriching the other. If nothing else, the tour will show the leaders of the two countries how much genuine affection there is between people on either side of the great divide and that, hopefully, will cause many to stop and ponder. [29]

Imran Khan, the legendary Pakistani cricketer, too argued: 'When the two countries are trying to become friendly, cricket plays a healing role, cricket becomes a cement in bonding the countries together.' [30] Saba Karim's comment is perhaps most revealing in this context: 'When the relation between the two nations is strained, sportspersons can act as ambassadors and go a long way to heal the rifts.' [31] It was thus obvious that the tour had had a political dimension as teams played in an emerging climate of rapprochement and peace. Even Colin Powell, the US Secretary of State, on his visit to India during the series in March, expressed the hope that the enthusiasm generated by the revival of cricketing ties would certainly have a positive impact on bilateral peace process. [32]

Sport, particularly cricket, between these two countries has always been played with nationalist fervour – and even fear. Many of the early tests between India and Pakistan were drawn, both teams showing an excess of caution, petrified of losing to their neighbour. A loss against any other team did not matter – both teams were habitual losers until the 1970s – but a defeat to their neighbour rankled deeply. Abbas Ali Beg's promising career is said to have been derailed because of an average run of scores against Pakistan, when a similar streak against any other side would not have mattered. Javed Miandad's last-ball six off Chetan Sharma still rankles in the Indian psyche as a low point for the *nation*. In every World Cup, Indians treated their game against Pakistan with as much importance as the tournament itself, not caring if they lost the cup as long as they beat Pakistan. When Pakistan lost the 1996 World Cup match in Bangalore, the house of their captain Wasim Akram was stoned.

Sport has always been described in terms of war. Games are often described as 'battles', teams are often said to have been 'routed', 'slaughtered' or 'demolished', in a vocabulary of alpha-male aggression. 'Sport is an unfailing cause of ill-will' – thus said George Orwell. In a celebrated essay written in 1945, Orwell argued:

> I am always amazed when I hear people saying that sport creates goodwill between the nations, and that if only the common peoples of the world could meet one another at football or cricket, they would have no inclination to meet on the battlefield. Even if one didn't know from concrete examples (the 1936 Olympic Games, for instance) that international sporting contests lead to orgies of hatred, one could deduce it from general principles. [33]

The point Orwell went on to make was that all sport was competitive and involved winning or losing, and thus pride. A sport between nations thus took on bigger proportions, as it involved national pride – much as war would. Indeed, Orwell was bold enough the question the very act of playing and following sport that is representational: 'as soon as the question of prestige arises, as soon as you feel that you and some larger unit will be disgraced if you lose, the most savage combative instincts are aroused.' [34] He did not of course suggest that 'sport is one of the main causes of international rivalry; big scale sport is itself, I think, merely another effect of the causes that have produced nationalism'. [35] Sport thus remains to Orwell 'a mimic warfare', 'bound up with hatred, jealousy, boastfulness, disregard of all rules and sadistic pleasure in witnessing violence'. [36] While many other bi-national rivalries exist in sport – the Ashes in cricket and Brazil–Argentina in soccer for example – none are quite so fierce and filled with 'ill-will' as that between India and Pakistan.

Media in the twenty-first century perhaps play the most important role in representing sport as a metaphor for war. Whenever India and Pakistan play each other in cricket, the media talk of the game as a metaphor for war – and perversely, with a sense of glee and anticipation. The feelings that India–Pakistan cricket inspires are extreme, and sentiments like pride and honour *are* affected by victory or defeat, much as they would be in a war. [37] Naturally, when India prepared for a full tour of Pakistan in March–April 2004, media representations began to mould the public imagining of the same in more ways than one.

For Indians and Pakistanis, the people of the other nationality have been dehumanized through decades of mutual distrust and nationalistic propaganda. That is why intellectuals in both countries stress the importance of people-to-people contact, so that the other can be seen as human again, and one can feel empathy with them. Cricket can definitely play a part in this process. It has been argued with some conviction that 'the more we see our opponents, the more we are exposed to their humanness, and the less the mythic differences seem'. [38] The Indo-Pak series promised and provided a unique opportunity to *humanize*, if not *normalize* the strained relations between the two nations. The cricketing skills on display, the emotions on the field, all draw people on one side towards the other side – and the appreciation can sometimes go beyond national pride. The spontaneous applause that the Pakistan team got from the Chennai crowds when they won the enthralling Test there in 1999 is a great example of this spirit. The cordial and hearty reception of the Indian team on its arrival in each city of Pakistan, the presence of sporting crowds at every venue cheering with passion on the occasion of every Indian victory with true sportsmanlike spirit and the overall attitude of friendliness and hospitality during the 2004 tour also provided a series of such desired occasions. [39] That exposure to cricketers and ex-cricketers from the other country can also help foster an ambience of mutual benefit is perfectly illustrated by *The Shaz and Waz Show*, jointly hosted by Ravi Shastri and Wasim Akram, two most popular Indian and Pakistani ex-cricketers on ESPN-Star Sports. If the two nations play cricket regularly, it seems, then perhaps it can move from being a metaphor for war to a vehicle of peace.

'Peace Tour', 'Feel Good' and Electoral Politics

Despite the enormous media hype on the tour, representing it as a diplomatic tool or a confidence-building measure in the normalization of relations between the two countries, it is important to keep in mind the confusion and hesitancy, speculation and sensationalism that preceded it. With the escalation of militancy in Kashmir in the mid-1990s, culminating in the Kargil War in 1999 just after the conclusion of the Pakistan tour of India, the Indian government imposed an embargo on Indo-Pak cricket series for a while. Interestingly enough, as Kingshuk Chatterjee has argued, the government seemed to manufacture a semi-consensus on the issue with relative ease 'as part of its nation-building project based on the premise of aggressive nationalism'. [40] All through 2003, the debate or what Chatterjee calls 'the lack of it' on the advisability of playing a series in Pakistan in 2004 recurred on the pages of newspapers and magazines and on TV channels. Even when the political and diplomatic relationships between the two countries improved enough to suggest a resumption of cricketing relations towards the end of 2003, the actual decision to clear India's tour of Pakistan, albeit again manufactured smoothly by the government, was fraught with many dilemmas.

The media tirelessly speculated during the months preceding the actual official decision to clear the tour [41] that the tour was in serious doubt. Although security reasons were cited in a media campaign pressing for postponement, the real fear was that any 'untoward incident' during the series would spoil the 'feel good' factor before the polls. [42] There were several arguments both in favour of and against the proposed tour. [43] Some held that the risk was simply not worth it: an attack or assault on the team by motivated parties would in a stroke destroy the peace process and set off a series of calamities. [44] Some reasoned that not touring would be the real sabotage of the peace process, preventing, as it would, the rare opportunity of thousands of people meeting thousands of people across the border and watching a game. [45] Yet some others argued that it was precisely because of the danger posed by thousands of people meeting thousands of people and watching a game that the tour must not proceed. [46] More prudent politicians such as L.K. Advani, the influential Home Minister and the veteran leader of the Bharatiya Janata Party (BJP), were in favour of shelving the tour until after the general elections slated to begin on 20 April. He sensed – but definitely not the people, as the polls would later show – this heavy ephemeral buzz, a 'feel good' factor sweeping through the nation, and what might a possible cricket loss to Pakistan on the eve of polls do to that? And would such friendly overtures towards Pakistan before elections make the party look too soft in the eyes of the voters? [47]

The Ministry of External Affairs, on the other hand, was in favour of the tour because it feared that a postponement of the tour, a key confidence-building measure, would hit the peace process and expose Vajpayee's peace initiative as hollow. As one newspaper correspondent reported:

> It would have vitiated the atmosphere ahead of the official level dialogue between the two countries, beginning on Monday. Calling off the tour would have also taken away the current diplomatic advantage that Delhi has over Islamabad, the foreign office held. . . . Going back on any confidence-building measure would have invited questions about India's intentions of improving relations, it believed. [48]

Naturally, therefore, Vajpayee's success in clearing the tour despite Advani's reservations about the same was seen as 'a loss of face for the home ministry'. [49]

More importantly, it was widely argued that when Atal Bihari Vajpayee, the Indian Prime Minister, ahead of his government's re-election, cleared the Pakistan tour, despite objections from several quarters including those by Advani, he was trying to utilize cricket as a tool for forthcoming election propaganda against his political rival Sonia Gandhi, the Congress leader. As Sachidananda Murthy points out:

> The cricket tour has much at stake for Vajpayee. If Sachin Tendulkar and company overcome the nasty surprises readied by Javed Miandad, the BJP will tout it as another shining example of the feel-good factor. Even if the result is disappointing, the success of the tour would be touted as vindication of the friendly hand extended to Pervez Musharraf. [50]

That it was Vajpayee's political strategy to clear the tour, however, occasionally got vehemently critiqued by a few in the media on purely cricketing grounds. As Ashok V. Desai maintained:

> Before the boys in blue left, I thought it made no sense as cricket, and all sense as Vajpayan politics. It was crazy to send our best cricketers to play in April, when the temperature in Multan would be touching forty. They had just returned from an exciting tour of Australia; only an election-crazy politician would send them into another gruelling series even before they had unpacked their bags. [51]

Yet others argued that postponing the series for the time being would mean having to play in May, 'in the most hellishly searing innards of summer, where cricketers and spectators alike would have fallen like flies'. [52] Moreover, both teams had a packed schedule of cricketing commitments beyond the summer. Some among the political circles therefore hinted at 'splitting the tour into two, holding only the Tests – "less excitable for the masses" – before the elections'. [53] Some others smelt a bane at the way expectations and preparations gathered momentum around the tour:

At the best of times, a tour to Pakistan is difficult because of the emotions involved. The pressures are political, diplomatic, emotional, and that's even before you get to the cricket. There is more the ruling coalition's hope that a successful tour will convert the electoral gains. That is a dangerous game to play given its glorious uncertainties. [54]

When the players met the Prime Minister before their departure for the tour, Vajpayee urged the Indian cricketers straightaway 'to not only win the matches in Pakistan but also win the hearts of the people there'. [55] He presented a bat to skipper Sourav Ganguly, on which was written 'Khel hi nahin, dil bhi jitiye' ('Not only the game, win hearts as well'). The placards waved around while Vajpayee met the team, featuring messages such as 'Best of Luck' and 'Atal ne diya cricket ka uphaar, India-Pakistan sadbhavana ka prachar' ('Atal's cricket gift spreads harmony in India and Pakistan'). [56] On the other hand, Priyanka Gandhi and Rahul Gandhi, representing the Congress outfit at the National Stadium in Karachi to watch India play, emphasized the need to develop people-to-people contact and cricket's potential role in the process. [57]

Many Indians were aware that this series might have major repercussions on the forthcoming elections. India's stirring performances in the one-day series led to animated discussion on whether the BJP would be back with a significant majority. As one commentator argued, 'It was as if every four or six hit by Ganguly's men counted for one more vote for the BJP. *India* was certainly *shining* and the "feel good" mood escalated no end.' [58] While the economic consequences of the tour were well understood, many also appreciated the government's decision to send the team ignoring electoral considerations. On the other hand, it was quite rightly pointed out that the decision was 'a well thought out electoral strategy'. [59] 'With three Muslims spearheading the Indian challenge in Pathan, Zaheer and Kaif, the liberal image of the BJP government was bolstered no end – a political masterstroke in election hour.' [60] However, the point that often begs for attention is that Vajpayee's decision might have been precipitated by purely cricketing considerations. Given India's consistently better performance on the field since the World Cup in February–March 2003, the team seemed to have a bright chance of beating the Pakistani team on its own soil. As Krishnamachari Srikkanth, former Indian captain, confidently argued on the eve of the tour: 'We are the favourites to win the series. Both batsmen and bowlers are at a higher confidence level having proved themselves in Australia.' [61]

When India won the first one-dayer, hectic appropriation followed within the political parties of India. Priyanka and Rahul Gandhi spent time in the Indian dressing room. Soon SMSs beeped to mobile phones in India: '*Bharat ko jitney ki sahi aas thi, Rahul aur Priyanka team ke paas the*! (India was in right mood to win as Rahul and Priyanka were with the team).' [62] The sender was 'Congress', though the party later claimed it to be a hoax. The BJP retaliated with its own SMS: '*Khel bhi jeeta, dil bhi jeeta. Shabash India!* (The match is won, hearts are won too. Hail India!).' [63] And Vajpayee got on to the phone to Ganguly. Vajpeyee rang him again on India's miraculous victory in the fourth one-dayer thanks to brilliant innings by Rahul Dravid and Muhammad Kaif. The Prime Minister, on the campaign trail, wooed Muslim voters in Uttar Pradesh by praising the 'splendid work done by one of your sons, Kaif'. [64]

It is beyond doubt that the series presented a great opportunity for people on both sides of the border to interact one-on-one. Everybody understood on the eve of the tour that there were bridges to be built and hearts to be won. In fact, it was a great chance for both nations to capitalize on the prevailing feel-good atmosphere. For example, Indian cricketers launched a polio eradication campaign in Pakistan and joined hands with the Ministry of Health to send a message across the country to that effect. Surely, the victory in Pakistan made the average Indian feel *better*. In fact, it was a lot more successful than the 'India shining' campaign of the BJP. Yet it did not probably have much to matter for the party in the subsequent election.

Indo-Pak Arch-Rivalry and the Cricketing Factor

It is axiomatic that over the years cricketing exchanges between India and Pakistan have been kept to a minimum primarily because of everlasting strained foreign relations. More than anything else, it has had a detrimental effect on the quality of cricket the two countries put on display on the rare occasions they play each other. The rarity of the occasion leads to an unusual hype and the pressure builds up to such an unrealistic extent that both teams approach the game in a completely negative frame of mind. As Asif Iqbal, former Pakistani cricketer, has noted, 'Avoiding defeat becomes the primary and overwhelming objective. The result is that both teams play at a level considerably below their full potential and in an atmosphere where fear of defeat is such a major component that often dull draws are the only outcome.' [65] With the progress in cricketing relations from the close of 1970s, some improvement took place in the 1980s as more matches were played and the approach to the game became more result-oriented. Yet thanks to another dry spell of series encounters in the 1990s, a fall-out of sensitive political relations, cricketing rivalry between the two became confined mostly to a few tri-series tournaments, a face-to-face Toronto meet in Canada for a few years and a match in the World Cup in every four years. Hence the on-field tensions and off-field perceptions around the Indo-Pak match became not only stiff but complex, particularly in the wider context of Indo-Pak diplomatic conflict over the Kashmir and associated terrorist infiltration issue as well as an unhealthy nuclear power rivalry in late 1990s. This complex cricketing jinx seems to be resolved with the decision of the Indian government to send its cricket team to Pakistan for a full tour in February 2004, albeit with numerous security conditions sorted out between the two cricket boards.

With a new season of hope beginning to unravel with India's tour, cricket was primarily looked on as more a diplomatic ploy to redress the domestic and foreign political priorities on the part of the Indian government than as a game that pits against each other two of world's most fascinating cricketing nations with temperamental cricketing skill and peerlessly passionate fanfare. As Sambit Bal, in a befitting editorial in *Wisden Asia Cricket*, argued:

> Given the bitter history these two nations share, every little thing that promotes goodwill is worth clutching at, but there is a danger here of overestimating the power of cricket. . . . But cricket is only a sport; it cannot be mistaken for diplomacy. The essence of sport is contest. Sportsmen cannot be expected to win and carry the candle of reconciliation at the same time. The life of an international cricketer is stressful enough; to burden him with national missions is stretching expectations. . . . Diplomacy should not hijack the main agenda of the tour, which is cricket. [66]

Specialist cricket commentators and experts were more concerned to focus on this overemphasis on cricket as diplomacy, politics or peace. Harsha Bhogle, for example, warned his readers at the outset:

> I fear too many people are under delusion that India are going to Pakistan on a political tour. If that feeling persists, India will lose. There is far too much talk about the business of cricket and the politics of the sub-continent and far too little about playing cricket. . . . The presence of our cricketers can be a political statement, but they must play cricket first. They can be ambassadors of peace they must be cricketers first. Merely landing in Pakistan will not be a victory, that is for politicians and poets, doing well and winning a cricket match will be. . . . And you certainly cannot have them [people] thinking that this is a tour where politics, diplomacy and the building of cultural bridges is paramount. It is not. It is about playing cricket first. Everything else must follow, it cannot lead. [67]

Bhogle's point has much to commend about it as it addresses the importance of the series in terms of purely cricketing skill and brain. The tour on the pitch was a time for the professionals and pragmatic people. It put on the agenda the uniqueness of preparation of an Indian team touring Pakistan. The Indian XI had to prepare well to contend with odds in Pakistan – the pace and bounce of the pitch, the reverse swing of the Pakistani pacers, the fierce spells of Shoaib Akhtar, oppressive security and many more. [68] The technical aspects of the game, therefore, should not be overlooked in the course of the apparent media hype of elevating sport to diplomatic/ political status. As S. Dinakar pointed out,

> An India-Pakistan clash is as much a test of nerves as skills. Mental strength or lack of it is often the decisive factor. India travels across the border with the confidence that it possesses a most accomplished batting line-up. And Pakistan waits with what has often proved a destructive bowling outfit. . . . Interestingly, while the sides' respective strengths could cancel each other out, how the supposed weak links – India's injury-hit bowling and Pakistan's largely inexperienced batting – fare could settle the issue. [69]

More importantly, this much-hyped blend of sport and diplomacy, cricket and goodwill inevitable brought forth another important relational reality – cricket and match-fixing. That India won the one-day series by the narrowest margin of 3–2 with some very close finishes in at least three matches gave some critics to see the shadow of match-fixing under which the series was played. In Pakistan itself, it was reported, it was a worm of suspicion that slowly grew through the series and on 24 March, the day of the final one-dayer, it became a faith. [70] People were seriously engaged in deciphering the list of 'mysterious moments' in the series to lend credence to their argument that 'the governments have mutually fixed it'. [71]

When the one-day series was poised at 1–1, Raju Mukherji, a former Indian cricketer, had already become suspicious of the true cricketing competition of the series. He wrote a newspaper article that opened with these words: 'Was the result of the first one-day international of the India-Pakistan revival series in Karachi a gift to a guest? And that of the second at Rawalpindi a return gesture on the part of the visitors?' [72] His objections came on purely cricketing grounds:

> In the first one-dayer in Karachi, the way the Pakistani batsman, Moin Khan, moved away to the leg side and converted two wide balls into legitimate deliveries, was enough to raise a few questions. In that eventful last over, Pakistan was actually in the driver's seat and appeared to have the match in its grasp. But in that absorbing over, Khan seemed to have had other, farreaching ideas. [73]

Mukherji wondered whether it was a fallout of the 'goodwill' both the Pakistani President and the Indian Prime Minister had been harping on. He concluded with a unique prayer: 'Now that the first two matches are over and the teams are at par, let us pray that the real cricket begins. Let us hope that from now on, the series is played in the spirit of competitive cricket and not in the spirit of gracious politics.' [74] Whether Mukherji's claim is justifiable or not is not really the important point here. Rather, that an ex-Indian cricketer could make such a claim midway through a tour certainly puts a question mark against the integrity of the cricketing fraternity of the two countries.

It was over the result of the fourth one-day international that a cloud of suspicion began to blossom. The International Cricket Council's anti-corruption unit rightly refused to say anything on the speculation, considering it unworthy of comment. When a journalist asked Rahul Dravid, one of the heroes of the match, 'What do you have to say about the impression this match was fixed?' he uncharacteristically reacted: 'Somebody get this guy out of here.' [75] To a similar question from a television channel, Pakistan's captain Inzamam-ul-Huq was reported to have said: 'Shut up.' [76]

Conclusion

Indo-Pakistan cricket, whatever its incidental nature or contextual relevance at one time or other, is at least in part a celebration of a common cricket culture. It takes on its political and commercial importance as much because of this common culture as because of the history of conflict. The knowledge, appreciation and enthusiasm for cricket are the pre-conditions for the eminence of this tie among global sporting rivalries. The media, however, are certainly not the only responsible parties. For broadcasters, sponsors and advertisers, the easiest way to maximize the return on their investment in cricket was to inflate its value by infusing it with extraneous emotional value. They were therefore tempted to hype the series as the ultimate confrontation, a contest of unique importance to the nation, as 'war minus the shooting', in George Orwell's words. That was where the cricket-loving public of both nations had a responsibility, 'to discipline the private sector super patriots, to insist on a sense of proportion'. [77] Manifestly, emotions run high in cricketing encounters between India and Pakistan. But the fund of mutual *goodwill* and *friendship* out there proved sufficient to handle these emotions, ensuring that mutual trust and reciprocal faith have come back at least in Indo-Pak cricketing relations. As Shaharyar Khan has observed of this 'most important, highly publicized and politically important cricket tour in Pakistan's cricketing history':

> The tour provided a memorable boost to bilateral relations and went a long way towards projecting Pakistan's image as a peaceful, moderate and progressive society. As the Indian High Commissioner, Shivshankar Menon, remarked, 20,000 Indian fans had gone back to India acting as Pakistan's ambassadors. Despite my anxiety at the beginning of the tour, cricket had acted as a genuine bridge of peace. [78]

It is now left to the policy-makers, diplomats and politicians of both countries to toe the line set by cricket when it comes to resolving outstanding issues in foreign relations.

Acknowledgements

While I planned this essay during the tour of the Indian cricket team in Pakistan in March–April 2004, I must remain thankful to two persons: Rahul Bhattacharya, contributing editor at *Wisden Asia Cricket* and Shaharyar Khan, chairman of the Pakistan Board (whom I never met), who have very recently produced two wonderful accounts (*Pundits from Pakistan* and *Cricket: A Bridge of Peace* respectively) on contemporary Indo-Pak cricket. Reading their works has been a real pleasure as well as immensely thought-provoking. This chapter resonates, if not reproduces, many of their views and comments. I also thank Anirban Mukherjee, my friend, for helping me with some interesting newspaper cuttings and absorbing comments on the cricket tour.

Notes

[1] Quoted in Bhattacharya, *Pundits from Pakistan*, 35 (emphasis added).
[2] Dev, *Straight from the Heart*, quoted in Dev, 'Beginner's Pluck'.
[3] Dev, *Straight from the Heart*, quoted in Dev, 'Beginner's Pluck' (emphasis added).

[4] Boria Majumdar, 'Willow Talk: Moolah and Mediation', *Sahara Time*, 13 March 2004, 22–3.

[5] India and Pakistan underwent Partition following independence in August 1947.

[6] Reddy, 'Pakistan Has a Lot to Gain', 19.

[7] For details, see Majumdar, 'Communalism to Commercialism'.

[8] A few years back, at a railway station in Godhra, Gujarat, two train compartments packed with Hindu political activists caught fire, killing almost all the passengers in those compartments. This incident triggered off a series of communal clashes in different parts of India, particularly in Gujarat, where the ruling BJP-led state government was held responsible for inaction to prevent this heightened communal assault on the Muslims, thereby hardening socio-political relations between the two communities and defaming India's secular face.

[9] In early 1999 India's successful nuclear test at Pokhran, reciprocated shortly by similar tests by Pakistan, led to heightened political tension in South Asian diplomatic relations.

[10] Cross-border infiltration into Indian Kashmir reached a peak in the late 1990s, culminating in a war between India and Pakistan in the mountainous range of Kargil adjacent to the Line of Control in mid-1999. The Indian army fought successfully to combat the infiltration and push back the Pak-sponsored army.

[11] For an interesting discussion on the complex interplay of identities – Hindu, Muslim or Indian – during an Indo-Pak cricket match in a World Cup, see Dasgupta, 'Manufacturing Unison'.

[12] Kalighat, a locality on the bank of Ganga in south Kolkata, is situated one of the most famous *Kali* temples of India, where thousands of devotees visit and pray to the mother goddess every day.

[13] 'Down with Pakistan'.

[14] *Outlook*, 31 March 2003, 32.

[15] *The Statesman*, 5 March 2003.

[16] *The Statesman*, 3 March 2003.

[17] Ibid.

[18] Ibid.

[19] *The Statesman*, 5 March 2003.

[20] D.V. Madhav Rao, Chennai, Letters to the Editor, *Outlook*, 31 March 2003.

[21] *The Statesman*, 3 March 2003.

[22] Quoted in Bhowmik and Kakodkar, 'Keeping the Faith'.

[23] Ibid.

[24] Brijnath, 'India-Pakistan', 9.

[25] Khan, *Cricket: A Bridge of Peace*, vii.

[26] Ibid., 92.

[27] Ibid.

[28] Thyagarajan, 'The Tour Should Pave a New Road', 29.

[29] Iqbal, 'Change of Pace', 36.

[30] *The Statesman*, 11 March 2004, 12.

[31] Saba Karim, 'The Soothing Balm That Sports Can Be', *The Staesman*, 25 Feb., 13.

[32] *Ananda Bazar Patrika*, 18 March 2004.

[33] Orwell, 'The Sporting Spirit', quoted in Verma, 'The Humanising Factor', 46.

[34] Orwell, 'The Sporting Spirit', quoted in Bhattacharya, *Pundits from Pakistan*, 16.

[35] Ibid.

[36] Ibid.

[37] Verma, 'The Humanising Factor', 46.

[38] Ibid., 47.

[39] Rameez Raja, CEO of the Pakistan Cricket Board, told *Wisden Asia Cricket* that the crowds for this series were the most sporting he had seen for any series in Pakistan, let alone one against

India: 'I mean, I have never in my experience seen Indian and Pakistani flags stitched together.' Indian vice-captain Rahul Dravid also maintained that 'Everywhere we went we have been cheered. The guys who fielded at the boundary kept saying how appreciative the crowd have been.' For further details on this aspect, see Bhattacharya, 'A Glow of Warm Feeling', 31.

[40] Chatterjee, 'To Play Or Not To Play'.
[41] The decision to go ahead with the series, which surprised many, came after a confidential meeting at the residence of the Prime Minister, Atal Bihari Vajpayee on 14 February. The meeting was attended by Deputy Prime Minister, L.K. Advani, External Affairs Minister Yashwant Sinha, Finance Minister Jaswant Singh and national security adviser Brajesh Mishra.
[42] *The Telegraph* (Kolkata), 15 Feb. 2004, 1.
[43] These arguments have been briefly but eloquently dealt in Bhattacharya, *Pundits in Pakistan*, 9, 13–14.
[44] Ibid.
[45] Ibid.
[46] Ibid.
[47] Ibid.
[48] *The Telegraph*, 15 Feb. 2004, 1.
[49] Ibid.
[50] Murthy, 'Icing on the Feel-good Cake'.
[51] Ashok V. Desai, 'How Sweet is My Carrot', *The Telegraph*, 27 April 2004, 12.
[52] Bhattacharya, *Pundits from Pakistan*, 9.
[53] Ibid. The hint at this possibility was given by the newspapers on the day the official decision to go ahead with the tour was declared. For details, see *The Statesman*, 15 Feb. 2004, 1; *The Telegraph*, 15 February 2004, 1.
[54] *Sahara Time*, 13 March 2004, 3.
[55] *The Statesman*, 11 March 2004, 1.
[56] Ibid.
[57] 'Pakistan Notebook', *The Sportstar*, 27 March 2004, 22.
[58] Boria Majumdar, 'Cricket turns global', *Sahara Time*, 3 April 2004, 17.
[59] Ibid.
[60] Ibid.
[61] K. Srikkanth, 'India Can Deliver the Goods', *The Statesman*, 25 Feb. 2004, 13.
[62] Bhattacharya, *Pundits from Pakistan*, 141. Also see *Ananda Bazar Patrika*, 26 March 2004.
[63] Bhattacharya, *Pundits from Pakistan*, 141.
[64] Ibid.
[65] Iqbal, 'Change of Pace', 36.
[66] Bal, 'It's Just a Game'.
[67] Bhogle, 'It's a Cricket Tour', 16.
[68] Ibid.
[69] Dinakar, 'Indian Batting and Pakistan Bowling', 11.
[70] Joseph, 'La Horde!', 50.
[71] Ibid., 51.
[72] Raju Mukherji, 'Cricket Killed with Goodwill', *The Telegraph*, 18 March 2004, 13.
[73] Ibid.
[74] Ibid.
[75] Joseph, 'La Horde!', 48.
[76] Ibid.
[77] Marqusee, 'Border Crossings', 68.
[78] Khan, *Cricket: A Bridge of Peace*, 187.

References

Bal, Sambit. 'It's Just a Game'. *Wisden Asia Cricket* 3 (4) (March 2004): 5.

Bhattacharya, Rahul. 'A Glow of Warm Feeling'. *Wisden Asia Cricket* 4 (5) (April 2004): 28–32.

——. *Pundits from Pakistan: On Tour with India, 2003–04*. London: Picador, 2005.

Bhogle, Harsha. 'It's a Cricket Tour, Not a Political One'. *The Sportstar*, 6 March 2004: 16–17.

Bhowmik, Saba Naqbi and Priyanka, Kakodkar. 'Keeping the Faith'. *Outlook*, 31 March 2003, 32–3.

Brijnath, Rohit. 'India-Pakistan: Why We Need to Remember This is Just Sport'. *The Sportstar*, 28 Feb. 2004: 8–9.

Chatterjee, Kingshuk. 'To Play Or Not To Play: Fabricating Consent over the Indo-Pak Cricket Series'. In *Sport in South Asian Society: Past and Present*, edited by Boria Majumdar and J.A. Mangan. London: Routledge, 2005: 277–94.

Dasgupta, Jishnu. 'Manufacturing Unison: Muslims, Hindus and Indians during the India-Pakistan Match'. In *Sport in South Asian Society: Past and Present*, edited by Boria Majumdar and J.A. Mangan. London: Routledge, 2005: 239–48.

Dev, Kapil. 'Beginner's Pluck'. *India Today* Collector's Edition (March 2004): 28–34.

Dinakar, S. 'Indian Batting and Pakistan Bowling Hold the Key'. *The Sportstar*, 13 March 2004: 11–17.

Iqbal, Asif. 'Change of Pace'. *India Today*, March 2004: 36–40.

Joseph, Manu. 'La Horde!' *Outlook*, 5 April 2004: 47–51.

Khan, Shaharyar. *Cricket: A Bridge of Peace*. Oxford: Oxford University Press, 2005.

Majumdar, Boria and J.A. Mangan, eds. *Sport in South Asian Society: Past and Present*. London: Routledge, 2005.

Majumdar, Boria. 'Communalism to Commercialism: Study of Anti-Pentangular Movement'. *Economic and Political Weekly*, 15 Feb. 2003: 656–64.

——. *Once Upon a Furore: Lost Pages of Indian Cricket*. New Delhi: Yoda Press, 2004.

——. *Twenty-Two Yards to Freedom: A Social History of Indian Cricket*. New Delhi: Penguin/Viking, 2004.

Marqusee, Mike. 'Border Crossings'. *India Today*, March 2004: 64–70.

Murthy, Sachidananda. 'Icing on the Feel-good Cake'. *The Week*, 14 March 2004: 34.

Nandy, Ashis. *The Tao of Cricket: On Games of Destiny and the Destiny of Games*. London: Viking, 1989.

Reddy, Muralidhar. 'Pakistan Has a Lot to Gain'. *The Sportstar*, 28 Feb. 2004: 18–19.

Thyagarajan, S. 'The Tour Should Pave a New Road to Constructive Friendship'. *The Sportstar*, 28 Feb. 2004: 28–9.

Verma, Amit. 'The Humanising Factor'. *Wisden Asia Cricket* 3 (4) (March 2004): 46–7.

The Golden Years of Indian Hockey: 'We Climb the Victory Stand'

Boria Majumdar

This article seeks to explore the glory years of Indian hockey. Now almost forgotten in the wake of the enormity of cricket's stellar popularity in India, it was hockey and not cricket that had provided India the most conspicuous sporting success on the world stage in the first half of the 20th century. The article delves into the history of those years when India reigned as the undisputed champions of the game winning six straight Olympic gold medals. The article explores the history of that meteoric success bringing to life the victories, personalities and controversies of those 'golden years'.

India claims to be the foremost in many things in the world. The world admits that she is foremost in hockey. [1]

Hockey, more than any other game, is etched in the Indian psyche. It is hockey that brings out the magic and mystery, the poetry and prose in Indian sport. [2]

'We Were Made Heroes'

One of the world's oldest sports, hockey predates the ancient Olympic Games by a little more than 1,200 years. However, the modern game of field hockey (for those distinguishing it from ice hockey) evolved in the British Isles in the middle of the nineteenth century. The British helped spread hockey globally, promoting it in parts of the empire as part of the civilizing process, and subsequently its popularity became especially visible in the Indian subcontinent by the early twentieth century. In colonial India, especially in the early decades of the twentieth century, hockey was as popular as cricket and football, the country's other passions. Even school and college magazines of the period are replete with descriptions of hockey matches, and they specifically draw attention to India's spectacular performance in the Olympics. [3]

In India, organized hockey started in Calcutta in 1885 when the first hockey clubs were formed. Within a decade the great tournaments that were to become the

Boria Majumdar, La Trobe University, Calcutta.

breeding grounds of the national team had been established. The Beighton Cup in Calcutta and the Aga Khan Tournament in Bombay were both set up in 1895. Having established itself in the east and west of the country, hockey moved north to the Punjab, first to the army cantonments, and then made its way into the Punjab University sports tournament in 1903. In the same year, Lahore started its famous Hot Weather Tournament. [4] These tournaments were to be the lifeline of Indian hockey all through its golden age. Writing of the Beighton Cup in 1952, the great Dhyan Chand, who cut his hockey teeth first in the army, and then with the Jhansi Heroes, observed:

> In 1933, the Jhansi Heroes decided to participate in the Beighton Cup hockey tournament. My life's ambition was to win the Beighton Cup, as I had always regarded this competition as the blue riband of Indian hockey. In my opinion it is perhaps the best organised hockey event in the country. Calcutta is indeed lucky that it has at least three or four first class hockey grounds on the maidan, and this is a great advantage to run a tournament on schedule. Instituted in 1895, this tournament has had a non-stop run. World Wars I and II did not affect the tournament. Threats of Japanese bombs and actual bombings in Kolkata while the hockey season was on also did not prevent the tournament from being held. That being said, it is sad to think that the tournament had to yield to the communal frenzy, which gripped the nation in 1946–47. [5]

Like the Bombay Pentagular in cricket, these tournaments helped in popularizing the game beyond the confines of army cantonments and the first attempts at forming a national association were visible in Calcutta in 1907–8. [6] The political chaos that engulfed Bengal after its partition in 1905, however, put paid to these efforts. The move was revived in the 1920s when C.E. Newham, president of the Punjab Hockey Federation, started a campaign to create a central organization to govern Indian hockey. This second attempt at establishing a nodal organization also ended in failure and it was not until November 1925 that a governing body for hockey was established.

The princely state of Gwalior was the new centre. Writing in 1959, this is how A.S. De Mello, describes the formation of the Indian Hockey Federation (IHF):

> In 1924, at the request of the now defunct Western India Hockey Association, Lieutenant Colonel Luard, who was then President of the Gwalior Sports Association, addressed all hockey associations, clubs and individuals interested in the game and invited them to a meeting in Gwalior. This meeting, which took place on November 7th, 1925, resulted in the official formation of the Indian Hockey Federation. [7]

At the inaugural meeting of the Federation, Gwalior, Bengal, Punjab, Sind, Rajputana, Western India, Punjab University and the Army Sports Control Board were represented. For the first two years Gwalior was treated as the headquarters, which was subsequently moved to Delhi in 1927. [8]

The formation of the IHF was a landmark event because it enabled international exposure for Indian players for the first time. Soon after its formation the IHF organized India's first international tour, the trip to New Zealand in 1926. The Indian team immediately made its mark and its wizardry proved to be a commercial success as well. The New Zealand Hockey Federation made a profit of £300 sterling after paying the Indians a healthy sum of £500. The Indians ended the tour with 18 victories in 21 matches, with just one defeat. They scored a total of 192 goals, conceding 24, at an average of 9.31 goals per match. Astonishingly, the Indians registered double-digit scores in as many as nine games. [9]

It was on this tour that Dhyan Chand established himself as the premier star of Indian hockey. For him, an enlisted sepoy in the army and a man not born into privilege, unlike some of his counterparts, the opportunity to represent India was an unexpected windfall. His outright delight is beautifully portrayed in his autobiography:

> It was a great day for me when my Commanding Officer called me and said: 'Boy, you are to go to New Zealand.' I was dumbfounded, and did not know what to reply. All I did was to click my heels snappily, give as smart a salute as I possibly could, and beat a hasty retreat. Once out of sight of the officer, I ran like a hare to reach my barracks and communicated the good news to my fellow soldiers. And what a reception they gave me! I lost no time in getting prepared for the trip. I was not a rich man, my earnings as a *sepoy* being only a few rupees a month. My parents were not rich either. All thoughts of outfitting and equipping myself in the proper manner for an overseas tour of this nature had to be given up for want of sufficient resources. I clothed myself as inexpensively as possible, and my main personal outfit was my military kit.... As soldiers, particularly those belonging to the Other Ranks [read lower ranks], it was a great experience for us. Prior to this tour we could never conceive of being feted and entertained at private houses and public functions in such a glorious and enjoyable manner. We were made heroes, and on my part, if I may put it quite modestly, I proved myself a great success and left behind a great impression. [10]

Riding on this success and encouraged by the colonial British government's support, the IHF applied for and subsequently obtained global affiliation in 1927. This was crucial to India's participation at the Amsterdam Olympic Games in 1928. It was in Amsterdam that India started its uninterrupted reign over the world of hockey for the next two decades.

'Can I See My Trousers in the Sun': The Beginning

Men's hockey first appeared at the 1908 Olympic Games in London. It reappeared in Antwerp in 1920, returning to stay from the 1928 Amsterdam games onwards. Women's hockey waited much longer, finally debuting in 1980. Between 1928 and 1956, India won six straight Olympic gold medals and 24 consecutive matches, a record likely to stand for the foreseeable future. Indians have won two more gold medals since, in 1964 and 1980. In fact, it was at India's insistence that hockey was reinstated at Amsterdam after being dropped from the programme of the eighth Olympiad in Paris in 1924.

A.S. De Mello – from whose autobiographical essay we have borrowed the subtitle of this chapter – writes that before leaving for Amsterdam, India's hockey players were 'confident that they would not disgrace themselves'. [11] At the same time they had not approached the games with any fantastic hopes. Jaipal Singh, who had a first-class degree from his native Ranchi and was then a student at Balliol College, Oxford, was appointed captain of the team. A Munda tribal from Chotanagpur, the forested plateau of Bihar, Jaipal is a fascinating character in Indian history, whose influence in later years extended far beyond the hockey field. As Ramachandra Guha writes, he later became the *marang gomke* or 'great leader' of the tribals of Chotanagpur and in the Constituent Assembly 'he came to represent tribals not just of his native plateau, but all of India'. It was his interventions in the Constituent Assembly that ultimately led to the reservation of seats for tribals in government jobs and in legislative bodies after independence. [12] Sent to Oxford by missionaries, Jaipal successfully led a team comprising Indians studying at British universities to Belgium and Spain and had earned a great reputation as a hockey player in the UK, as is evident from his numerous profiles published in the *World Hockey* magazine. When the team for Amsterdam was announced it included Jaipal, S.M. Yusef and the Nawab of Pataudi Senior, who were already in Britain. Thirteen players sailed from Bombay, nine of them Anglo Indians, to lead India's challenge at the 1928 Olympics. [13] However, before they sailed for London, there was a last-minute alarm when it was revealed that because of insufficient funds only 11 of the 13 selected players could undertake the tour. The shortfall, contemporary reports revealed, was Rs15,000. That the crisis was serious was evident when the federation announced that in case sufficient funds weren't garnered Shaukat Ali of Bengal and R.A. Norris of the Central Provinces would not accompany the team. In the end it was largely owing to the munificence of the sports-loving public of Bengal, who organized public collections to make up the funding shortfall, that the two players were able to make the trip. [14]

While he became better known in later life as a prominent parliamentarian and Adivasi leader, Jaipal thus describes his hockey career in the UK in his memoirs:

> The effect of the tours of Indian students I conducted every year with the help of Aga Khan, 'Kanji' Baroda, Patiala, Bhopal and other Indian royalty was the formation of the Indian Hockey Federation. . . . India decided to send a team to the Amsterdam Olympiad in 1928. I was still at Oxford a probationer for the Indian Civil Service. . . . As after 1926 I could not play for the University team, I played for the Wimbledon Hockey Club. . . . As at Oxford I continued to receive publicity in the London press. [15]

In a clear reflection of how haphazardly that first Olympic team was put together, and also of the times, he goes on to narrate the strange manner in which he was appointed captain of the Indian team:

> One early evening two Britishers, Colonel Bruce Turnbull and Major Ricketts, both of the Indian army, called at the Church Imperial Club. Turnbull was Secretary of

the Army Sports Board in India and Ricketts was his lieutenant. I stood them drinks. They told me the Indian hockey team was coming the following week on its way to Amsterdam. 'We want you to captain the team,' I agreed but told them I would have to get leave from the India Office for absence during term time. I did not get leave! I decided to defy the ruling and face the consequences. [16]

Jaipal met his team when its boat docked at Tilbury on 30 March 1928. Having lived in England for a few years by now, he was unimpressed by what he saw as their rustic 'untidy dress and crude demeanour'. The team was put up in a pension at South Kensington and Jaipal invited them a couple of times to the well-known Veeraswamy's Restaurant on Regent Street: 'It was expensive to feed them. The Indian dishes were Hyderabadi but not cheap.' Soon after arrival the players started addressing Jaipal as 'skipper', though he was yet to accept the offer formally. In the first few practice sessions Shaukat Ali and Dhyan Chand caught Jaipal's attention. Shaukat played for the Calcutta Customs and could adopt in any position. Dhyan Chand, a Lance Naik in the Indian army, had made his name in New Zealand scoring the bulk of the goals for the Indian Army team in 1926. Dhyan Chand, Jaipal states,

> was humble. He had only one pair of trousers. I took him to Austin Reed on Regent Street. We went downstairs. Trousers galore were shown. 'Can I take them upstairs and see them in the sun?' That finished me. I told Shaukat the story. 'What else do you expect of a Lance Naik?' he laughed. [17]

The Indians played a series of matches in London against leading club sides and haphazardly put together national teams such as the Anglo Irish. Dhyan Chand scored in almost every game. India's last engagement in England was at the Folkstone Easter Festival, where it beat the English national team 4–0 and a team calling itself the Rossalians 18–0. Following these victories the British and French press in unison suggested that the Indians were favourites for the hockey gold in Amsterdam. [18] And they weren't wrong.

'The World's Best Centre-Forward': Amsterdam 1928

At Amsterdam the onus was on the hockey team to lead the Indian challenge. The athletes, Chawan in the 10,000 metres, Hamid in the 400 metres hurdles and Murphy in the 800 metres, had failed to qualify for the second round. In hockey India played its first match against Austria, winning 6–0, an encounter reported in detail at home. Already Dhyan Chand was being described as the 'world's greatest centre forward'. As *The Statesman* put it:

> The Indian Hockey team has successfully surmounted the first obstacle towards the prize for which they journeyed to Europe. India defeated Austria 6–0 with the

world's greatest centre forward Dhyan Chand giving another masterly exhibition. He scored all 3 goals in the first half. After the interval Dhyan Chand scored the fourth goal. The fifth was obtained by Shaukat Ali while Gately secured the last goal. [19]

Dhyan Chand eventually scored 14 of India's 29 goals in Amsterdam.

The very next day *The Statesman* published another detailed report on India's 9–0 win over Belgium. The space allotted to the report was nearly double compared to the first, an indication of the growing popularity of the team back home:

> All India followed up their brilliant victory over Austria by defeating Belgium 9–0. The point about today's victory was it proved India can pile up goals even if Dhyan Chand does not think it necessary to improve his goal average. In his skilful manner he worked out scoring possibilities yet tapped the ball either to Feroze Khan or Marthins. Seaman, whose clever stick work on left wing has been the feature of the tour, bewildered Belgium's goalkeeper twice. Allen in India's goal did not have much to do. Jaipal Singh was brilliant and Penniger did all that was required of him with polish. [20]

Subsequently the Indians beat Denmark and Switzerland to set up a title clash with hosts Holland on 26 May 1928.

When the Indians trounced Holland 3–0 in the final, the press back home went ballistic. *The Statesmen* had an entire report titled 'How India Won Honours' and went on to suggest that 40,000 people went into ruptures over the brilliant exhibition of hockey displayed by the Indians in the final. It reported that despite having to reconstruct the side in the absence of Feroze Khan, who had broken his collarbone in the clash against Denmark, and Shaukat Ali, who was down with flu, India won comprehensively. [21] Interestingly, the report does not mention the absence of captain Jaipal Singh, who had for personal reasons walked out of the team before the semi-final. This is one of the most enduring mysteries of the tour and perhaps the first known political controversy within the national hockey team. Jaipal too is remarkably silent about this discord in his memoirs, one that had raised doubts over who had actually captained the final victory–Singh or Penniger. Singh left the Olympic team on the eve of the semi-final and did not take part in the final either. He refused to discuss the issue ever again in public and until new evidence emerges, the mystery of Jaipal and why he walked out of that first Indian Olympic victory will remain unresolved. [22]

Coming back to the victory, *The Statesman* report quoted above also hit on another intriguing aspect of those years of Indian dominance at the Olympics: 'It is no empty title, for the critics are of the opinion that even if England had been competing in the Games, honours would have gone to India, though possibly not with the record of not conceding a goal remaining intact.' [23] The colony had won in Europe but the colonizer was absent. In fact, there was a rumour in Olympic circles that England had initially entered a team for the Olympic hockey competition at Amsterdam. According to this rumour, after the 4–0 drubbing they received at the Folkestone festival at the hands of the Indians, the English were scared of losing on an international stage to their 'colony' and withdrew from the event. That there is some truth to this rumour is evident from Dhyan Chand's recollections:

> I reiterate that this is mere hearsay (that England dropped out of the Amsterdam Games fearing the Indians), although we fondly hoped that at least in future Olympics we would have the honour of meeting Great Britain and showing them how good or bad we were. It is my regret that this hope was never realised so long as I participated in Olympic events. [24]

The British hockey team never participated in the Olympics until 1948, by which time India was an independent nation. [25] When India beat Great Britain 4–0 in the 1948 games, it unleashed great celebrations in the newly independent nation and the win contributed to national self-confidence and self-belief. [26]

It was in Amsterdam that the legend of Indian hockey was created. Even the Dutch papers praised the team with generosity: 'So agile are the Indians that they could run the full length of the hockey field, juggling a wooden ball on the flat end of the hockey stick.' [27] Britain may not have participated, but soon after the win the viceroy, Lord Irwin, sent a telegram to the team manager B Rosser: 'Please convey to Jaipal Singh and all members of his team my heartiest congratulations on their magnificent victory. All India has followed the triumphal progress throughout the tour and rejoice in the crowning achievement.' [28] This telegram, which mentions Jaipal as captain, finally laid the captaincy debate to rest.

India scored 29 goals in Amsterdam without conceding even one, and averaged more than five goals per match. Interestingly, the Olympic hockey competition was played in May, while the actual Olympiad, including the opening ceremony and other events, took place two months later in July. As a result, the victorious Indian team did not have the good fortune of enjoying the Olympic atmosphere, the rituals of the opening ceremony and the subsequent ambience of the Olympic village.

In London, the victory became a source of great nationalist celebration for the Indian community. Indian women organized a tea party in their honour and presented them with turbans. Interestingly, as Jaipal pointed out, 'The Anglo Indians never wore them!' [29] They were also entertained to lunch at Veeraswamy's by Dr Paranjpe, a member of the Indian Council. And when the team reached Bombay it was welcomed by a huge throng of adoring fans. Mole Station overflowed with a wildly cheering crowd trying to get a glimpse of the new heroes. In audience was Dr G.V. Deshmukh, the Mayor of Mumbai, who was there to accord the team a civic reception, and a representative of the Governor of Mumbai, who sent a congratulatory message. [30]

Jaipal, who had broken his term at Oxford without leave to play in the Olympics, paid a personal price for the victory. He returned to Oxford after the festivities were over, only to be confronted with angry dons. As he put it: 'I was told that as I had broken term I would have to stay for one more year. Captaining India to world championship was no prize for the British. I resigned from the ICS and refused to pay back 350 pounds. I was not put in gaol.' [31]

Jaipal's resignation from the ICS after that first hockey win left an enduring legacy far beyond the hockey field. He gradually moved into politics and became the leader of the Adibasi Mahasabha in 1938. The man who had looked down in derision at Dhyan Chand for his rustic manners now became the champion of India's tribals. He held the view that the tribals were 'the original inhabitants' of the subcontinent– hence the term *adibasi* or *adivasi*. As Ramachandra Guha has pointed out, Jaipal went on become the greatest defender of tribal rights in the Constitutional Assembly and his interventions were erudite as well as spirited, as for instance when he opposed the prohibition of alcohol which had been inserted as a Directive Principle. Alcohol, for him, was part of the daily and ritual life of the tribals of India and denounced the ideas as an interference:

> With the religious rights of the most ancient people in the country... it would be impossible for paddy to be transplanted if the Santhal does not get rice beer. These ill clad men... have to work knee-deep in water throughout the day, drenching rain and in mud. What is it in the rice beer that keeps them alive? I wish the medical authorities in this country would carry out research in their laboratories to find out what it is that the rice beer contains, of which the Adibasis need so much and which keeps them [protected] against all manner of diseases. [32]

Jaipal's hockey adventure led to his premature departure from the ICS, but the ICS's loss was independent India's gain. It was Jaipal who first initiated the demand for a separate tribal state of Jharkhand, which was ultimately carved out of Bihar in 2001.

Loans of Glory: En Route to Los Angeles 1932

Global economic depression, starting from the great Wall Street Crash in 1928, meant that India, Japan and the United States were the only entrants competing for hockey honours at the Los Angeles Olympiad in 1932. However, that does not take away from the fact that the Indians were far superior to any of their contemporaries. With a view to defending the title won at Amsterdam, the IHF tried to pick the best team possible for the 1932 Olympics and organized an inter-provincial trial in Calcutta in March 1932. Only Dhyan Chand picked himself automatically. Based on performance at the trials, the appointed representatives of the provinces affiliated to the federation picked the rest of the national team led by Lal Shah Bokhari. G.D. Sondhi was appointed manager and Pankaj Gupta the non-playing captain and assistant manager of the touring side.

The effects of the depression were also felt in India and the IHF found it exceedingly difficult to raise funds necessary to undertake the tour. In the end, funds were raised from a diverse range of sources: contributions from Viceroy Lord Willingdon, the governors of the provinces, a few of the princely families, public collections by the nation's sporting public and proceeds from exhibition football and hockey matches played in Calcutta, Bhopal, Bombay, Madras, Bangalore Singapore and Colombo. Even these were not enough to cover the entire expense but at least they allowed the team to leave Indian shores. [33]

Picking the team was the easy part, but sending it overseas was a huge financial challenge. To cope with the financial shortfall, the federation undertook a loan of Rs7500. It organized exhibition matches for the national team at Colombo, Madras, Bombay, Delhi and Lahore on the team's homeward journey and hoped that proceeds from these matches would wipe out the debt entirely. A sports goods dealer from Sialkot, Uberoi and Co., chipped in by supplying the players with hockey sticks and balls. The sticks, it is evident from players' memoirs, were the very best available globally.

Despite the challenges, the IHF was reluctant to forgo the opportunity of international glory. A measure of the obstacles faced by the IHF in sending the team is borne out by the reminiscences of Pankaj Gupta:

> Before the Los Angeles Games, I, in my capacity as Hony Secretary of the Indian Hockey Federation and Mr A.M. Hayman, the President, had more than our share of headaches. First there was the question of finance and secondly it was debatable whether it was worthwhile sending a team to play against such weak opposition as that provided by the USA and Japan. Several meetings were held and the IHF took a bold decision, prompted by the fact that if India did not take part the event might be deleted from the Games and possibly not revived...I am glad that we, in the larger interest of international glory, decided to send our team. [34]

In the same article he emphasized Bengal's contribution in promoting hockey in India and declared that

> it might be news to many that most of the money at the earlier stages of India's participation in Olympic hockey came from Bengal. I must not be misunderstood when I refer to Bengal, which I have not done from any parochial angle but public memory is always short and history and tradition should not be forgotten. [35]

He went on to state that in his opinion the best Indian team ever produced was the 1932 Olympic team, which played on consecutive days despite having to undertake overland third-class travel on the continent to meet expenses. [36]

India's newly picked team played its first pre-Olympic tour match at Bhopal on 15 May against a team from the Aligarh University. The national team won easily, scoring five goals each on either side of half-time. On 16 May it played the Bhopal team, beating it 8–2. While at Bhopal the team was accorded royal treatment as guests of the Nawab. Prince Rahid-uz-Zafar Khan, who made a contribution of Rs1000 towards the tour fund, organized a reception in their honour. At the time of the visit, the Nawab of Bhopal was away on official work and sent the team the following message:

> I extend a most hearty welcome to the members of the Olympic Hockey Team on their visit to Bhopal and my keenest regret is my absence from my state on this occasion. But my inability to show you and your team hospitality in person will not diminish the cordiality, which my state will offer you on my behalf, or the sincerity of my good wishes for the success of your mission. Our Indian team represents the true spirit of sportsmanship in India and carries with it the good wishes of all people. We are confident that all of you will... keep the flag flying in all the countries you include in your tour. Your sporting achievements will... add further glory to the fair name of India and enhance its reputation among the nations of the West. [37]

This message is indicative enough of the respect accorded to the players by the Nawab. For players such as Dhyan Chand and Roop Singh, men from under-privileged and humble backgrounds, the game was a means to social respectability and, as in football and cricket, princely patronage played a crucial role.

The communal riots in Bombay, though, cast a deep shadow on the team when it moved to Bombay for three matches between 19 and 21 May. Attendance at these games was affected by the riots and the from here the players moved on to Bangalore, Madras and then Colombo. Travelling around the country, raising money for their Olympic journey, the guiding principle for these players was the idea of 'national self-respect'. As skipper Lal Shah Bokhari put it in a message issued to the people in Madras, 'I can assure my countrymen that we will bring respect to India and we will maintain our tradition as World's Champion Hockey playing nation'. [38]

The money-raising drive did not end in India. En route to Los Angeles, the team played exhibition games at every port it docked. The only aim was to raise the money to wipe out its loans. Everywhere, the players' exhilarating stick work left dazzled onlookers in their wake. Watching them play in Ceylon, for instance, the governor declared in awe, 'Is it really over? I feel I have been watching your team play for only five minutes.' [39] From Colombo the team set sail for Singapore on board the steamship Haruna Maru. The final destination of the pre-Olympics tour was Japan, where the Indians beat an unofficial Japanese team by 11 goals on 20 June. Having won hearts in Tokyo, the Indians proceeded to defend their crown at Los Angeles.

Their arrival in America was greeted with much fanfare, with Indians settled in California coming out in large numbers to fete the team. The citizens' forum of San Francisco organized a civic reception in honour of the Japanese, Philippine and Indian Olympic athletes when the boat carrying the Indian team stopped in San Francisco for two days on 6 July 1932. At the reception the mayor presented a key of the city to each delegation. Finally, after a 42-day voyage the Indians arrived in Los Angeles. Once settled, they were all praise for the Olympic village and the training facilities at the University of California Los Angeles. What had especially impressed the Indians was the wholesome food on offer in the Olympic village. [40] Local newspaper reports in the US mentioned that while the Indians indulged in light exercise, the US and Japanese teams practised all day long to improve their skills. [41]

Indians in America: The Real Action

The first Indians in action at the Los Angeles games were the sprinters M. Sutton and R Vernieux. Both athletes performed well and were successful in making it to the British Empire team picked to face the Americans after the Olympics. This was the first occasion when Indian athletes had made it to the empire team. [42] While the Indians acquitted themselves well in athletics, in swimming N.C. Mallick lost out in the 400 metres freestyle competition, coming fourth in his heat. However, his timing was considerably better than what he had clocked at home, a remarkable achievement in a short span of time.

In hockey, India's preparations did not proceed to plan, with Hammond and Jaffer down with muscle strain and Lal Shah, the captain, badly hurt above his nose following an injury in practice. Penniger joined the injured list on 2 August when he emulated Lal Shah and suffered a stick contact resulting in a split in his eyebrow, requiring stitches to be put in place. Finally, a day before the first encounter against Japan, India's goalkeeper R.J. Allen, who had distinguished himself at Amsterdam by not conceding a single goal, suffered a strained muscle that forced him out of the contest. Hind, the reserve goalkeeper, replaced him. [43]

11–1

In the opening match of the hockey competition at Los Angeles the Indians overwhelmed the Japanese by 11 goals to one. If contemporary reports are anything to go by, India's clinical display mesmerized the Japanese, who had no answer to the deft stick work and ball control exhibited by the Indians. Dhyan Chand scored four goals while Roop Singh and Gurmit Singh scored three goals each. Carr scored the final goal for India after a brilliant solo run. The match reports mentioned that the Indians would have fared better but for the soft turf to which they were still not fully accustomed. [44]

Having beaten the Japanese by a convincing margin, the Indians were inevitably thought to be certainties to retain the gold they had won at Amsterdam. Their confidence was evident when they decided to make a series of changes to the team in the match against the US to ensure that all 15 players in the squad played a hand in the victory. Olympic rules necessitated that a player had to play a part in the competition to be entitled to a medal. [45]

24–1

The match against the US, which saw the Indians make a mockery of the Americans by beating them 24–1, was thus reported back home:

India has retained the world hockey championship. Today, before a crowd that sat amazed at the skill of the Indians, the US suffered a defeat by 24 goals to 1. It was greatly expected that India would win easily but not even her most optimistic admirers thought goals would come at the rate of one in every two minutes. The Americans worked hard but the game was a revelation to them. Amazingly clever stick work of the Indians, the perfect understanding between forwards, the manner in which half backs came up to support and strengthen each attack, the flick passes of both forwards and halves–all these were new to the Americans who often were so spell bound by these tactics that they could only stand and gape at their nimble opponents. Roop Singh scored 12 goals and Dhyan Chand 7, Gurmit Singh scored 3 and Jaffer and Penniger 1 each. [46]

In the immediate aftermath of the victory there were spectacular scenes of jubilation when India's flag fluttered at the summit of the stadium and the band played the national anthem of British India. Newspapers across the world paid tribute to the incalculable superiority of the Indians and surprisingly did not express astonishment at the magnitude of the score, which was an international record. Rather, newspapers in the US expressed satisfaction that the US was able to score a lone goal against the mighty Indians. [47] The US captain's comment that for the most of the game 'they were chasing shadows' aptly summed up the nature of the encounter. Finally, a special broadcast was arranged to comment on India's incomparable prowess in hockey and pay tribute to the Indian team's exceptional conduct and widespread popularity. [48]

The Viceroy, who had helped in raising funds for the team, sent a congratulatory message as well: 'I am delighted and proud to learn of the splendid victory of our hockey team. Please give all members of the side my warm congratulations upon retaining World's Championship.' [49] The director of the Olympic village wrote the following message to Pankaj Gupta:

The Indian team being in the village longer than any of the others became part of the family. On behalf of all my associates and myself here I want to thank you, and through you the entire Indian delegation, for the splendid cooperation you gave us in the operation of the village. [50]

Not surprisingly, after the final, the Indian community in Los Angeles went berserk. Many contributed generously to raise a pool of $400 needed to enable the Indians to travel around the country exhibiting their skill. The post-Olympic tour lasted for almost a month. [51]

'He is an Angel'

India started its post Olympic tour at Philadelphia with a rematch against the United States on 20 August. This time round the final score was a wee bit more respectable for the United States, with the Indians winning 20–1. The visit to Philadelphia was followed by a return visit to California before the Indians embarked upon a tour of

Europe. Again financial considerations were paramount here. When in Los Angeles, the advantages of returning via Europe were considered by the Indian delegation. Pankaj Gupta was determined to make this happen and did a great deal to obtain quotations for rail and steamer fares. Upon knowing the Indian intention to travel through Europe, the German Hockey Association made the Indians a generous offer if they played a certain number of games in the continent. The Indians accepted the offer as it did not involve a substantially higher expenditure than if they returned via Japan. [52]

The Indian Olympic team played nine matches in Europe on its way back and won each one of them. Europe was a logistical nightmare, as reported by the president of the IHF:

> Every member of our party enjoyed the tour immensely, notwithstanding the strenuous travel we had to undertake. To play the match at Budapest on 15 September, we had to travel by bus from Vienna to that city and back, a distance of 500 kilometres. We left Vienna at 10.30 am, arrived at Budapest at 5 pm, played at once, and returned to Vienna at 2 am the following morning. [53]

The Indians received their warmest reception at Amsterdam. People at the Dutch capital were jubilant to have the team back in the city. Old acquaintances such as Mr Leming, attaché of the Indian team four years earlier, organized a civic reception for the Indians in which the players were presented with the local mascot – a monkey. [54]

Contemporary reports make it clear that Dhyan Chand was an idol in the hockey world of Europe. Germany held him dearest, calling their best hockey player 'the German Dhyan Chand'. At Prague a young lady insisted after the match on kissing India's hockey wizard, a demand that made him extremely uncomfortable. 'He is an angel,' she declared before kissing him. In Germany the Indians met the German national team in Munich, beating them 6–0. After the match the Indian contingent presented a stick signed by the entire squad to their hosts at the German Hockey Federation. [55]

In all, the Indian team played 28 matches on tour, including eight in India, and scored a total of 263 goals.

The Problem of the Rupee

The Olympic title or the spectacular display put up on numerous occasions across the world weren't enough to solve the financial crisis plaguing Indian hockey. At the start of the tour the team was short of the estimated expenditure by Rs8,000–10,000. The contributions received as a result of matches played at various places on the way to Los Angeles had made up a large part of this deficit. However, expenses in America proved way in excess of the estimate and transport charges for excess baggage throughout the tour weighed heavily on the touring party. Added to these was the extra expenditure incurred in Europe to play a series of exhibition matches in several

European countries. As the IHF president put it, 'We all took too much luggage with us. This involved us in avoidable expenditure in transport charges. This is a matter that should receive careful attention in subsequent tours.' [56]

On tour the expenses were met from the special tour fund and by drawing upon the few thousands from the main account of the federation. At the end of the tour the final debt stood at a substantial Rs12,000. To pay up the money drawn from the federation account, the team was forced to issue a plea to sports fans and sporting clubs back home to come forward and make a donation to the tour fund.

Interestingly, the managers of the team were determined the get the accounts of the tour fund audited at the earliest instant and were also keen to publish a summary of the receipts and expenditures incurred to ensure transparency. [57] Whether this was eventually done is not known.

The 'National' Game: What Was Special about Hockey?

Why was India so good at hockey in those early years? Commenting on the Indian success at Amsterdam, the manager A.B. Rosser declared in his report that

> The success of the Indian team was due to positional play, combination of forwards with halves, likewise of halves with backs, the tackle back, quick movement and first time passes, deft stick work both in attack and defence, frequent use of hand to stop the ball and the feint to baffle the defence. [58]

From this description it is evident that the Indians were sound in the basics and adept at tactics and strategy.

The managers of the 1932 Indian touring team further developed Rosser's analogies. They argued that because the grounds in India were hard and fast, they allowed the Indians to develop a fast game. Also, the Indians were supple in their wrists, making possible the dribble, and playing in light footwear enabled quickness of foot movement. Swami Jagannath, a player, organizer and subsequently a professional hockey umpire, offered a similar explanation:

> The chief factors which contribute to the success of the Indians in the field of hockey are the extensive plots of land available as playing fields, heavy rainfall over only a short period of the year giving generally dry and hard grounds, the light physique of the people and the supple movements of their bodies. [59]

The comparatively low cost of practice was another reason behind India's supremacy in world hockey.

Writing in the 1960s, C.D. Parthasarathy argued that it was only when a series of rule changes were introduced and a series of amendments passed that India's superiority was challenged. For example the introduction of free hit for 'bully' made skill secondary. Also the new penalty corner rule introduced in the 1950s made goal scoring easier, rendering ineffective the natural Indian flair with the ball. Gradually, crisp and sharp short passes and the dribble, a feature of India's play, gave way to long and powerful hits and first-time passes. Soon, power counted more than precision and the Indians lost out, unable to adapt the innovative techniques of the Europeans. [60]

However, none of these explanations convincingly clarify the reasons behind the Indian superiority or subsequent decline in hockey. This is because even after the rule changes were introduced the Indians won silver at Rome in 1960 and gold at Tokyo in 1964.

Rather, it can be suggested that the most striking feature of the successful Indian tours in 1928 and 1932 was the absence of divisions among players or officials on the lines of class, caste or economic privilege. In 1932, the entire touring party with the exception of G.D. Sondhi stayed together at the Olympic village. This also included the president of the IHF, A.M. Hayman. In his review of the tour, Hayman singled out this sense of camaraderie and fellow-feeling among the players and officials as the central factor that contributed to India's continuing dominance in world hockey. He ended his report with the words:

> I have been with the Olympic team throughout the tour. I lived with the players at the Olympic village at Los Angeles. I entered into all their frolic and fun. I have never lived with better companions. At all times and in all places everyone of them behaved as a true sportsman and gentleman. [61]

It was this feeling of camaraderie among players that held the Indian team together during its amazing run of six consecutive Olympic Gold medals between 1928 and 1956 and explains why India could do it in hockey but was unable to scale similar heights in cricket or football in the 1930s or 1940s.

It is perhaps worth suggesting that the camaraderie was a product of the players' backgrounds and professions. Unlike in cricket, where the princes always held the upper hand because the players were dependent on them for patronage, in hockey the players were mostly professionals in other fields, with an innate sense of discipline governing their lives. Hockey players who weren't part of the army were professionals employed by institutions such as the railways and on most occasions had graduate degrees, which helped to inculcate in their minds the importance of self-restraint and moderation.

A study of the class composition and professions of the players of the 1932 Indian Olympic team helps substantiate this point. While the captain Lal Shah Bokhari was a member of the Punjab Provincial Service, the goalkeeper Richard Allen James worked for the Port Commissioners in Calcutta. Eric Pinniger, who captained the team in the absence of Jaipal Singh at Amsterdam, worked for the North Western Railway, as did his second-in-command Arthur Charles Hind. Others employed by the railways included Carlyle Tapsell (Bengal Nagpur Railway), William Sullivan (Central India Railway) and Richard John Carr (East India Railway). Dhyan Chand, as mentioned earlier, was a Lance Naik in the army while Roop Singh, Muhammed Jaffer, Aslam Bagga, Masud Minhas and Gurmit Singh were either in college or had just finished their bachelor's degrees from well-known institutions such as the Chief's College or Islamia College in Lahore. [62] In hockey there were none like Lala Amarnath or Mushtaq Ali who could rise to prominence because the Maharaja of Patiala and the Nawab of Bhopal accorded them patronage.

In sharp contrast to the rosy picture painted by the hockey team, the Indian cricket team that toured England in 1932 was a divided house. The sharply divided nature of the team is portrayed in *Twenty-Two Yards to Freedom: A Social History of Indian Cricket:*

> The team that was initially united under Patiala's leadership was deeply divided by the end. Soon after the tour was over, Vizzy donated a pavilion to the newly built Ferozeshah Kotla Stadium in Delhi, naming it after Lord Willingdon. These efforts to curry favour with the Viceroy were successful, and though Patiala was elected chancellor of the Chamber of Princes in 1933, his influence over Indian cricket was on the wane. [63]

Mihir Bose also draws attention to this deep-seated internal discord in his seminal work on the history of Indian cricket:

> Willingdon's hostility to Patiala had coincided with the waning of the latter's cricket power. He had been the kingmaker of the 1932 tour, but in the winter of 1933–34 he was pushed to the sidelines. The emergency Board of Control meeting in Delhi on 1 May 1933 showed that the associations, which had once survived because of his generosity were now turning against him. [64]

That the scenario had not improved is evident from a letter written by Mushtaq Ali to his mentor C.K. Nayudu when on tour in England in 1946. Written on 1 August 1946 from the Carlton Hotel in Taunton, the letter goes thus:

> Now Sir I must tell you something from this end, how Indian cricket is and how we are doing in this country. In my humble opinion this tour is worse than 1936, the same old trouble: no team work at all. Every member of the team is for himself. No one cares for the country at all. Amarnath is the cause of all these things. Pataudi is a changed man... and is very much against the Indian players. C.S. Nayudu plays in the team not as a bowler but as a fielder only.... Whenever a county player is set for a big score you will find the Indian captain back in the pavilion. As a captain he is worse than a school boy.... I am very much fed up with him as are the other members of the team. Believe me Sir, the second Test match was ours after such a nice start. We collapsed because he sent in Abdul Hafeez at No 3 instead of going in himself.... I think Merchant is a much better captain than this fellow. [65]

In football too the picture was similar, evident from the tremendous infighting between provincial football organizations in the lead up to the formation of the All India Football Federation in 1937. It started when the Indian Football Association (IFA), based in Calcutta, unhappy with its role as a regional institution, aimed to govern the development of football in the whole country, posing as the governing body for soccer in India. It was as a mark of protest against such intentions of the IFA that other state associations for soccer formed the All India Football Association (AIFA) in 1935. The formation of the All India Football Association in September 1935 triggered the commencement of a bitter struggle between the Indian states, Bengal on the one hand and the western and northern Indian states on the other, for assertion of supremacy over the control of the game. Unfortunately for Indian football, players too were drawn into this conflict and were forced to take sides. When the Chinese Olympic team visited the country for a series of charity games before the Berlin Olympiad of 1936, there was a huge dispute over the venues and also over the players picked to represent India against the Chinese team. That there was an overwhelming majority of Bengali players in the team did not go down well with soccer players from northern and western India.

In fact, it was only when the representative of the Army Sports Control Board, a key player in the whole controversy, decided to strike a compromise between the provinces by taking the initiative to form the All India Football Federation that the conflict came to an end. Eventually the army was forced to issue a circular to all soccer associations of the country declaring that a conference would be held at Simla in May 1937, where the All India Football Federation would finally come into existence. While this solution was not something Bengal would have wanted ideally, it was the best result under the circumstances. Bengal was in no position to alienate the Army Sports Control Board, whose support was key to the survival of the IFA. The IFA tried its best to postpone the formation of the AIFF to September but the army board held firm. In a personal letter sent to the Maharaja of Santosh, the president of the IFA, the representative of the Army Sports Control Board declared his intentions to go ahead with the formation of the AIFF at Simla in May 1937, solving the crisis that had plagued the fortunes of soccer in India for almost a decade. [66]

In hockey, there were none of the early administrative and political divides that the other two games experienced. The players, unsullied by administrative wrangles, played as one unit. The hockey team rose to national prominence for its performances on the international stage as a 'national' team. It was this nationalist link that bounded it in the early years. While the politics of nationalism operated in both cricket and soccer, [67] neither of these two games produced triumphs of the 'national' team. The great 1911 victory of the Calcutta-based Mohun Bagan club over the British East York Regiment is seen by a number of historians as not just a sporting but also a nationalist milestone that spurred on the *Swadeshi* (indigenous) movement. [68] By the 1930s, the noted literary figure Sajani Kanta Das had noted that three things personified Bengali colonial identity: Mohun Bagan, Subhash Chandra Bose and New Theatres. [69] Yet soccer's triumphs were not the triumphs of a 'national' team in the way that hockey's was and soccer remained enmeshed in regional rivalries between Bengal and other provinces until much later.

In sharp contrast, the astonishing success rate of Indian hockey in the late colonial and early postcolonial period, when it won six successive gold medals at the Olympics between 1928 and 1956, turned that game into an icon for the nationalist sentiment as a whole. So much so that when the IOC toyed with the idea of dropping hockey as an event in the 1952 Helsinki Olympics, India offered to host the event separately in New Delhi. The success of the Indian hockey teams in beating Western teams demonstrated to the nationalists that Indians could compete on equal terms with the West. The success of the Indian hockey teams was such that after independence the Ministry of Sport, not surprisingly, chose hockey as the official 'national game' of India.

Onwards to Berlin

Beyond a shadow of a doubt India had established herself as the world's foremost hockey-playing nation by 1932. At the same time, there is little doubt that the absence of leading European and Australasian nations at Los Angeles had diluted the impact of the Indian triumph. In fact, their absence at LA had transformed India's title defence at Berlin in 1936 into something far more significant than a quest for another Olympic gold. That the Indians were in no mood to relinquish their hold on the world title was evident when on its second tour to New Zealand in 1935 the team stunned the world, winning all of the 48 games played. The Indians scored a record 584 goals and conceded just 40. It was indication enough that India was ready to take on Europe at Berlin. What makes the Indian dream run at the Nazi Olympiad especially momentous was that for the first time in history the legendary Dhyan Chand was appointed captain, an appointment that hinted at the decisive collapse of the privilege barrier in hockey.

Notes

[1] A.M. Hayman, President, Indian Hockey Federation, 1932, in 'Review of the 1932 Olympic expedition by the President of the IHF', File OU MO 01 14 36, CIO CNO IND CORR, Olympic Studies Center, IOC Museum, Lausanne (hereafter 'Hayman Review 1932').
[2] Rajdeep Sardesai, *Sunday Times of India*, 1992.
[3] The magazines of the Presidency and St Xavier's Colleges in Calcutta between 1920 and 1940 are full of praise for the Indian hockey team's performance at the Olympics.
[4] For details see 'We Climb the Victory Stand: Hockey in *Excelsis*', in De Mello, *Portrait of Indian Sport*.
[5] Dhyan Chand, *Goal*, published in *Sport and Pastime*, 1952. The book has been digitized and is available at http://www.bharatiyahockey.org/granthalaya/goal/, accessed 10 Sept. 2007.
[6] For details see De Mello, 'We Climb the Victory Stand', 82.
[7] Ibid.
[8] Ibid., 83.
[9] For details see Parthasarathy, 'Indian Hockey: Rise and Fall'.
[10] Dhyan Chand, *Goal*.
[11] De Mello, 'We Climb the Victory Stand', 85.
[12] Guha, *India After Gandhi*, 115–16.

[13] Subroto Sirkar, 'They Came…They Played…They Conquered', *World Hockey*, 13 March 1995, 8.

[14] For details see; Dhyan Chand, *Goal*.

[15] Notes from Jaipal's Singh's Memoirs passed on to us by Amar Singh, then secretary of the C.C. Morris Cricket Library, Pennsylvania in 2001. Amar Singh, Jaipal Singh's son, passed away in 2002. Jaipal Singh's memoirs were later published as an edited collection by Rashmi Katyayan in 2004 by Prabhat Khabar Publications, Ranchi.

[16] Katyayan, *Lo Bir Sendra*, 35.

[17] Private papers of Jaipal Singh passed on by Amar Singh. Quoted in Katyayan, *Lo Bir Sendra*, 35–7.

[18] Dhyan Chand, *Goal*, section on the 1928 Amsterdam Olympiad.

[19] *The Statesman*, 19 May 1928, 11.

[20] *The Statesman*, 20 May 1928, 11.

[21] *The Statesman*, 29 May 1928, 14.

[22] Personal interview with Amar Singh, C.C. Morris Library, 2001.

[23] *The Statesman*, 29 May 1928, 14.

[24] Dhyan Chand, *Goal*, section on the 1928 Amsterdam Olympiad.

[25] Great Britain did not participate in the hockey competition for the 1932 and 1936 Olympics. The games were not held thereafter until 1948, due to the Second World War.

[26] A series of reports were published in the *Times of India* commenting on the significance of this victory against England in 1948. It was considered a great gift from the team for the people of the newly independent nation.

[27] Parthasarathy, 'That Golden Age'.

[28] Quoted in Parthasarathy, 'Indian Hockey: Rise and Fall'.

[29] Katyayan, *Lo Bir Sendra*, 37.

[30] For details, see Dhyan Chand, *Goal*, section on the 1928 Amsterdam Olympiad.

[31] Katyayan, *Lo Bir Sendra*, 38.

[32] Guha, *India After Gandhi*, 115–16.

[33] Hayman Review 1932, Olympic Studies Center.

[34] Gupta, 'India's Hockey Supremacy', 37–8.

[35] Ibid.

[36] Ibid.

[37] Quoted in Hayman Review 1932, Olympic Studies Center.

[38] Ibid.

[39] Ibid.

[40] Ibid.

[41] Quoted in *The Statesman*, 2 Aug. 1932, 11.

[42] *The Statesman*, 9 Aug. 1932, 11.

[43] *The Statesman*, 4 Aug. 1932, 11.

[44] *The Statesman*, 6 Aug. 1932, 12.

[45] Mentioned in Hayman Review 1932, Olympic Studies Center.

[46] *The Statesman*, 13 Aug. 1932, 9.

[47] *The Statesman*, 14 Aug. 1932, 12.

[48] Ibid.

[49] Hayman Review 1932, Olympic Studies Center.

[50] Ibid.

[51] Hayman Review 1932, Olympic Studies Center.

[52] Ibid.

[53] Ibid.

[54] Ibid.

[55] Ibid.

[56] Ibid.

[57] Ibid.

[58] Quoted in Parthasarathy, 'That Golden Age'. The original report is housed in the International Olympic Museum, Lausanne. File OU MO 01 14 36, CIO CNO IND CORR, Olympic Studies Center, IOC Museum, Lausanne.

[59] Quoted in De Mello, 'We Climb the Victory Stand', 93–5.

[60] Parthasarathy, 'That Golden Age'.

[61] Hayman Review 1932, Olympic Studies Center.

[62] Ibid.

[63] Majumdar, *Twenty Two Yards to Freedom*, 44.

[64] Bose, *History of Indian Cricket*, 80.

[65] The entire letter is published in Majumdar, *The Illustrated History of Indian Cricket*, 84.

[66] For details, see Majumdar and Bandyopadhyay, *Goalless*, ch. 4.

[67] For Indian cricket and the nationalist imagination, particularly in colonial India, see for instance, Guha, *Corner of a Foreign Field*, and Majumdar, *Twenty Two Yards to Freedom*.

[68] See for instance, Bandyopadhyay, '1911 in Retrospect'.

[69] Majumdar and Bandyopadhyay, Introduction to 'A Social History of Indian Football', 122.

References

Bandyopadhyay, K. '1911 in Retrospect: A Revisionist Perspective on a Famous Indian Sporting Victory', *Soccer and Society*, 6 (2005): 27–47.

Bose, Mihir. *History of Indian Cricket*, revised and updated edn. London: Andre Deutsch, 2002.

De Mello, Anthony S. *Portrait of Indian Sport*. New Delhi: Macmillan, 1959.

Guha, Ramachandra. *Corner of a Foreign Field: The Indian History of a British Sport*. New Delhi: Pan Macmillan, 2002.

——. *India After Gandhi: The History of the World's Largest Democracy*. New Delhi: Picador, 2007.

Gupta, Pankaj. 'India's Hockey Supremacy'. *Sport and Pastime*, 10 May 1958: 37–8.

Katyayan, Rashmi, eds. *Lo Bir Sendra*. Ranchi: Prabhat Khabar Publications, 2004.

Majumdar, Boria. *Twenty Two Yards to Freedom: A Social History of Indian Cricket*. New Delhi: Penguin-Viking, 2004.

——. *The Illustrated History of Indian Cricket*. New Delhi: Roli Books, 2006 [also London: Tempus, 2006].

Majumdar, Boria and Bandyopadhyay, Kausik. *Goalless: The Story of a Unique Footballing Nation*. New Delhi: Penguin-Viking, 2006.

——. Introduction to 'A Social History of Indian Football: Striving to Score'. London: Routledge.

Parthasarathy, C.D. 'Indian Hockey: Rise and Fall'. *Sport and Pastime*, 16 Feb. 1963.

——. 'That Golden Age'. *Sport and Pastime*, 23 Feb. 1963.

'The Wood Magic': Cricket in India – A Postcolonial Benediction

Somshankar Ray

Cricket in India has unquestionably become the de facto national game and has therefore come to corner the lion's share of the public attention as well as financial and infra-structural support, while other games to varying degrees languish for want of support and following.

By comparing the fortunes of the Indian national teams of cricket, with football and hockey, this article tries to explore the reasons behind this singular pre-eminence of the national cricket team at the expense of all other sports.

Success has a thousand fathers, defeat is an orphan. [1]

A look at the contemporary sporting scene of India undoubtedly reaffirms the continued relevance of the above time-tested adage. Here cricket monopolizes every bit of public adulation and resultant financial spin-offs while other games, with the partial exception of soccer, languish in stepmotherly treatment. The sort of attention that cricket commands in India is showcased by headlines such as 'The Dream of a Billion Comes True', which a leading Bengali daily carried on the opening page after the Indian cricket team completed a Test series victory over the eternal *bête noire* Pakistan. [2] Now, how could cricket, or more specifically the national cricket team, succeed in becoming the most important vehicle of the popular expression of Indian nationalism? This paper will attempt to answer this query by comparing the annals of the national cricket side with that of the all-India units of other major sports such as football and hockey. Here it will be shown how cricket managed to keep pace with the varying priorities of the Indian nationhood while the rest gradually lagged behind.

Rolling the Pitch

1926 may be singled out as the year of first major convergence between cricket as a pastime and cricket as a nationalist assertion. By that time, the formation of a

Somshankar Ray, Vidyasagar College for Women, Kolkata.

representative Indian cricketing constellation had become increasingly viable. This was because by the middle of the 1920s, not only in the cricket field but also in the arena of politics, the definite concept of an Indian nation was at last emerging. In 1929 the Indian National Congress passed the *Purna Swaraj* resolution, which asked for complete political independence for the entire country from the British, and in 1930 Mahatma Gandhi triggered off the Civil Disobedience Movement to achieve that goal. This struggle was certainly more 'national' in its nature than those of 1905 and 1921. For the first time the peasantry, constituting the overwhelming majority of the Indian populace, participated wholeheartedly in the nationalist exertion under the unifying guidance of a single party. A million of them courted arrest throughout the country. Even more strikingly, Indian women joined this struggle in an unprecedented fashion and suffered with their male counterparts. This assertion of an Indian nationality was preceded by the formation of an 'all-India' cricket team which took the field against the MCC at Bombay on 16 December 1926. The stories of the Indian nation and of its cricket team were moving hand-in-hand.

India's connections with cricket, however, can be traced back to a period much earlier than 1926. A few decades ago Berry Sarbadhikary had dwelt on theories regarding the presence of cricket in India at least from the days of Alexander the Great, or even earlier. [3] More recently, Raju Mukherjee has argued that cricket originated in this subcontinent during the mythical epic age. [4] If anything, these hypotheses attesting to the existence of cricket in South Asia even in the hoary past prove the fascination of the modern inhabitants of the region with this game. Cricket in its recognizable form arrived in India with the Union Jack and by the dawn of the nineteenth century it was being played in all the British-Indian presidencies, i.e. Calcutta, Bombay and Madras. Alongside major bureaucrats such as Lord Harris, lesser officials such as Peter McWilliam also did their bit to spread the game in India. [5] The first Indian community to get interested in this exercise was the Parsis of Bombay, who were commercially and socially close to the British. They organized tours to England in 1886 and 1888; in 1892 they met the combined might of the Europeans of Bombay Presidency in the maiden first-class match on Indian soil. However, the Parsis, owing to their social exclusiveness, could not actually Indianize the sport.

This job was left to the native princes, who controlled one-third of the country during the colonial days. From the 1920s these indigenous rulers took an increasing interest in cricket. But even before that, the princely order had produced the first major Indian cricketing figure, Jamsaheb Ranjitsinhji of Nawanagar (1872–1933) universally known as 'Ranji'. Over the years fierce debates have raged over the 'Indianness' of Ranji's achievements. [6] He has been derided as an Anglophile retrograde despot who disdainfully remarked: 'Duleep [his nephew] and I are English cricketers.' Some others, on the other hand, have highlighted his less publicized services to Indian cricket such as the spotting of the fast bowler Amar Singh and his acknowledgement of the Indian Test team's potential in 1932. Whatever be the case, his stupendous 24,692 runs at an average of 56.37 runs, including 72 centuries on the

English first-class circuit and his Test debut century in 1896, indeed served to bolster the battered Indian psyche during the high noon of colonialism. Still, the systematic patronage of Indian cricket by the princes was heralded by the house of Patiala. The lead was followed by rulers of states such as Cooch Behar, Natore, Bhopal, Jath, some *jagirdars* of Hyderabad and importantly the prince of Vizianagaram. Now why the potentates chose to extend patronage to cricket is a moot point. Possibly they understood cricket as the sport of the English gentleman, upholding the notions of social hierarchy and therefore worth cultivating. [7] Indeed the Englishmen posted in India during the late nineteenth and early twentieth century preferred cricket over other imported games like football and hockey as it had an amateur tradition promoted by the upper and middle classes. So cricket was a good medium of socializing with British officials. However, not all principalities aided cricket with a pro-British mindset. Men such as prince Jagadindranarayan Ray of Natore often chose cricket as a field where the foreign conquerors could be fought on even terms. [8] Also the aristocratic supporters of cricket were mostly minor chieftains who often found other means of colonial socializing such as polo and hunting (*shikar*) too expensive and therefore settled for cricket, which was both patrician and affordable. Significantly, the comparatively large native states of Hyderabad, Travancore and Gwalior never became major cricketing powers and Indore became one only at the fag-end of the British Raj.

By the turn of the twentieth century, Indians had already started enjoying cricket along with football and hockey like other indigenous spectacles or '*tamashas*', and the involvement of the rulers (so important in a traditional society) had invested the game with an edge over the others, which later became almost permanent. Interestingly, though patronized by the princes, right from the eighteenth century cricket drew a substantial plebeian group of spectators. Thus cricket's mass appeal in the 1970s and 1980s was not really a sudden development. By 1926, when the MCC first decided to send a squad to India, cricket was being played by Indians cutting across class and communal lines in the presidency towns and the princely centres. The 1911 'All-India' side touring England had representatives from all major communities and, almost unbelievably, included an 'untouchable', Palwankar Baloo. [9] The MCC tour of 1926–7 (ironically, sponsored by the English community of Calcutta) indicated that Indian cricketers were now capable of competing with the best; also that the natives were able to raise an Indian XI of their own and thus prove that Indian national unity overrode regional and religious factors. The former was proved by C.K. Nayudu, who smashed an epic 153 against the visitors at Bombay; the latter was showcased by a representative all-India team at the same venue that held the English to a high-scoring draw. C.K. Nayudu, as scholars such as Mihir Bose have claimed, was in a sense a true Indian cricketer as he was by birth a South Indian, learnt his cricket in central India and earned his fame in western India (in the community-oriented Pentangular tournament in Bombay). Also, he was not a prince but a commoner. So quite justifiably he became the first cricketer who made the game popular throughout the nation. In 1994, long after 'C.K.' had passed away, the then Prime Minister of India, the late Narasimha Rao, fondly recalled his leaning for Nayudu during his childhood days.

After the heroics of Nayudu events progressed speedily for Indian cricket. The captain of the touring side A.E.R Gilligan was satisfied with the standard of Indian cricket and with his encouragement the governing body of Indian cricket, the BCCI, was formed in 1928 and was admitted to the Imperial Cricket Conference the next year. [10] After some usual princely melodrama, the Indian selection side finally stepped on to the Lord's pitch on 25 June 1932 to appear for its first 'official' Test, led fittingly by Nayudu. A chequered journey was about to begin.

It would be appropriate to place the rise of the Indian national side in the wider context of sporting development in the entire Third World. The 1920s also saw, in the other deprived parts of the planet, the ascent of similar sporting squads such as the Uruguayan soccer side and the West Indies cricket team. Uruguay, a tiny country with just two million inhabitants, produced a crack football team that won the Olympic gold in 1924 and 1928 and then hosted and annexed the first-ever FIFA World Cup in 1930. The psycho-social importance of these victories was underlined by this remark of a Uruguayan official in 1966: 'Other countries have their history, Uruguay has its football.' More significant from the Indian point of view was the evolution of cricket among the coloured populace in the West Indies and South Africa. [11]

So, as in India, in other parts of the globe also cricket was becoming a vehicle for the expression of popular identities. However in India cricket was still not the sole sporting spokesman for the Indian nationhood. Other athletic challengers were also appearing on the horizon. The most important of these was hockey. Although the oldest hockey tournament in India, the Beighton Cup, started in Calcutta in 1895, followed by the Agha Khan Cup in 1896, it captured national imagination only around 1928. A year earlier India had become the first non-European country to enter the International Hockey Federation. After that a national team was formed to participate in the Amsterdam Olympics of 1928. At first financial inadequacy threatened the departure of the team for the meet, but ultimately the hockey-lovers of Bengal raised the requisite amount. [12] This showed the popularity of hockey at that stage. This must have been enhanced by the performance of the team in the Olympics themselves, where, led by Jaipal Singh, India won all their matches without conceding a goal and thereby netted the gold medal. With this started the journey of one of the most successful sides in the history of team sports. India won six consecutive Olympic golds up to 1960. Before India achieved independence, the hockey team had won two more golds in the 1932 and 1936 Olympiads, which was a wonderful tonic for a subjugated people. In fact in the 1932 Los Angeles competition India thrashed hosts USA 24–1, till now a record, while in Berlin in 1936 Dhyan Chand is said to have earned the admiration of Adolf Hitler.

Another game competing with cricket for public attention was soccer. This sport became popular among the Indians of Calcutta around 1865, owing to the efforts of Nagendraprasad Sarbadhikary. Association football always had the potential for patriotic adulation, as right from the late nineteenth century there was an undercurrent of hostile competition between the British and the native clubs of Calcutta both on and off the field. Also at that stage Calcutta was the capital of the Indian Empire and the nursery of the nascent Indian nationalism. [13] So naturally an incident on the soccer field could easily assume wider implications. By the time the IFA was formed in 1893 as Bengal football's governing body, the game had taken off among the natives, as is evident from the establishment of clubs like Sovabazaar, Nationals and Aryans. Still the IFA had only one Indian member initially in Sarbadhikary and the IFA shield was considered a preserve of the Europeans. Things started getting even murkier as a new Bengali club called Mohun Bagan (established 1889) started creating ripples in Calcutta. In 1904 it won its first major title, the Cooch Behar Cup, and other triumphs followed. The foreign rulers knew now they had a match and the manhandling of the Mohun Bagan players by the Gordon Highlanders' footballers in 1909 showed that they cared. However the issue of colonialism versus nationalism came to the forefront in 1911 when Mohun Bagan entered the IFA Shield final as the first Indian club.

Bengal was then in the grip of the Swadeshi agitation, which ushered in the modern era in India's freedom struggle. So the 29 July confrontation between Mohun Bagan and the East Yorkshire Regiment quickly assumed the status of a proxy war. The match reportedly attracted a crowd of 80,000. Naturally the celebrations were unprecedented when the indigenous outfit actually pulled off a legendary victory. The triumph made news in places as far as London and Singapore. [14] However some remarks made in a few Indian newspapers regarding this breakthrough revealed the impact of this event on the national psyche. Next day's *Amrita Bazaar Patrika* commented: 'May God bless the Immortal Eleven of Mohun Bagan for raising their nation in the estimation of the Western people by their brilliant feat.' The *Weekly Moslem* observed that Mohun Bagan's success had heartened all Indians irrespective of their religious affiliations.

Bengal Muslims, however, soon had their own champion to cheer for. Mohammedan Sporting had been established between 1887 and 1891. But it had done little of note until the 1930s in the football circuit. In 1932 S.A. Aziz took over the management of the club and vigorously recruited Muslim players from length and breadth of India. The result went beyond the wildest dreams of its supporters as Mohammedan annexed the Calcutta League title for five consecutive years from 1934. The reaction of the Muslims (of not only Bengal but even outside) was delirious. [15] A section of Indian society that had felt clueless under the British had found its icon. Later Mohammedan's triumph transcended communal barriers and joined the myths surrounding India's struggle for freedom.

Thus soccer was a genuine competitor to cricket for being the agent of Indians' general nationalist feeling, though the concept of a national football team had not yet taken off properly. Actually until 1947 cricket had failed to take a decisive lead over other sports as the 'all-India' cricket side could not win a single official Test until then. So the Indians were left to celebrate only individual excellence amidst collective disappointment on the cricket field. Mihir Bose has recounted how Lala Amarnath was felicitated by the patricians and the plebeians alike after scoring India's maiden Test century in 1933. 'India hailed a hero', he remarked. [16] Significantly, the team lost the Test comprehensively.

The Opening Session

The case more or less remained the same for the few initial decades of the chronology of free India. As the country began its journey towards independent development, the priorities of the nation also changed. Now the need for anti-colonial patriotism was gone and the vision to build a progressive society was the need of the hour. In the sporting arena also India required some successes that would instil confidence in a freshly liberated people and present a bright image abroad. One has to admit that the cricket team largely failed to do so. Here a thought can be spared about how the colonial games such as football, hockey and cricket could retain their relevance in a postcolonial society. It would have been natural if after freedom the traditional Indian sports had staged a comeback. However, India had no indigenous outdoor amusement that could appeal to the masses cutting across class and region, especially to more sophisticated and affluent urban spectators. *Gilli danda*, possibly a primitive variant of cricket, could never replace its English cousin, in spite of a derisive suggestion in 1959–60 that the Indian cricket side should better play *Gilli danda* as it was being ominously whitewashed in the cricket field by the West Indies and England. Wrestling did have deep roots in traditional Indian culture, and even modern India won an Olympic medal in this sport (in 1952 by K.D. Yadav); yet somehow it failed to attract the cosmopolitan audience.

So cricket, football and hockey survived as public recreations even after political emancipation. The new ruling elite also did not disapprove of these entertainments as the Indian elite had always appreciated the blissful aspects of British civilization while decrying colonial exploitation. India's poet laureate Rabindranath Tagore also distinguished between the 'great Englishmen' and the 'mean Englishmen' and praised the former. Also the postcolonial elite could appreciate that popular Occidental games had the potential to bring in the recognition necessary for an emerging nation from a varied international community. This was beyond mere country merriments with their restricted appeal. So the imperial sports continued in democratic India and were harnessed to bolster the profile of this newly independent land. Hockey and football achieved this object as India continued to reign supreme in Olympic hockey until the mid-1960s, though right from 1952 the newly born Pakistan gave its older brother a run for its money, showing the evil effect of the partitioning of resources. The football team too made its proper debut on the international scene in the 1948 London Olympics. Though much could not be achieved at the world level, India quickly became a heavyweight in the Asiatic arena. On 10 March 1951 an emotional triumph was recorded when the soccer side won a gold medal in the inaugural Asian

Games (an Indian brainchild). For a newly independent nation it was a truly cherished moment and it is said that even Jawaharlal Nehru, the first Prime Minister of the land, personally pepped up the squad. [17] After a temporary eclipse, the football outfit entered the Olympic semi-finals in 1956, becoming the first Asian pack to do so and performed gallantly in the next edition in 1960. In the Asian context, it finished runners-up in the Merdeka tournament (in 1959 and 1964) and the Asia Cup (1964) and actually won the Asian Games gold in 1962. India by then had gathered a genuine constellation of talented footballers whose ability would remain unmatched in India's entire football history. India then had heroes in other sporting activities as well, such as Ramanathan Krishnan, who reached the Wimbledon semi-finals in 1961 and 1962, and Milkha Singh, who was the best short-distance runner of Asia at his peak.

The cricket team, though, failed to set such standards. From 1947 to the mid-1960s its performances oscillated between mediocre and horrible, especially on foreign soil. Throughout this period Indian cricket remained a story of personal heroics, of a Subhash Gupte, Vijay Hazare or a Vinoo Mankad amidst general ruin. However, it would be wrong to assume that cricket failed to create any occasion when the entire Indian psyche could identify itself with the game. One such poignant moment came on 10 February 1952, when India won its maiden Test match, and that too against the erstwhile master, England. As Partab Ramchand recollects, after that victory 'messages poured in from all over the country – including President Rajendra Prasad and Prime Minister Nehru – and the world'. [18] Another such occasion came in the West Indies in 1953. There the gallant fight put up by the Indian cricket side arrived as a tonic for the Indian settlers who were being increasingly sandwiched between the African-Americans and the whites. Mihir Bose has recorded the testimonies of a number of Caribbean Indians to drive the point home. [19] Suren Capil Deo has recalled: 'The effect of the visit of this, the first, Indian cricket team was to coalesce the Indian community. ... The 1953 tour came as a culture shock. Suddenly they (the Negroes) found that the Indians could play cricket and compete with the West Indians.' Ivan Madray, a future Test player, recalled the morale boost he received from the form of the Indian drove: 'I became more dedicated to my cricket; I played with a new courage.' However, despite playing this crucial role in helping the Indians to find their feet both at home and abroad in a postcolonial world, the overall picture for the cricket team remained bleak. In fact it remains a wonder how it could retain a fair amount of popularity amongst the common Indians. Along with this, one must remember that cricket was a game that could be played out on fields and streets by its admirers. So after watching their heroes in action, the children and youth of India could imitate them vigorously on the local pitch (be it a patch of green or even a lane between two blocks of buildings), and just one bat and a single stump sufficed as equipment for a match involving 22 players. Also, because cricket was a team sport, in such a local contest virtually all youngsters of the area could participate (with their parents as spectators), thus creating a solid support base for the game.

Unnoticed by many, wheels of change had started revolving in a direction favourable to cricket by the mid-1960s. Actually, from then India started its long downhill journey in other sporting activities while the worst days of cricket gradually were over. In 1964 the Indian football team failed for the first time to qualify for the Olympics. After that it could never win back its place in 'the greatest show on the earth' and thus got removed from the world stage (being formally amateurs, the Indians did not participate in the other world-level tournament, the FIFA World Cup). Also in the 1968 Olympics India was out of the final, and settled for the bronze for the first time in hockey. In cricket, however, things started to look up. Under the charismatic leadership of M.A.K. Pataudi the Indian band started playing attractive crowd-pulling cricket. The fielding standard began to improve, while in the bowling department an unprecedented array of four spinners of outstanding calibre came together – namely B.S. Bedi, B.S. Chandrasekhar, E.A.S. Prasanna and S. Venkataraghavan . The effect of these factors was not immediately evident as India lost all its Test matches in England and Australia in 1967–8, but the way the Indians contested the ground in Leeds and Brisbane proved that they were shedding their 'dull dogs' image.

The Middle Overs

Individual brilliance finally translated into collective success in 1971 when the Indian team, under a fresh skipper, Ajit Wadekar, conquered its traditional *phobia exotica* and vanquished the West Indies and England on their own soil. No less significant was the emergence of Sunil Gavaskar, India's new opening bat, in the series against the West Indies. In cold statistical terms, in a career stretching to 1987, he became the first batsman in the world to total 10,000 Test runs and also scored the most number of Test centuries. But his contribution went beyond these. Most importantly, during his long career he could instil pride and self-esteem among the Indian batsmen by definitely exorcizing the notion that they were too chicken-hearted to play hostile fast bowling. As an opener he scored runs in an era when genuine pace bowling reached a peak throughout the cricketing world. Also his authoritarian position in Indian cricket, achieved by 1978, sealed the dominance of the middle class and other ordinary citizens, at least in the cricket field. [20] This achievement of his assumes extra proportion in the context of the changing face of Indian nationalism. The 1970s were a turbulent time for the Indian nation. In the words of Prof. Ranajit Guha, 'disillusionment caused by failed possibilities' had made the Indians, especially unemployed middle-class youth, restive, leading to disturbances such as the Naxalite frenzy (an extremist movement that affected parts of India in the 1960s and 1970s), the movement of Jaiprakash Narayan (a wide ranging socio-political movement to protest against the alleged malpractices of the then central government) and the National Emergency. But at the same time all was not lost. In 1971, alongside Indian cricket, the Indian army also came of age by winning its most remarkable victory over Pakistan. In 1974 India went atomic as well. These bellicose measures boosted the flagging spirit of the Indians. So the mood in the 1970s remained, again in the language of Guha, 'one of anxiety suspended between despair and expectation'. [21]

Thus the India of 1971 was vastly different from that of 1952. In 1952, when India secured its maiden Test victory, public opinion did not go overboard in praise of the triumph and only politely acknowledged it. Being members of a newly independent land, the Indians of the 1950s cherished realistic hopes for future development of the country and the people. The nation focused on the up-and-coming industries and public works and not on sports. But the mood of the 1970s was certainly dissimilar. Most of the expectations generated in 1947 remained unfulfilled and a bulging population only added to the Indians' woes. This apart, India was falling behind the advanced countries in every field of human activity, ranging from the intellectual to the cultural. So the country was in search of icons who could offer them assurance in a turbulent situation. Recently Rahul Dravid has argued that it was from the 1970s that India became a true first-rate cricketing power. [22] In the batting section, Gavaskar was ably complemented by G.R. Visvanath, who was later joined by Dilip Vengsarkar and Mohinder Amarnath. Significantly, all of them averaged over 40 in Tests, a mark of consistency unmatched in Indian cricket till then. The bowling bracket continued to be dominated by the spinning quartet whose guiles were universally acknowledged. The Indian fielding also looked up considerably owing to the presence of exponents such as Abid Ali and Eknath Solkar. Naturally the constellation captured the public imagination and the victories gained by it were celebrated vociferously. This was expected, as cricket brought beleaguered citizens much-needed optimism and no significant intellectual exercise was required to appreciate the cricketing successes. This author has heard from the elders of his family how even the University at Burdwan, then a small town far away from Calcutta, declared holidays to celebrate the cricketing conquests of 1971. Though the cricket flock could not repeat the feats of 1971, the good mix of players did enough throughout the decade to suit the mood of the populace. Tony Greig, once reminiscing about his 1976–7 tour of India, wrote of Indians as 'people, who love cricket like no others I have ever seen'. [23] Table 1 reveals how the Indian cricket team gained in consistency from the 1970s and created a constituency of its own.

From the 70s, therefore, the national cricketing side could bring much coveted laurels to a pressurized populace, and thus succeed in making the game the most potent arena of expressing the general desire to see India victorious. The central

Table 1 India's progress in Test cricket over the years

Time Period	Total Tests	Victories	Win percentage
1932–'46	10	0	0
1947–70	106	15	14
1970–99	214	46	22
2000–	55	21	39

government led by Mrs Indira Gandhi was not lethargic in exploiting these wins for its own purpose. It tried to use the multi-regional cricket team as a safety valve through which various socio-economic tensions could be harmlessly dissipated. This contrast with 1952 again attested that 'sporting nationalism has always been most intense where there is a general feeling of insecurity or inferiority'. [24]

Beginning in 1978, the popularity of cricket in India touched fresh heights. In that very year, interestingly in a series versus arch-rivals Pakistan only, India at last unearthed a bowler who could be called 'express' according to international terminology – Kapil Dev. [25] In Indian cricket lore, he is the sole rival of Sunil Gavaskar in terms of social significance. It was with his advent that cricket took its most critical step in becoming the merriment of the masses in India. As a cricketer he was the ideal hero of the commoner, an attacking pace bowler and a hard hitter who matched Viv Richards and Ian Botham. To appreciate him, one need not get into the intricacies of a googly or a floater, or have the monumental patience necessary to evaluate an ideal innings by a Bombay batsman. Besides, his personal appearance, including the famous Palmolive smile and his family background, were apparently as simple as his game plan. Therefore, as the collaborator for his autobiography Vinay Verma, has noted,

> The rickshaw-puller whose life expectancy is no more than 40, is fuelled by this man's exploits. The man pulling a two-ton load on a hand cart is happy when Kapil blasts a quick 50. . . . The teeming millions of India need a blood and guts fighter to carry their banner for them. [26]

Indian cricket had always been affected by the 'filtration effect' as the tendency to follow the game first gripped the top level of the society – i.e. the rulers and the businessmen – and then influenced the middle strata during Gavaskar's reign. Now during the 1980s the Indian multitude finally became passionately hooked on the game, largely owing to Kapil's presence. Also there were some other auspicious factors that helped to make cricket firmly the 'game of the people' in this decade.

The most important of them was the advent of one-day cricket in India. Actually India had participated in this shorter version of the sport since 1974. But its record until 1980 was so dismal that the Indian crowd paid little attention to it. Despite improvement in its Test record in the 1970s, the Indian team proved to be surprisingly slow learners in this format. The batsmen either defended clumsily or attacked quixotically, the bowlers normally bowled outside the off stump, allowing easy scoring opportunities, and the fielding remained terrible. The sole victory over a Test-playing nation, up to 1980, came in 1978 against Pakistan. This was a little shocking as one-day cricket was not alien to the Indian domestic scene. The Talim Shield had been there for a long time, and limited-overs competitions such as the Deodhar Trophy for the zonal teams and the Wills Trophy for the provincial sides had been introduced in 1973–4 and 1977–8 respectively. However, from 1979 a breeze of change started blowing over the Indian cricket field. Then a number of utility all-rounders such as Roger Binny made their debuts, and along with Kapil they formed the nucleus of a potentially successful one-day side. It was in the 1980–1 tour down under, as Sunil Gavaskar once elaborated, that the Indians finally grasped the essentials of the shorter format. [27] There they had to play ten one-dayers on the trot, and the Indian cricketers appreciated that the one-day international (ODI) fashion was indeed here to stay. This realization helped India achieve its first ODI series win, over England in 1981–2, and a morale-boosting victory against the West Indies in early 1983. Still, as the one-day World Cup of 1983 arrived, India under Kapil was not given a ghost of a chance.

It has been recounted times out of number how the Indian squad made idiots out of the pundits by conquering the world on 25 June 1983. The success was certainly important, but the social impact it had was even more fundamental. As Mike Marqusee had noted, the final match, contested between India and the West Indies, two dark-hued sides, was extremely interesting from a sociological point of view. [28] For hundreds of thousands of South Asians and Caribbeans, the contest at Lord's marked a fleeting moment of triumph over a hostile society which consciously looked down upon them. Marqusee has especially marked the hysteric reaction of an Indian factory worker as India gradually progressed towards the prize from a seemingly hopeless position. The fervour of his countrymen back home was even more ecstatic. The Prime Minister. Mrs Gandhi, announced to the world 'we can do it', while India's legendary singer Lata Mangeshkar composed a number in the team's honour. But more decisive was the reaction of the common man. Within a few months of the World Cup triumph Indian small towns such as Jamshedpur and Guwahati, situated in areas not known for their cricketing prowess, produced capacity crowds for one-dayers held there. Most of these supporters must have come from the same proletarian social background as that of Marqusee's factory worker. Actually, limited-over cricket had combined the virtues of a day-long entertainment, which the Indians liked (as mentioned earlier) with the promise of a result. This was irresistible for the average Indian fan. In the next couple of years India, owing to its combination of a deep and varied batting line-up with a number of effective all-rounders, won three more one-day crowns, including the 'World Championship of Cricket' in Australia – a.k.a. the Benson and Hedges Cup (1985). This tournament opened up a new vista for the Indian spectator. The WCC was telecast live on television, which was gradually making its appearance in India. The superb coverage, by Channel Nine, of the matches played with white balls by the players in coloured apparel, simply bowled over the cricket buffs in the subcontinent. Since then, television and cricket went into a honeymoon that continues with increasing passion. By 1985 the Indians, almost universally, had been won over to the cause of cricket and even the highest in the land used the game as an expression to confirm India's relevance in a competitive world.

The Final Hour

It was only in 1987 that the Indians succeeded in making cricket an instrument for flexing its muscle in a global order which tended to treat its dark-skinned members in a step-brotherly way. That year India did not win any major laurels but hosted (along with Pakistan) the cricket World Cup. This was important, as the World Cup was looked upon as the special preserve of England, which was supposed to be the nerve-centre of a cricket world that was certainly less egalitarian than that of soccer or athletics. But what the Pommies and the Kangaroos failed to discern was that by then in terms of both the number of supporters and the amount of sponsorship money the subcontinent had outstripped them. The bid to host the World Cup thus rapidly became a classic postcolonial showdown with the once underprivileged countries demanding their place in the sun. The power equation was always dominant in this episode as the plan to organize the World Cup occurred to N.K.P. Salve, the then president of the BCCI, only after he had been shabbily treated by MCC officials in 1983 still steeped in colonial values. After India and Pakistan had made their bid, England ridiculed the offer by citing the traditional theory of socio-economic backwardness of India. Ultimately India pulled it off by guaranteeing a larger sum of money. There was nothing sentimental about it (in old colonial terms, cricket was enmeshed in a whole lot of gentlemanly perceptions) as the erstwhile dependency simply flexed its youthful muscles to show the former master its rightful place. India and Pakistan could offer an aggregate prize-money of £99,500 while England came up with only £53,000. What was more startling was the conviction among the Indians about the correctness of their position. R. Mohan, a leading Indian cricket writer, had asserted:

> The tens of thousands who will flock to the grounds in the four weeks of the World Cup are the one great reason why the Cup is being held here. Bringing the cricket to them represents a higher justice than a blind allegiance to the centre of a once great empire.

Anil Ambani, the executive director of the Reliance Industries, the official sponsor of the competition, added confidently: 'We will show the world that India and Pakistan are capable of jointly making it a grand success.' [29] In the actual event India lost in the semi-finals but even the English could not deny that India had organized a superb World Cup. Massive crowds watched all the proceedings including, significantly, the final contested by two foreign teams, Australia and England.

While we delineate the emergence of cricket as the soporific of the masses in India, some attention should also be paid to the prolonged decline of the two major rivals of cricket, hockey and football. In 1968 India had been definitely knocked off the hockey pedestal. The seven-times gold medallist had to remain content with a bronze in that year's Olympiad. Another bronze followed in 1972, and then in the 1976 Montreal Olympics India drew a blank for the first time by finishing seventh – the nadir had been reached. After that India has failed to reach the semi-finals of Olympic hockey even once except in 1980 (when the field was miserably restricted for political reasons). The causes of this catastrophic collapse of India's premier sporting institution are varied. Some of them were beyond India's control, however. In the 1976 Olympics the playing surface was changed from natural grass to AstroTurf.

Naturally to cope with this factor such surfaces had to be introduced at domestic level as well. This was beyond economically backward India, who quickly fell behind. Another cause was the increasing interest of the European nations in hockey. From the late 1960s Germany, Netherlands and Australia provided stiff competition for India. Being financially well off, they adopted AstroTurf more efficiently. From 1988 the Occidentals have established a monopoly over the Olympic gold while dominating the hockey World Cup as well. But possibly a more important reason for the disaster for Indian hockey lies within the country's system for this sport. During the Munich Olympics of 1972 it was clear that the Indian team had fallen prey to internal bickerings and a lack of cohesion. Both the senior players and the federation bosses were responsible for this. The coach of the Indian hockey team, K.D. Singh 'Babu', submitted a report to the then central government underlining the growing factionalism within Indian hockey. But no steps were taken to remedy that. The infighting within the hockey establishment reached its peak at the next Olympics in Montreal, when the players led by Ajitpal Singh openly rebelled against the tour manager R.S. Bhola. The players accused the manager of deliberately practising the 'divide and rule' policy, while the official blamed the players for gross indiscipline. [30] Predictably, India performed horribly in the competition. Again, two commissions were set up to prepare reports regarding the debacle and again nothing came out of them. Intra-federation conflicts have continued to plague Indian hockey since then and one of the recent examples of this was the dramatic sacking of the national coach, Rajinder Singh, before the Athens Olympics.

Like hockey, football had also started fading from the popular psyche by 1987. The Indian soccer side had begun walking backwards from 1964. The pace had quickened in the 1970s and by the 1980s it was in the base of the pit. In the 1970s, when cricket was establishing its hold on the popular psyche, the football team failed to bring any solace to success-starved Indians. It performed miserably in the 1974 and 1978 Asiads. But there was a glimmer of hope in the early 1980s as a national soccer outfit of considerable talent emerged and played creditably during 1982–4. Sadly, Indian football could not hold on to this new lifeline, largely owing to official inefficiency. In the 1986 Asiad India lost all its football matches. Also the arrival of television exposed the Indian spectators to top-quality foreign soccer and ruthlessly laid bare the shortcomings of indigenous practitioners. Soccer, like cricket, was a game that could be actually played by its supporters and was easy to understand. But the sorry state of the Indian team forced soccer to lose out to cricket in India. It remains a matter of speculation what could have taken place if the football side had built upon the promise shown in 1982.

The ordinary Indian, then, was left with no alternative other than to root for the cricket team whose exploits were world-class and lit up his otherwise mundane life. The other sport where India started creating waves from the 1980s was chess. But chess could not produce the effect of a 'spectacle' on the popular mind. In a cricket stadium, surrounded by other vocal partisans, the least politically conscious individual could identify with the nation as symbolized by some young athletic men. It was impossible that a game of chess contested by two completely static persons present in a theatre with limited spectator capacity would generate the same impact. Also to grasp the subtle moves of a Vishwanathan Anand or Dibyendu Barua one had to perform considerable cerebral labour. Thus by 1987 the national cricket team became the most significant vehicle of the popular expression of Indian nationalism. Since then the domination of this squad over the Indian mind has progressively increased.

The globalization of the Indian economy since 1991 seems to have aided this process. The partly open market policy followed by the government has led to an increase in the subscribers to private TV channels. Realizing the impact of television, various other companies have rushed in to advertise their wares on the small screen and as they found the cricketers to be the most recognized stars in the country they have quickly adapted the latter as endorsers and models. This again enhances the appeal of the members of the national cricket team among the common people of India. Thus it seems that a highly profitable circle has been established for the national cricketers. However there is an ugly side to the adulation the cricketers receive. During the 2003 World Cup, when Indian stars such as Sachin Tendulkar and Saurav Ganguly failed to meet their countrymen's expectations at the initial stages, the fans reacted sharply by burning the effigies of their idols and even attacking their houses. [31] Still, such incidents only show the intensity with which the Indians identify with their cricket team, and victory in cricket is treated as the triumph of the nation itself. In the 1996 World Cup, India beat arch-rivals Pakistan in a high-pitched encounter. Next day a leading English daily carried a simple banner headline on the first page: 'VICTORY'. It was as if all our patriotic aspirations had come true in a day.

Conclusion

Sport is a medium that is appreciated by both the high and the low of a community. So it is common for a nation to seek glories in the sporting sphere as all its members could readily participate in the resultant joy. Such victories make the citizens surer of their position in the broader world. In India, which continued to evolve as a nation state in the postcolonial world, cricket fulfilled this role. Cricket could bring in the success that made a commonplace Indian, always subject to immense socio-economic uncertainties, feel proud and equal to other peoples. For a 'generation-y' youngster (his social status being virtually immaterial here) cricket may actually be a way of life – more powerful than India's traditional cultures – but this was not the case throughout history. As explained in this essay, cricketers could keep pace with the changing *zeitgeist* of the Indian Leviathan by scoring international successes at crucial moments, unlike participants in other sports. From a tonic during the freedom struggle, a booster in the nation's early years, to a balm in the turbulent 1970s and 1980s, cricket could satisfy the shifting demands of the Indian people. Then from 1987 cricket became the only means through which the Indians could dictate terms to the world. The history of the subsequent period is not dealt with in detail here, as no real novel development has taken place in the cricket field after 1987. Only the stranglehold of cricket has increased as India continues to remain marginal in other major sporting events such as the Olympics. This explains the week long celebrations in the country after Abhinav Bindra won India's lone gold at the Beijing Olympic Games. But how long will this scenario last? The question is relevant as suddenly, during the last half- year, fresh icons in various other sporting activities have started emerging such as Rajyabardhan Rathore, Sania Mirza, Pankaj Advani and Narain Kartikeyan. [32] So, for how long will cricket remain the sole field of power for the Indians? Only time can tell.

Notes

[1] Tacitus.
[2] Banner Headline of *Anandabazaar Patrika* (Kolkata), 17 April 2004.
[3] Sarbadhikary, *A Century of Tests*, 307.
[4] Mukherjee, 'Not A Very Different Ball Game', *The Telegraph* (Kolkata), 20 Oct. 2004.
[5] For the career of Peter McWilliam, see Mangan and Bandyopadhyay, 'Imperial and Post-Imperial Congruence', 66–96.
[6] For Ranji see Frith, 'Had Gavaskar been an Englishman', 59.
[7] Mukherjee, 'It's Still the Same Old Game', 34–7.
[8] For a fuller treatment of J. Ray's career, see Majumdar, *Twenty-Two Yards to Freedom*, 33–6.
[9] Guha, *Spin and Other Turns*, 31–4.
[10] Mihir Bose puts 1929 as the year of India's admittance to the ICC (Bose, *History of Indian Cricket*, 61). However the 2004 *Wisden Almanack* puts it at 1926.
[11] As in India, cricket was brought to the West Indies by the British. It was soon played with enthusiasm by both white- and dark-skinned settlers. By 1891 an inter-territorial competition had taken off there. However, as the twentieth century progressed cricket and Caribbean social aspirations became more closely interlinked. Despite the abolition of slavery in 1838, the lot of African-Americans in the initial years of the century was certainly unsatisfactory. They became more restive after the First World War, during which many of them had the opportunity to watch the outside world as soldiers. So they too were searching for a medium that would give vent to their desire to assert themselves. Cricket fitted that role as it was a field in which the Negroes were well versed and at the same time a victory there would certainly stick a finger up the white master's nose. Hence the adulation surrounding George Headley and Learie Constantine, the two early heroes of the West Indies cricket team which gained Test status in 1928. This extract penned in 1963 by the Trinidad born Nobel laureate V.S. Naipaul would focus on the importance of cricket in Caribbean society: 'Who is the greatest cricketer in the world? The question came up in a General Knowledge test one day in 1940. ... I wrote, "Bradman". This was wrong; the pencilled cross on my paper was large and angry. "Constantine" was the answer to this one' (Cited in Guha, *The Picador Book of Cricket*, 432). Cricket became a carrier of popular suppressed emotion in some more areas also in the first half of the twentieth century. In South Africa, Britain promoted cricket at the beginning of the century in a bid to bring the 'Briton and Boer' together, but significantly cold-shouldered the majority coloured and dark populace. Undeterred, the latter organized their own cricketing circle, though at first divided along communal lines, e.g. 'Bantu', 'Indian', 'Malay' and 'Coloured'. As the unfortunate and cruel policy of apartheid gripped South African society from 1948, the cornered indigenous people cheered lustily for the visiting foreign sides in the cricketing arena.

[12] Thyagarajan, 'The Romance Continues', 49–54.
[13] Information regarding Indian football used in this essay is taken from Bhattacharya, *Kolkatar Football*; Bose's *Stories from Indian Football*.
[14] See Saha, 'Ekadase Suryodaya'.
[15] Bhattacharya, *Kolkatar Football*, 196 and 199. There the author records the joyous reaction of the Muslims of all sections to Mohammedan's triumphs. This was embodied in the rhyme "Hail to thee, Mohammedan Sporting. Today we are the lords, and others are subordinates." (translation mine). This shows how Mohammedan was quickly made the flagship of the then Muslim revivalism in the broader society. Also later the Muslim League ministry openly backed the club.
[16] Bose, *History of Indian Cricket*, 85.
[17] Bose, *Stories from Indian Football*, 45–6.
[18] Ramchand, 'An Appointment With History', 50–2.
[19] Bose, *History of Indian Cricket*, 193–6.
[20] For an account of the rise of Gavaskar, see his autobiography, *Sunny Days*.
[21] From Guha, *A Subaltern Studies Reader*, xi.
[22] 'Batting 80', special cricket pull-out, *Anandabazaar Patrika*, 31 March 2005, 6.
[23] Greig, *Test Match Cricket*, 91.
[24] Guha, *A Corner of a Foreign Field*, 349.
[25] Interestingly, India's immediate neighbour Pakistan, which shared a common sporting history with India until 1947, could build up a formidable fast-bowling tradition, from Fazl Mahmood in the 1950s to Shoaib Akhtar of today.
[26] Dev and Verma, *By God's Decree*, foreword.
[27] Interview with Sunil Gavaskar in *The Sportstar*, 6 Jan. 1996, 32–5.
[28] For Mike Marquesee's treatment of the 1983 World Cup see his *Anyone But England*, 226–30.
[29] Cited in *The Sportstar*, 10 Oct. 1987, 6 and 69.
[30] For more information on the decline of Indian hockey, See 'Vishesh Krida Sankhya' [Sports special], *Desh* (1988), 141–2 and 168–70.
[31] *Wisden Cricketers' Almanack* (2004), 962.
[32] For an article on the new challengers to cricket see Gautam Bhattacharya, 'Cricket's Monopoly Over' [in Bengali], *Anandabazar Patrika*, 27 March 2005, 20.

References

Bhattacharya, Rakhal. *Kolkatar Football*. Kolkata: Prabhabati, 2002 (reprint).
Bose, Jaideep. *Stories from Indian Football*. New Delhi: UBSPD, 2003.
Bose, Mihir. *History of Indian Cricket*. London: Andre Deutsch, 1990.
Dev, Kapil and Vinay Verma. *By God's Decree*. Sydney: Harper and Row, 1985.
Frith, David. 'Gavaskar jodi ingrej hoten' ['Had Gavaskar been an Englishman']. In *Anandabazar Patrika Cricket World Cup Commemorative Volume*. Kolkata: 1987.
Gavaskar, Sunil. *Sunny Days*. Kolkata: Rupa & Co, 1976.
Greig, Tony. *Test Match Cricket*. London: Hamlyn, 1977.
Guha, Ramachandra. *Spin and Other Turns*. New Delhi: Penguin Books, 1994.
——. *A Corner of a Foreign Field*. London: Picador, 2002.
——, ed. *The Picador Book of Cricket*. London: Picador, 2001.
Guha, Ranajit. *A Subaltern Studies Reader*. New Delhi: Oxford University Press, 1997.
Majumdar, Boria. *Twenty-Two Yards to Freedom*. New Delhi: Penguin Books, 2004.
Mangan J.A. and Kausik Bandyopadhyay. 'Imperial and Post-Imperial Congruence'. In *Sport in South Asian Society – Past and Present*, edited by Boria Majumdar and J.A. Mangan. London: Routledge, 2005.

Marquesee, Mike. *Anyone But England*. New Delhi: Penguin Books, 1994.

Mukherjee, Raju. 'It's Still the Same Old Game'. *The Sportstar*, 23 Dec. 1995: 34–7.

Ramchand, Partab. 'An Appointment with History'. *The Sportsworld*, 12–18 Feb. 1992.

Saha, Rupak. 'Ekadase Suryodaya' [The Dawn in [Nineteen] Eleven]. In *Desh Pujabarshiki*, Kolkata: Ananda Publishers, 1991.

Sarbadhikary, Berry. *A Century of Tests*. Kolkata: Cricket Library, 1964.

Thyagarajan, S. 'The Romance Continues'. *The Sportstar*, 25 Dec. 1999: 49–54.

Wisden Cricketers' Almanack. Hampshire: John Wisden and Co., 2004.

The Culture and Politics of Local Sporting Heroes in Late Colonial Bengal and Princely Orissa: The Case of Santimoy Pati

Projit B. Mukharji

Instead of studying the histories of national or elite club teams, this article seeks to explore the social and cultural forces that shaped local sporting heroes in mid-twentieth century India. Using a prosopographic approach the article uses a case study of a single talented student-sportsman, Santimoy Pati, growing up in colonial Bengal and Princely Orissa in the closing years of the Raj to explore the reasons why young people took to sport, the nature of their sporting exploits and the ways in which their sporting activities helped to shape their social lives. Though focussed upon a single life-story, through it, this micro-historical study touches upon the broader political, social and cultural currents of the day.

It also highlights that the culture of youth sport of the day was not specifically related to any particular sport but inspired the same youth to take up multiple sports. Such varied sporting interests were moreover often highly politicized and sportsmen saw their sporting activities as part of a larger nation-building process. However the precise doctrinaire form of the politics espoused by youth sportsmen could and did vary widely.

Though the history of sports in South Asia has often served as a critique of the more elitist preoccupations of political or social history, it has, at least in South Asia, fallen prey to its own brand of elitism. [1] Histories have revolved around national teams or premier clubs. In the case of individuals it has focused on the stars that have appeared for these elite teams.

Sport, however, never was, and is still not, limited to the few club or national teams. Sports stars are not merely those who eventually make a living or a name out of their sporting exploits. Sports stars are to be found in every village, school or street. Every village has its star strikers, every street its mighty batsman.

Projit B. Mukharji, Newcastle University.

The politics of the archives, however, results in an almost total erasure of such plebeian heroes from the historical memory of the community. Occasionally they crop up in the anecdotes of local old-timers, or perhaps in old photographs, yet for the most part their stories are lost; their sporting heroics forgotten.

Yet these forgotten performances are more than simply of antiquarian interest. As micro-historians have suggested since the 1970s, the individual lives and experiences are crucial to re-constructing the past. [2] In fact nowhere is prosopography more apt as a method than in the case of studying local sporting heroes. After all what makes the local sports heroes great are precisely their specific socio-historical contexts. It is because their exploits struck a chord and resonated with their viewers and fans that their exploits were enjoyed and remembered. However the micro-historical approach has often been criticized for making much of singular cases. [3] Without going into a protracted discussion of these objections, we might clarify that in the present case the approach used is not that of traditional prosopography but rather a modified and de-centred approach that – in our view – answers such objections adequately. Instead of being based upon a single or singular written document as the source of information on a singular life – as is the preferred technique of micro-historians – we have based our narrative on local memories – verified wherever possible by such rudimentary written documentation as exists. Character certificates and personal references along with school and college leaving certificates have thus verified the account mostly reconstructed through oral history. Thus the individual life studied has been available to us as narratives of social memory constructed as a compilation of socially viable and resonant images, making a strict distinction between the individual/singular and the social/plural slightly blurred. This blurring occurs as the individual may have actually adopted socially valuable roles and role models from his immediate cultural and social milieu thereby giving these images a 'reality'; while another equally tenable possibility is that the stellar life may have actually been remembered locally through identification with other similar images. There is no way to decide. Yet it is this unresolved tension between the individual and the social – between the singular and the commonplace – that gives our approach its grounding in social history as well as micro-history and hopefully adequately answers the criticism of atypicality.

Using the these tools this paper will therefore try to look at the role of college sports and sports stars in Orissa and Bengal in the tumultuous years immediately leading up to the Independence of India in 1947. Through a single micro-historical case study of student sports star Santimoy Pati (Figure 1) in the last two-and-a-half decades of the Raj, we will try to locate the culture of youth sports and the identities of the student sportsmen within the larger context of the times. [4]

The School Years

Orissa had, along with many other areas which came under British rule in its early years, administratively formed part of the British Bengal. In 1912 following the

Figure 1 Santimoy Pati in his Calcutta University Blue blazer and tie.

annulment of the Partition of Bengal, Bihar and Orissa were separated from Bengal and constituted in to a new province. Subsequently the province was again split, finally giving Orissa its long-sought administrative autonomy in 1936.

Politically, Orissa was divided among a number of petty, semi-independent principalities on the one hand, while on the other British Orissa was placed under a commissioner. Apart from the big feudal chiefs, there were also a number of smaller zamindars. [5] Like in neighbouring Bengal, sub-infeudation and expanding families had reduced many of these zamindars to the status of petty landholders. With one foot in land, their sons often tried to supplement their ever-diminishing incomes through small governmental jobs and professions. It was this new Oriya middle-class that had spearheaded the Oriya language campaign in the late nineteenth century which eventually brought the province autonomy. The language movement in its early years was often built around eloquent critiques of people from neighbouring states, especially Bengal, filling up the lower-level government jobs, thus depriving the Oriya middle classes. The Oriya Bhodrolok class, thus formed from the lesser gentry but also showing characteristics of a professional middle class, came like its counterpart in Bengal to invest heavily in the education of its wards, particularly boys. [6]

Santimoy Pati was born in 1922 in a family of small Brahmin zamindars in Keshiari in the district of Midnapore. [7] Santimoy's father, Sureshwar Pati, held lands on the Orissa-Bengal border. Being a largely tribal area, the social and ritual status of the Patis had ensured that they continued to wield sufficiently more authority in the area than their holdings alone would suggest. However, by the 1920s, even if not by economic necessity, culturally it was almost assured that young Santimoy would be given a thoroughly modern education. Though he was initially educated in Midnapore, by the age of nine he had been externed from the district of

Midnapore because of his involvement with nationalist revolutionaries in the area. Thereafter he travelled to Baripada, the capital of the princely state of Mayurbhanj, where an uncle of his worked as a civil surgeon. At Baripada, the young Santimoy joined the Baripada High School. It was here that both his political as well as his sporting interests came into full bloom. [8]

By the 1920s educational institutions were sites for multiple cross-cutting ideological investments in sports. From the middle of the nineteenth century, British authorities had sought to indoctrinate students in sports such as cricket, football and so on. It was an ideologically inspired elaboration of the larger 'civilizing mission' of colonialism, but probably also drew on pedagogical ideologies in metropolitan Britain that sought to produce good empire-builders by inculcating an ethos of 'muscular Christianity'. [9] This imperial origin however did not preclude its popular appeal, and it soon caught the people's imagination. Soon afterwards it was sought to be appropriated by Indian educators, whose commitments were usually not towards fashioning colonial subjects but rather towards the building of the future of the community. With the rise of nationalism, this project metamorphosed into the building of future citizens – though there remained considerable ambiguity and overlap about which nation they sought to cultivate. As we shall see in the case of Santimoy Pati, the ideological leanings could finally also veer towards communism.

It is not our intention to study the larger discourses on sports and politics. Instead, a prosopographical approach in fact allows us to interrogate the myriad ways in which these multiple ideological investments in sports in educational institutions of the time actually affected individual sporting personalities.

Baripada was the capital of the princely state of Mayurbhanj and directly ruled by the Bhanj family with support from the British government. The Baripada High School was originally established by the Maharaja Krushna Chandra of Mayurbhanj along with some 37 other schools he established in the region. Mayurbhanj was one of numerous petty, semi-independent kingdoms in the region and controlled much of the lands along the border of Orissa and Bengal. Krushna Chandra had originally not been in line for the Mayurbhanj throne. Yet upon his uncle King Srinath Bhanj's death in 1867, despite strong opposition from the dead king's widow, the young Krushna Chandra obtained the throne through the strong support of the paramount British official of the region, T.E. Ravenshaw. [10] Throughout his reign Krushna Chandra painstakingly cultivated his close relationship with the British government. Principally this meant cultivating the close relationship with Ravenshaw, which had brought the throne to Krushna Chandra. Ravenshaw also happened to be an enthusiastic educator and, in his capacity as the commissioner of the Cuttack Division, he encouraged, supported and funded the founding of numerous educational institutions. Ravenshaw's own views on education, however, were largely shaped by his belief in the necessary connection between the spread of education and good governance. He represented perhaps a more humane aspect of Macaulay's infamous wish to produce a class of Indians educated in English who would mediate between the British overlords and their Indian subjects. [11] Writing in the aftermath of the devastating famine of 1866, Ravenshaw had bitterly complained that

> No other province in the Presidency was so deficient of intelligent and public spirited residents who would appreciate the facts, bearing on the prospects and means of the people and who could give practical information to the authorities as would have been the case in any district of Bengal proper and in carrying out remedial measures. [12]

Education was thus seen as the way to produce informed mediators who would supply the government with the information necessary for good governance. Further, as the eminent historian (and Santimoy Pati's son) Biswamoy Pati points out, these and other apparently philanthropic institutions built by Krushna Chandra often added to the woes of the subjects since they were funded through additional cesses. [13]

The Baripada High School, set up in 1889, was thus founded to produce a class of students who would play a subordinate role in government. There is not much that is known to us today about the sporting ideologies that informed sporting activities in the school's early days. Chances however are that the administrators would have been inspired by very similar ideologies as those identified in some of the larger metropolitan schools and colleges of the day. Following the foremost historian of the 'games ethic', James Mangan, we know that

> [t]he game was considered by the colonizers to carry a series of moral lessons, regarding hard work and perseverance, about team loyalty and obedience to authority and, indeed, involving concepts of correct physical development and 'manliness'. As such, it was used as a key weapon in the battle to win over local populations and begin transforming them from their 'uncivilized' and 'heathen' state to one where they might be considered 'civilized' and 'Christian'. [14]

Having said this, however, it must be conceded that Boria Majumdar has convincingly highlighted the implicit difference – or at the very least ambivalence – between the British officials with their ideologies of sports and the maharajas, who while superficially seeming to toe their line often nursed secret aspirations of doing the British down in their own game. [15] Krushna Chandra, however, was too much of a loyalist – he is known to have given lavish feasts for instance to commemorate British military victories elsewhere in the subcontinent – to infer any 'secret agenda' on his part until any actual evidence of such is found. [16]

Whatever the ideologies that inspired him, by the age of 13 the young Santimoy was an avid sportsman and won the All Indian States Athletic Championship. [17] Santimoy, however, was already deeply involved in politics. At the age of nine, the local police had suspected of him having links with the local underground nationalist militants. [18] His house had been searched and he had been placed under house arrest, greatly embarrassing his staunchly loyalist father. After the victory at the provincial championships, once again he ran into trouble with the local police.

The loyalist local gentry of the day were doubly suspicious of militant nationalists. On the one hand any suspected involvement with the militants – whether real or imagined – made the British establishment frown upon them; while on the other hand the militants often preyed upon loyalist gentry, looting their treasuries to finance the militant campaigns. Santimoy's father – the staunchly loyalist Sureshwar – having long despaired of his son's actions therefore immediately reported his son to the police upon suspicions of the latter's being a 'Swadeshi dacoit'. [19] Thus in the months following Santimoy's provincial glory, he was once again hunted by the police acting upon the report of his own father. A search of his room by the police revealed a copy of Rajani Palme Dutt's *India Today*. [20] The book at the time was considered a nationalist manifesto and had been proscribed by the government. Its recovery from the boy's room earned him therefore a short stint at the Midnapore district jail.

Upon release from jail he found himself without a home, as his father refused to let him back. He was, however, sheltered by an uncle of his who was a civil surgeon at Baripada. Appearing for his matriculation examinations under such circumstances, not surprisingly he barely passed his examinations, receiving a third division. [21] Without his family's support and with poor academic results, there were few avenues open to the local sportsman. [22] It was then that one of his father's employees (*gomastha*) volunteered to help. The employee knew of the keen interest that the principal of the biggest college in the vicinity – the Bankura Christian College – took in sports, and he undertook to mention the young sportsman's plight to the principal. Principal W Bailey was a professor of history at the college and was not known to be particularly fond of the nationalist agitators. He was, however, keen to see the college sports teams do well and had an immense appreciation of sportsmen. Upon hearing of Santimoy's plight, he immediately mentioned that the college was playing a crucial football match the very next day and its regular striker was indisposed. Principal Bailey promised that if he was convinced by the boy's performance on the field in the crucial match, he would be admitted into the college without any further questions.

Santimoy played the match on the following day and scored thrice before half-time, thus earning himself a place at college despite his poor results and police record. [23] Principal Bailey continued to support the youngster as he performed on the sports pitch in several different sports. By the time he graduated he had represented his college in cricket, football, volleyball, hockey, tennis and badminton. [24]

The College Years

In between his multiple sporting commitments, however, Santimoy's political activities continued. When the Bengal famine struck in the 1940s as a result of the Second World War food shortages, Santimoy plunged into the kitchen relief movement started by the Communist Party of India. [25] Principal Bailey kept supporting him as long as he kept up his sporting performances.

There are a lot of similar examples across the Bengal presidency of the day: young men from staunchly middle-class backgrounds risking their futures for their political actions. However, what is interesting is that these men did not actually indulge in full-blown political careers. Instead they practised a kind of politically inspired social activism. More often than not this strenuously physical commitment to political ideals went hand in hand with sports. Sports was a preparatory skill, as it were, that helped these young men develop their physical prowess to then be used in the politically inspired social activism they undertook.

Along with the famine, however, during the war came the Royal Air Force. The RAF set up a number of forward bases in the region, including one in Bankura town itself. It was in these RAF years that the custom of playing regular Sunday matches between an RAF and a BC College team arose. It must have arisen partly out of the soldiers' need to kill time as well as perhaps to smooth the relations between the encamping airmen and the locals, already reeling under shortages and famine. Whatever the reasons for starting, it soon became an eagerly awaited weekly local fixture. Stories still circulate of how the barefoot college team repeatedly defeated the better equipped and booted RAF team. [26] There is of course no way today to find out what the real scores were. There is no way to ascertain whether the college boys really won as many matches or whether local lore has – over the years – retouched and embellished the memory. What is important, however, is to note that this minor weekly fixture, which was too informal to have been preserved in any written record, has yet been remembered with such enthusiasm by the locals. Moreover as Boria Majumdar and Kaushik Bandyopadhyay have pointed out in their brilliant study of the history of Bengali football, Indian nationalism of the time was not merely a political project – its socio-cultural dimensions, which perhaps pre-dated the political project, were as conspicuous. Football particularly 'became a rallying point for anti-colonial consciousness and an instrument by which to establish oriental superiority'. [27] While direct spectatorship of Anglo-Bengali footballing clashes in Calcutta were often limited by small stadiums and very few tickets being made available to Indian spectators, in the informal setting of small-town Bankura the games were played on open fields allowing all and sundry to watch. [28] Majumdar and Bandyopadhyay have rightly highlighted the tremendous effect the maidan clashes in Calcutta had – despite the difficulties of actually watching the game – in stoking a national consciousness and a confidence in being equal to the colonizers. We can only imagine how much more effective actually seeing the matches would have been in Bankura.

By all local accounts, however, these Sunday encounters were spectacular events with people from the neighbouring villages turning out in their hundreds to witness the match. [29] It was perhaps these spectacular events that elevated the college sportsman to the status of being a local celebrity of sorts and a leader among his peers. His popularity may have also helped him in his political work as an organizer and activist. Principal Bailey described his social and political activities by saying that he 'supported movements for the assistance of poor students and for the inauguration of village famine relief work'. [30] His organizational skills are repeatedly mentioned even later during his days as a university student in Calcutta. Lieut. D.K. Chowdhury, the organizer of physical education at Calcutta University, mentioned that 'apart from his abilities as an athlete and player he is an able organizer'. [31] His election as secretary of the College Athletic Committee also attests to his role as a student organizer and leader. [32] After university, while studying for his law degree, he was once again elected as the general secretary of the College Athletic Club. [33]

What is interesting, then, is the number of ways in which Santimoy's interest in sports intersected with his political work. First, he seems to be typical of a youth culture where young men combined an avid interest in sport in general with a very physical commitment to rural uplift, local welfare and so on – in short, the actualities of nation-building. The ideal of the healthy young man cultivating his physical strength and stamina through sport and then using it to build a better and stronger nation seems to have reverberated with many like Santimoy. Significantly, he was interested almost equally in all the sports on offer at college and not merely any one sport. This too is typical of the time – when a generalized cult of the sportsman seemed to have been more popular than a particular interest in any one sport. [34] Second, it was the appreciation of his sporting prowess that earned him a degree of immunity from official scorn. Despite his overt links with the communists and his enthusiastic activities in their support, he retained his place in college and the support of his professors – all of whom wrote glowing references for him in later life – through his consistent performance on the field. Finally, it was his charisma on the field that drew others around him and gave him the role of a leader.

There is enough evidence to suggest that Santimoy's role was in no way an isolated phenomenon. The hugely successful 1961 silver-screen Bengali blockbuster *Saptapadi*, starring the matinee idols Uttam Kumar and Suchitra Sen, portrayed a very similar character. Krishnendu – played by Uttam Kumar – is a young medical student in Calcutta. He is originally from a small village and has rebelled against his orthodox father. He brings to the college a certain rustic physical strength as well as a simple honesty. However, his character develops through his overwhelming prowess on the sports field and his repeated clashes with white students. His professors – mostly British – however are full of appreciation for him. He excels in all sports and bests his British and Anglo-Indian rivals time and again in games as diverse as tennis and football. He is also committed to nation-building and eventually leaves Calcutta to work among 'those who most need medical help' – far away from the big cities. The film is perhaps predictably set in the late 1930s and early 1940s. It remains one of the classics of mainstream Bengali cinema. The huge popularity of the film merely underlines the lasting appeal of such social roles even after more than a decade since independence. [35]

Numerous similar stories are to be found in a set of anonymous memoirs, published as a collection, by some of those who had had to leave East Bengal after the

Partition in 1947. These anonymous memoirs are mostly of those who had been in their youth in the late 1930s and early 1940s. The reason these texts are interesting is that unlike other memoirs of the time they are not written by either career politicians or those trying to highlight their own participation in larger epoch-changing events. As anonymous writings they show how those with no interest in the larger narratives of nationalism and overtly political nationalism still participated enthusiastically in activities they saw related to nation-building. Once again the stories often tell of vigorous young men excelling at sport and manfully using the strength and stamina developed in the sports field to build a nation. [36] Abha Sinha's memoirs quoted above also mention how a veteran nationalist activist in the area – Surjyo Guho Thakurta – started a gymnasium to train the local nationalist youth in physical culture. Later one of Sinha's own uncles who had been a student at the gymnasium (*byamer akhada*) even started a 'Swadeshi Circus Party' with the aim of inspiring other young people of the area to take up 'physical cultivation' (*shorir chorcha*) as a way of doing *swadeshi*. Some of the young women of the village joined these camps and Sinha mentions that some of them even started weight training. Sinha's family, however, were devout Gandhians and her memoirs glowingly recall Gandhi's visit to the area and their involvement in the local reception given to him. [37]

However, even more interestingly, Santimoy's political views veered increasingly towards the left. While the physical culture of nationalism – particularly in early-twentieth-century Bengal – has been reasonably well documented, its connections to the left movement remain under-investigated. [38] Left-wing movements had been developing in Bengal along with other parts of the subcontinent throughout the early decades of the twentieth century and predictably developed their own cultural forms as well. These however have been curiously under-researched. Physical culture – and sports as a part of it – has too often been simplistically equated with the strident forms of neo-Hinduism of the time. The communal divide that apparently tore the world of Calcutta football in two in the 1930s has further strengthened this connection between physical culture/sports/communalism. [39] The regular and conspicuous physical education programmes of the right-wing Hindu Rashtriya Swayamsevak Sangh (RSS) have also led to the increasing identification of physical cultivation solely with right-wing politics. [40] What Santimoy's life tellingly highlights is that the culture of cultivating one's body through an avid participation in sports did not have any necessary connection with any particular brand of politics. There were several contending moral investments in the sporting youth culture of the day. What was unique to the historical situation in mid-twentieth century Bengal was the politicization of this culture itself. Sport was not seen to be an end in itself. Sport stars translated their participation in sports as a social act and sought to then use the individual skills they honed on the sports field for social ends. This was not necessarily linked to nationalist politics alone and definitely not merely to Hindu nationalism.

This oversight is perhaps in part due to the lasting preoccupation of the Marxists themselves with the economic sphere alone and the refusal of the more orthodox among them to acknowledge that there are indeed several *Marxisms*. Yet, as Rajarshi Dasgupta has pointed out, '[c]ommunist discourses and practices, however, remain deeply affected by subjective preoccupations, emotions, aspirations and imagination of the people who embrace it'. [41] Dasgupta further points out that the breach between a strict doctrinaire form of Marxism and those more comfortable with cultural engagements occurred in the middle of the 1940s as a radical faction came to control the CPI. Yet, Dasgupta argues, the cultural continuities between an earlier generation of 'nationalist-terrorist revolutionaries' and the young Communists remained all too obvious in the radical poetry of the times.

In fact Dasgupta's study of Marxist culture in Bengal also raises another interesting issue – especially for our present purpose. He has commented on how hagiographic memorialization of revolutionary terrorists such as Kshudiram Bose, who was hanged at the age of 14, is strikingly similar to the memorial narratives of mid-century Bengali Communists such as the poet Sukanta. He sees in these hagiographic memorial narratives the image of a 'committed, creative and courageous life, both simple and heroic'. [42] Santimoy's life as it is remembered today also deploys a number of easily recognizable images that 'telescope' various very similar narratives. There is of course the image of the socially committed, vigorously sporting and self-less young middle-class – *madhyabitta* – boy: much like Krishnendu from *Saptapadi*. Then there is the image of the barefoot Bengali/Indian footballer playing against the booted British players – an image immortalized by reports of Mohun Bagan's legendary 1911 victory of the IFA Shield, but also visible elsewhere. [43] The image of the 13-year-old revolutionary being hounded by jail is reminiscent of course of Kshudiram himself.

These images then raise interesting methodological questions about reconstructing Santimoy's life. While the bare 'facts' of his life – such as his participation in several sports, his internment, his achievements on the field etc – are easily verifiable, the cultural and emotional meanings and resonances these 'facts' had in their times cannot be verified within a strictly historicist framework. Growing up in an age where such stories would have been a glamorous part of oral youth culture, one possibility is that Santimoy may well have consciously moulded his own life according to these stories – played the socially sanctioned roles of a sportsman, local hero, political activist and so on. Another possibility is that irrespective of whether he consciously or unconsciously adopted these roles, the people around him may have made sense of his activities through the images they knew so well. A final possibility is that his memories may well have been slotted into – or 'telescoped' to use Dasgupta's phrase – into these popular images. It is thus not merely Santimoy's sporting exploits that we have been studying here, but rather the matrix within which they are recollected and remembered.

Michael Taussig's fascinating approach has highlighted the relevance of images as ways by which people experience and articulate their lives. It is through tracing these images that Taussig has suggested that it might be possible to the gain an empathetic understanding of the historical epoch under consideration. [44] Arguing from a very different position, E.P. Thompson has also championed an 'imagist history'. Though Thompson's imagist history is of greater relevance to historians of ideas, its use in social history in general cannot be ruled out. [45] By tracing these, therefore, we gain an understanding of the role and social meaning of sports that is not limited to the life of Santimoy Pati the individual – but indeed encompasses the entire socio-historical epoch in which he lived.

Another aspect that begs further elaboration is the degree to which sport 'helped' Santimoy in very practical ways. In an age when sporting superstars were a far cry, Santimoy's career clearly shows how even at the lowest levels of sporting stardom sports could open doors that would otherwise have been locked. Santimoy's academic career seems to have blossomed despite his poor results. Even in an age when the 'sports quotas' of today were unheard of, Santimoy managed to get into college – as we have seen – despite a third division in his marticulation examinations. After having studied economics at college he enrolled in a master's course in economics but also attended history lectures – especially those of the renowned Marxist historian of the day, Prof Susobhan Sarkar, at Calcutta University. [46] He followed up his university education by obtaining a degree in law from the University Law College, Calcutta, though he did not go on to practise law. Throughout these years he remained an active sportsman and an avid sports organizer. In 1949 his principal at the law college described him as an 'all round sportsman' and mentioned that he had won the college sports championship consecutively for the last three years. [47] His political activities continued unabated and as the final years of the Raj drew to a close he was in and out of jail twice more. However he also managed to win first his college colour and finally his university blue at the time, thereby assuring his continuation at the university. [48] Even after he finished his education as a struggling unemployed young man disowned by his father, he was helped by Oriya Muslim painters in Calcutta, who had maybe known him since his sporting days, to sell paint. [49]

Such social mobility through sports was in no way unique to Santimoy. Once again his life here is typical of larger trends. Radha Prasad Gupta – an eminent amateur historian, archivist and translator as well as an alumnus of Ravenshaw College – speaking of his days as a student in Cuttack in the early decades of the twentieth century mentioned similar instances. [50] The striking similarity of Gupta's life and reminiscences are further accentuated through his own politically inspired social and intellectual commitments. Gupta's own cultural identity too remained – like Santimoy's – anxiously and exuberantly straddling both Oriya and Bengali cultural spheres. Such 'in-between' identities – a consequence of the overlapping histories of geographically, politically and socially contiguous areas – has often been lost in the studies of elite teams where regional and sub-regional ethnic identities are often at the forefront. [51]

Yet another remarkably similar instance of career advancement through sport from slightly further afield in Bangalore emerges from the little-known memoirs of Anglo-Indian Patrick Brian Sweeney. In a world where only the lowest administrative jobs were reserved for the Anglo-Indians, Sweeney, a not-too-promising student, rose to the higher echelons of the colonial administration, serving in India and Africa by sheer dint of his sporting success. [52] Like Santimoy moreover, both Gupta's anecdotes as well as Sweeney's memoirs speak of a wide range of sporting interests. The 'sportsman' was thus often a composite identity – a youth playing several sports well and not specializing in any one. This sporting personality moreover was often considered to be of a morally superior mettle and hence given admission to educational institutions as well as jobs that otherwise they could seldom have aspired to.

The moral investment in sports therefore often materially aided the young sportsman in his life. Even more interestingly, sporting success precipitated a liminal identity for the sportsman himself. While on the one hand his sporting prowess on the field – as witnessed by others – sometimes, as we have seen, stoked anti-colonial nationalism, on the other hand the good sportsman disarmed many a staunchly colonial official, drawing instead appreciation and praise for his skill and dexterity. The physical equality that sporting encounters demonstrated between the colonizer and the colonized communicated different messages to different observers. Yet this much is indubitable, that it did often gain the sportsman the favour and appreciation of many on both sides of the colonial divide.

Conclusion

Moving away from the usual focus of sport's historians on national teams and the premier clubs, we have tried to look at the smaller heroes. Sports heroes who do not usually appear in the historical archives of the nation but remain vibrant in the memories of people in the areas they played in.

Recent years have seen a significant efflorescence in the academic literature on non-historical narratives of the past – memories, myths and so on. [53] This has supplemented the growing awareness of the partial and political nature of the historical archives. If we are to move away from the elitist preoccupations of the historical archives, we must find a way of utilizing what one scholar has called the 'romantic archives' of memory and sentiment. [54]

Though the prosopographic approach centres the individual's experiential world, in this case the nature of the archives and the necessary dependence on social memory forces us to once again de-centre the individual's experience. Shared social images structure the experiential world of the individual as well as the social memory of that life. Our analysis therefore regularly fluctuates between the individuality of the prosopographic method and the sociality of imagist history.

Through such a dialectic analysis there emerges a sporting culture that is highly politicized but often ambiguous about its political agenda. A cult emerged of youth sports that was invested with a social concern. The young developed a composite sporting identity, trying their hands at as many sports as they could. They saw their sporting success not as an individual achievement but as a way of serving their societies. The content of their political visions that informed precisely how they would serve their societies, however, varied largely and it would be wrong to assume that all politicization of physical culture necessarily led to the formation of 'fascist bodies'. [55] As Santimoy's case shows us, the ethic of cultivation of sporting bodies could as easily translate into left-wing politics of various hues.

Sporting success also materially affected the social context within which the sportsmen operated. While sporting success on the one hand made heroes out of the stars, allowing them to play leadership roles in their local societies, their success also earned them the support of some of their British superiors. Thus not only did they emerge as charismatic local organizational leaders but their careers often benefited from their sporting success. It also earned them a certain immunity from the government's scorn. Santimoy's career adequately shows that despite his repeated brushes with the law, as well as his poor academic results, his career did not suffer owing to the support he earned from his college and university teachers through his stellar sporting success.

Acknowledgements

I am deeply indebted to Dr Biswamoy Pati for sharing his father's life, memories, pictures and documents with me. Of course I remain solely to blame for any inadequacies in understanding that life. I am also grateful to Prof Waltraud Ernst for her suggestions.

Notes

[1] For an excellent and eloquent espousal of the role of sports history as a necessary counter-weight to the elitism of the majority of political history, see Majumdar, *Twenty Two Yards to Freedom*.
[2] For a good recent micro-historical work see Ginzburg, 'Latitude, Slaves and the Bible'.
[3] Cf LaCapra, 'The Cheese and the Worms'.
[4] Since this is a prosopographic study based on principally on the life of a single sportsman, it will not be possible to comment upon, say, the sporting lives of sporting women at the time.
[5] Pati, 'Interrogating Stereotypes'.
[6] Acharya, 'The Linguistic Movement in 19th Century Orissa'.
[7] Dr Biswamoy Pati, personal communication, 9 March 2008.
[8] His outstanding athletic career at school is mentioned in a reference written for him by Lieut. D.K. Chowdhury, university organizer of physical education, Calcutta University, dated 7 April 1949. His political career at school was mentioned by Dr Biswamoy Pati in a personal interview on 20 June 2007 and again in a personal communication dated 2 Feb. 2008.
[9] Mangan, *Athleticism in the Victorian and Edwardian Public School*.
[10] Samal and Nayak, 'Maharaja Krushna Chandra Bhanj'.
[11] Dehury, 'T.E. Ravenshaw and the Spread of Education'.
[12] Quoted in ibid.
[13] Pati, 'Interrogating Stereotypes', 169.
[14] Mangan, 'Soccer as Moral Training', 41.
[15] Majumdar, *Twenty Two Yards to Freedom*.

[16] Cf. Samal and Nayak, 'Maharaja Krushna Chandra Bhanj'.

[17] Dr Biswamoy Pati, personal communication, 1 Feb. 2008.

[18] The extreme youth of the militants was one of the characteristic features of the militant revolutionary tradition in colonial Bengal. The legendary Kshudiran Bose was hanged at the tender age of 14 after his failed attempt to assassinate a British official. Cf. Heehs, *The Bomb in Bengal*. Usually, however, younger boys were used to pass messages and arms. A small memoir from Barisal, for example, gives an account of a ten-year-old working as an informer and arms carrier for revolutionaries: see Sinha, *Dorponey Borisal*, 45–6.

[19] 'Swadeshi dacoits' and their vexed relationship with the local landlords are sensitively portrayed in Rabindranath Tagore's famous novel *Ghare-Baire*, later made into a critically acclaimed motion picture by Satyajit Ray. Sinha also mentions 'swadeshi dacoits', see Sinha, *Dorponey Borisal*, 46.

[20] Dr Biswamoy Pati, personal interview, 20 June 2007.

[21] Certificate of matriculation issued by the Patna University, dated 14 Sept. 1939.

[22] Though Santimoy's academic results would perhaps not appear to be especially poor by contemporary Western criteria of academic performance, throughout the ninteenth and twentieth centuries the enormous cultural value that came to be attached to university education and performance in competitive examinations would have made it highly likely for these results to be seen in quite poor light in the region under discussion. The importance of degrees and results in getting jobs in an increasingly over-saturated middle-class job market may have been at the heart of the exaggerated social criticality and heightened academic expectations. Cf Bhattacharya, *Sentinels of Culture*.

[23] Dr Biswamoy Pati, personal interview, 20 June 2007, and personal communication, 2 Feb 2008. Also verified by personal communication from historian Prof. Amit Gupta, 'Towards Freedom', Indian Council of Historical Research, New Delhi, 3 Feb. 2008.

[24] Though he had played all these games in college regularly, he officially represented his college team in only football, tennis and hockey. Prof W. Bailey, personal reference for Santimoy Pati dated 8 Oct. 1946; Prof Jitendra C Banerjea, personal reference for Santimoy Pati dated 30 July 1946.

[25] Bailey, personal reference.

[26] Prof Amit Gupta, personal communication, 3 Feb. 2007.

[27] Majumdar and Bandyopadhyay, 'Race, Nation and Performance', 40.

[28] For actual viewership details, see Majumdar and Bandyopadhyay, *A Social History of Indian Football*.

[29] Oral testimonies collected by Prof Amit Gupta, communicated via personal communication, 3 Feb. 2008.

[30] Bailey, personal reference.

[31] D.K. Chowdhury, personal reference.

[32] Ibid.

[33] J.M. Banerjee, principal, University Law College, personal reference for Santimoy Pati, 16 Aug. 1950.

[34] One recalls of course the career of the legendary Chuni Goswami, who captained both the Mohun Bagan football team as well as the Bengali Ranji cricket squad. Majumdar has mentioned this phenomenon of composite sporting interests in *Twenty Two Yards to Freedom*.

[35] Kar and Dutt, *Saptapadi*.

[36] Basu, *Chhere Asha Gram*.

[37] Sinha, *Dorponey Borisal*, 34–5 and 36–7.

[38] Particularly gender historians have documented the attempts by the Bengali youth of the day to rid themselves of 'self-image of effeteness' through vigorous physical culture. Cf Chowdhury, *The Frail Hero*.

[39] Cf Dimeo, 'Football and Politics in Bengal'. Majumdar and Bandyopadhyay have challenged this view, pointing out that other considerations often drove the politics of football clubs and communalization alone cannot explain it. In fact they show that communalism itself might have been a foil to thwart the immensely successful Mohammedan Sporting Club of the 1930s: Majumdar and Bandyopadhyay, *Goalless*.

[40] McDonald, 'Physiological Patriots?'

[41] Dasgupta, 'Rhyming Revolution', 80.

[42] Ibid., 85.

[43] Majumdar and Bandyopadhyay, for instance, mention a painful incident when a well-known Bengali coach tied his talented young nephew to a bedpost and repeatedly kicked him with boots on his shins, in order to make the youngster lose the fear of the British boots. Majumdar and Bandyopadhyay, 'Race, Nation and Performance', 2.

[44] Taussig, *Colonialism, Shamanism and the Wild Man.*

[45] Thompson, *Witness Against the Beast.*

[46] His CPI cell-mates included Ranajit Guha and Amalendu Guha, both of whom would go on to become eminent radical thinkers and professors.

[47] A Chaudhoori, officiating principal, University Law College, Calcutta, personal reference for Santimoy Pati, dated 29 March 1949.

[48] J.M. Banerjee, personal reference.

[49] Dr Biswamoy Pati, personal communication, 5 Feb. 2008.

[50] Gupta had been born in Cuttack in 1921, a year before Santimoy, and was the grandson of the first Indian principal of the Ravenshaw College. He had a distinguished career as a professor of mathematics at Presidency College, but history and literature remained his first loves. He translated literary classics energetically between Oriya and Bengali and became a veritable mine of historical material on the early history of the region. For a good biography of Gupta, see Jack, 'A Raconteur of Life's Little Tales'. Gupta discusses the sporting culture at Ravenshaw College in particular and Cuttack in general in a series of interviews recorded by the BBC. Allen, *Plain Tales from the Raj*. I am indebted to Boria Majumdar for this reference.

[51] Cf. Dimeo, '"Team Loyalty Splits the City in Two"'.

[52] Patrick Brian Sweeney, 'A Game Warden's Permit For A Corpse', MSS/Eur D1169, OIOC, British Library.

[53] Cf. Nora, 'Between Memory and History'.

[54] Chakrabarty, 'Romantic Archives'.

[55] Much of the literature on the politics of South Asian physical culture derives its theoretical frame from Holocaust studies and therefore often use the denomination of 'fascist bodies' to delineate politicized and cultured bodies. Cf McDonald, 'Physiological Patriots?'

References

Acharya, Pritish. 'The Linguistic Movement in 19th Century Orissa'. *Orissa Historical Research Journal* XLVII (1) (2004): 83–9.

Allen, Charles. *Plain Tales From the Raj*. Oral biography compiled for the BBC. MSS/Eur R1-075, OIOC, British Library.

Basu, Dakshinaranjan comp. and ed. *Chhere Asha Gram*. Calcutta: Jignasa, 1975.

Bhattacharya, Tithi. *Sentinels of Culture: Class, Education and the Colonial Intellectual in Bengal.* Delhi: Oxford University Press, 2005.

Chakrabarty, Dipesh. 'Romantic Archives: Literature and Political Identity in Bengal'. *Critical Inquiry* 30 (3) (2005).

Chowdhury, Indira. *The Frail Hero, Virile History: Gender and the Politics of Culture in Colonial Bengal.* Delhi: Oxford University Press, 1998.

Dasgupta, Rajarshi. 'Rhyming Revolution: Marxism and Culture in Colonial Bengal'. *Studies in History* 21 (1) (2005): 80.

Dehury, Dinabandhu Dakshinaranjan. 'T.E. Ravenshaw and the Spread of Education in Orissa'. *Orissa Review*, April 2005: 40–6.

Dimeo, Paul. '"Team Loyalty Splits the City in Two": Football, Ethnicity and Rivalry in Calcutta'. In *Fear and Loathing in World Football*, edited by G. Armstrong and R. Guilianotti. Oxford: Berg, 2001.

——. 'Football and Politics in Bengal: Colonialism, Nationalism, Communalism'. In *Soccer and South Asia: Empire, Nation, Diaspora*, special issue of *Soccer & Society*, 2 (2) (2001), edited by Paul Dimeo and James Mills: 57–74.

Ginzburg, Carlo 'Latitude, Slaves and the Bible: An Experiment in Microhistory'. *Critical Inquiry* 31 (3) (2005): 665–83.

Heehs, Peter. *The Bomb in Bengal: The Rise of Revolutionary Terrorism in Bengal 1900–1910*. Delhi: Oxford University Press, 1998.

Jack, Ian. 'A Raconteur of Life's Little Tales'. *Outlook Magazine*, 3 April, 2000.

Kar, Ajoy and Utpal Dutt, directors. *Saptapadi* (film). Calcutta: Alochhaya Studios, 1961.

LaCapra, Dominick. 'The Cheese and the Worms: The Cosmos of a Twentieth Century Historian'. In *History and Criticism*. Ithaca, NY: Cornell University Press, 1985.

McDonald, Ian. 'Physiological Patriots? The Politics of Physical Culture and Hindu Nationalism in India'. *International Review for the Sociology of Sport* 34 (4) (1999): 343–58.

Majumdar, Boria. *Twenty Two Yards to Freedom*. New Delhi: Viking Books, 2004.

Majumdar, Boria and Kaushik Bandyopadhyay. 'Race, Nation and Performance: Footballing Nationalism in Colonial India'. In *A Social History of Indian Football: Striving to Score*. London: Routledge, 2006.

——. *Goalless: The Story of an Unique Footballing Nation*. New Delhi: Penguin Viking, 2006.

Mangan, J.A. *Athleticism in the Victorian and Edwardian Public School: The Emergence and Consolidation of an Educational Ideology*. Cambridge: Cambridge University Press, 1981.

——. 'Soccer as Moral Training: Missionary Intentions and Imperial Legacies'. In *Soccer in South Asia: Empire, Nation and Diaspora*, edited by Paul Dimeo and James Mills. London: Frank Cass, 2001.

Nora, Pierre. 'Between Memory and History: Les Lieux de Memoire'. *Representations* 26 (1989) (special issue memory and counter-memory): 7–24.

Pati, Biswamoy. 'Interrogating Stereotypes: Exploring the Princely States in Colonial Orissa'. *South Asia Research* 25 (2) (2005): 166–82.

Samal, J.K. and P.K. Nayak. 'Maharaja Krushna Chandra Bhanj'. In *Makers of Modern Orissa*, N.p: Abhinav Publications, 1996: 126–59.

Sinha, Abha. *Dorponey Borisal*. Kolkata: Kalimata Pustokaloy, 1998.

Taussig, Michael. *Colonialism, Shamanism and the Wild Man: A Study in Terror and Helaing*. Chicago: University of Chicago Press, 1991.

Thompson, E.P. *Witness Against the Beast: William Blake and the Moral Law*. Cambridge: Cambridge University Press, 1993.

Fair's Unfair: Simulations of Consumption and Career in Indian Advertising

Anisha Datta

This essay looks at how a recent television commercial simulates and plays on the dominant aesthetic, careerist, consumerist, nationalist and entertainment/leisure desires of consuming female subjects in India. The product advertised here is a fairness (bleaching) face cream, 'Fair & Lovely'. The advertisement appeals to a set of prevalent gender and colour prejudices by 'seducing' the careerist and consumerist desires of educated young Indian women. Depicting the life of an 'ordinary' consuming subject from an unknown city neighbourhood to the globalized information highways of satellite television, the advertisement projects a hyperreal world in which gendered occupational barriers have apparently withered away, courtesy of commodity consumption. The advertisement is critically analysed as a pastiche of seductive simulacra concerning the desire for 'fairness' in the midst of 'unfair' cultural prejudices, social contradictions and apolitical commercial ideologies.

Introduction

Against the backdrop of a globalized capitalist economy and postcolonial modernity, contemporary Indian metropolises are sites of prolific production and consumption. Since the mid-1980s an intensified and highly visible consumer culture has emerged in urban spaces and there has been an unprecedented proliferation of media and mediated images in everyday life. Advertisements are the symbols of India's globalized and deregulated economy and its main consumers are the upwardly mobile middle class. India has a huge middle-class population of approximately 250–350 million with growing purchasing power, reflected by the remarkable increase in purchase of consumer durables in the last decade. Recently, the global real-estate consulting group Knight Frank ranked India fifth in the list of 30 emerging retail markets. In its India Retail Market Review Quarter 2006, the global consulting group

Anisha Datta, University of British Columbia.

Knight Frank ranked India fifth in the list of 30 emerging retail markets. The report states that organized retail makes up 3% of the US $230 billion retail industry in India and is projected to attain a size of US $23 billion (a 20% growth rate) by 2010. [1] In this essay, I will undertake a feminist and postcolonial deconstruction of a 'Fair & Lovely' face cream advertisement in order to unpack how this advertisement appeals to a set of dominant gender and aesthetic prejudices by seducing the careerist and consumerist desires of educated young Indian women. [2]

Baudrillardian Moments

At the outset, I would like to point out two classic Baudrillardian moments that I experienced while I was surfing the website (www.agencyfaqs.com) from where I accessed this advertisement. The 'agencyfaqs' website aptly reflects how production and consumption intersect with and reconstitute each other in the new media of the World Wide Web, and that too on a global scale. It is a website where the advertising agencies are advertising their products, primarily targeting potential client corporations; and at the same time it is a site for pure entertainment and leisure for a casual Internet surfer. And in the role of a casual surfer I chanced upon this website and this particular advertisement. Secondly, this website represents the extreme ephemeral and episodic nature of form that characterizes the postmodern world. The site uploads any new ad's audio/visual form, which they call the streaming version, as well as the still image-frames which are termed the storyboard. But the streaming version can be accessed only in the first few days, when the new ad is being beamed over the television channels and hence still 'live'. After which it is withdrawn from the website, and then one can only find the storyboard version of the same advertisement – which by now has been reduced to the status of 'file picture'. This reflects the transient existence of any mass-circulated sign today, be it fashion, news item or advertisement.

The Narrative Unpacked

The narrative of the advertisement revolves around an educated young woman with a passion for cricket, the most popular sport in India, who aspires to be a TV cricket commentator (see image Figures 1 to 8). The advertisement also depicts the hyperreal journey of an 'ordinary' young woman from an unknown city neighbourhood to the globalized information highways of satellite television and 'live' cricket matches.

Mainstream Hindi films (commonly referred to as Bollywood films) and cricket are the two pillars of India's *national* popular culture. The story of Indian cricket, which begins with the first mention of a cricket match played by British sailors in Cambay in 1721, is a story of its gradual indigenization. Since India's victory in the World Cup Cricket tournament in England in 1983, cricket has emerged as a huge corporate business in India in terms of match sponsorship, product endorsement by cricket players and the revenue generated through telecast rights and advertisements shown during telecast cricket matches. [3] Cricket in India is popularly portrayed in chaste terms, as being a social unifier cutting across class and regional boundaries, a civilizing agent and a national cultural bond striving to overcome religious, caste and language divisions. Since the mid-1980s, there was a significant change in the nature of cricket consumption with the spread of viewership through television, which has taken cricket out of its urban confines to the villages and small towns. During the last World Cup Cricket tournament in February 2003, 79.9 million Indians tuned into live cricket telecasts, of which 36.5 million – that is close to 50 per cent – were female viewers. [4] In the words of cricket historian Guha, cricket has become a vehicle for the playing out of nationalist feeling. [5] India's success in the game can also be viewed as the reappropriation of cricket by a former British colony, a typical phenomenon of the 'Empire striking back'. The indigenous adoption of cricket also reflects certain ideas of self-cultivation, manliness and self-worth. The game became a mirror through which a (middle class) [6] Indian identity assessed itself.

However, it is to be noted that even today, cricket commentary in India is overwhelmingly a male domain, as is the case with all other televised sports. Therefore, the aspiration of the girl in the advertisement indicates a definite breaking of new ground, a detraditionalizing move, as she wants to make a foray into a traditionally male occupation. Commentators have always been men and often these days one finds images of former (male) cricketers wielding the microphone on TV instead of the willow and the ball. Thus the advertisement projects a hyperreal world in which gendered occupational barriers have apparently withered away, courtesy of commodity consumption.

Let us now look into the first image in some detail: the woman is walking into an expansive cricket field dressed in a three-piece suit, *salwar kurta*, which is a typical dress of young working women in urban India. The shot of the woman walking into the huge field in the image is quite significant, as it can be read as the allegorical representation of the woman's entry into the juggernaut world of a high-profile career and conspicuous consumption.

Moving on to a later image in frame five (Figure 4), she is seen to be practising mock commentary while watching a cricket match on the TV. Keeping in mind the present status of cricket in India, the advertisement *simulates* the fusion of commerce and leisure/entertainment by representing the woman watching cricket on TV, commentating and using as well as advertising the product Fair & Lovely. In this image, she is also shown to have dark skin tone compared to her sister. It is the most hyperreal and *commercial* moment in the whole narrative, when her sister introduces her to the Fair & Lovely cream. It's an advertisement within an advertisement. This image frame is an example of Baudrillarian hyperreal. It's a simulation of the TV image and reality in which the relation between the signifying system and the reality gets ambivalent. The real is now an effect of the television commercial. The dialectical dynamics between the advertising image and reality are blurred in the process and the subjects turn indifferent towards it. What are left are merely signifying practices of becoming 'fair' (light skin toned), having the coveted and successful career of cricket commentator, breaking the glass ceiling, consuming more and promoting more consumption. Thus this image aptly reflects the closed circuit of commercial simulacra where advertisement, commodity, cricket, TV, entertainment, career aspiration and consumption all play into each other to produce the seductive hyperreal. [7]

Why Fair's Unfair?

Secondly, the advertisement appeals here to a set of prevalent gender and aesthetic prejudices by 'seducing' the careerist, consumerist and aesthetic desires of educated young Indian women. The young woman has a talent for commentary. But she is not born with a fair (light) skin complexion and hence not considered 'conventionally' beautiful by dominant Indian aesthetic standards. This desire for fair skin is well reflected in the images of lead actors/actresses in the other domain of Indian public culture – the mainstream Hindi Films. Also a casual browsing of the matrimonial columns in Indian newspapers and Internet sites makes it evident that when searching for a bride, fair/light skin tone becomes the most important aesthetic consideration. In the advertisement this aesthetic desire is kept minimally explicit. However, the metamorphosed image of the woman [8] does carry the seductive message which is sufficient for the consuming female subject to understand that a 'fair and hence lovely' look is absolutely essential to get a job 'in front of the TV camera', where visual appeal matters a lot. Note that in the advertisement the girl sends a videotape of her portfolio to the TV company. *Thus the surface and appearance that is the skin tone becomes as important (if not more so) as the substance that is the woman's commentating skills.* In the process both the woman and 'Fair & Lovely' face cream attain *sign value.* Also note that it is men who select her for the job, which directs our attention to the androcentric nature of the culture and economy.

Most importantly, it has to be noted that the ascribed and natural skin colour of the girl is transformed with the help of a *chemical* technology, the bleaching cream, whereby she achieves a new and perceptibly lighter skin tone. [9] Thus in consumer capitalism nothing is impossible and the collapse of difference between the true and the false is replaced by the hyperreal. The advertisement narrates and interpellates a typical manifestation of a (post)modern self, where one must constantly work on oneself through a kind of self-therapy with the aim of achieving new sign values. The woman is not merely an object of consumption here. She is also an active subject of production and consumption.

Detraditionalization and Retraditionalization

In the narrative, the woman and her family successfully dispose of the traditional mindset that sport commentary is a 'masculine' profession. Nevertheless, the other more deeply entrenched gender and aesthetic prejudices could not be subverted. Traditionally, fair/light skin tone is equated with beauty and particularly feminine beauty in India. The issue here is also how dark- and light-skinned status-coding is both pre- and postcolonial. The earliest Vedic text *Rig Veda*, scripted by Indo-Aryan language speakers and dating back to 1500–1000 BCE. has a few references to non-Indo-Aryan language speakers *Dasa*, who were compared to demons, being black-skinned (*Krisha-tvach*) and speaking a strange language. [10] However, historians such as Romila Thapar caution that Indo-Aryan 'refers to a language group and not to race, and language group can incorporate a variety of people'. [11] Unfortunately, nineteenth-century Orientalist scholars and British census officials concocted a theory of Aryan race invasion of ancient India. Such discourses also racialized the words *Arya* and *Dasa* as well as the caste system. [12] In present-day India, innumerable shades of brown, black and lighter skin tones can be found across the spectrum of class, caste, religion and ethnic groups. However, even in the fourteenth-century CE Vaishnavite literature of Bengal (India), one finds that *Gourango* (i.e. fair skin complexion) is more aesthetically appealing to the poets such as Vidyapati and Chandidas. [13] Finally, India's colonial encounter with a 'white race' in the eighteenth century simply seems to have reinforced this already existing aesthetic obsession with fair skin. Though new ground is broken in the narrative of the advertisement when the woman gets the 'non-traditional' job, 'tradition' is re-established 'in the last instance' with the aid of a retrogressive and gendered idiom, the 'fair and lovely' aesthetic myth and the (post)modern capitalist logic of self-therapy and material success.

In India, 'fairness' face cream is especially targeted at young women aspiring to get a job or get married, the category of women for whom looking beautiful is essential to be marketable, be it in the job or the arranged-marriage market. The 'fairness' cream market size in India is currently estimated at Rs6.5 billion or US$140 million. [14] Though many young men in India also aspire and eventually become TV sport commentators, air stewards, fashion models and so on, so far 'fairness' cream advertisements have never explicitly targeted them, which again suggests how the culture of 'looking fair' is overtly gendered.

Conclusion

To conclude, the advertisement appeals to a set of prevalent gender and aesthetic prejudices by 'seducing' the careerist and consumerist desires of educated young Indian women. Depicting the life of an 'ordinary' consuming subject from an unknown city neighbourhood to the globalized information highways of satellite television, the advertisement successfully projects a hyperreal world in which gendered occupational barriers have apparently withered away, courtesy of commodity consumption. The commercial is a pastiche of 'seductive simulacra' [15] concerning the aesthetic desire for 'fairness' in the midst of 'unfair' cultural prejudices, social contradictions and apolitical commercial ideologies. In this maze of the hyperreal, the deep ideological resonances are reduced to mere spectacles. The absorptive capacities of consumer capitalism once again emerge as the winner. And the critical question, which gets muted, is the following: how can we identify the structures of domination when apparently no one is dominating? [16]

Girl Becomes Cricket Commentator: The Storyboard

Figure 1 A shot of a girl in a cricket field. The camera moves into flashback where...
Source: agencyfaqs (www.agencyfaqs.com/www1/advertising/storyboards/Fair_&_Lovely/
1530.html). Reproduced here by permission.

Figure 2 The girl is doing commentary for the cricket being played in her street.
Source: agencyfaqs (www.agencyfaqs.com/www1/advertising/storyboards/Fair_&_Lovely/
1530.html). Reproduced here by permission.

Figure 3 Cut to the shot where she is delivering the commentary for her college match.
Source: agencyfaqs (www.agencyfaqs.com/www1/advertising/storyboards/Fair_&_Lovely/
1530.html). Reproduced here by permission.

Figure 4 The girl is at home commentating for a match on TV when a Fair & Lovely is transferred to her by her sister.
Source: agencyfaqs (www.agencyfaqs.com/www1/advertising/storyboards/Fair_&_Lovely/1530.html). Reproduced here by permission.

Figure 5 In the next shot she sends a tape for an audition following a job of a cricket commentator.
Source: agencyfaqs (www.agencyfaqs.com/www1/advertising/storyboards/Fair_&_Lovely/1530.html). Reproduced here by permission.

Figure 6 Finding it good, the selection team approves her name for the job.
Source: agencyfaqs (www.agencyfaqs.com/www1/advertising/storyboards/Fair_&_Lovely/1530.html). Reproduced here by permission.

Figure 7 Finding her as a professional commentator, people including her family find her commendable.
Source: agencyfaqs (www.agencyfaqs.com/www1/advertising/storyboards/Fair_&_Lovely/1530.html). Reproduced here by permission.

Figure 8 Musical Voice Over: Fair & Lovely, *zindagi roshan kare*. [Fair & Lovely brightens up life.]
Source: agencyfaqs (www.agencyfaqs.com/www1/advertising/storyboards/Fair_&_Lovely/1530.html). Reproduced here by permission.

Acknowledgements

I would like to thank Thomas Kemple for his suggestions on an earlier draft of this essay, and Indranil Chakraborty who helped me to locate the agencyfaqs website. Thanks to agencyfaqs who granted me the permission to reproduce the advertisement images here.

Notes

[1] http://www.knightfrank.com/ResearchReportDirPhase2/11113.pdf, accessed 29 August 2008.
[2] See the *Fair and Lovely* face cream's eight advertisement images (Figures 1–8) in this essay.
[3] A feature in *Hindu Business Line* reported that in 2001, India played four one-day international cricket matches and over 450 brands advertised on TV during the live telecasts of these matches. The number of spots purchased during the period was over 16,000. See Nithya Subramanian, 'Cricket as Always is Top Scorer in Rating, *Hindu Business Line*, 3 June

2002, available online at http://www.blonnet.com/2002/06/03/stories/2002060302100100.htm, accessed 15 October 2005.

[4] From Adex World Cup Brand Barometer, available online at www.indiantelevision.com/tamadex, accessed 15 October 2005.

[5] See Guha, *A Corner of a Playing Field.*

[6] The addition in brackets is mine. See Majumdar, 'Politics of Leisure in Colonial India'.

[7] See Baudrillard, *Selected Writings.*

[8] Compare image in Figure 5 to that in Figure 8.

[9] See the image in Figure 8.

[10] Thapar, *Ancient Indian Social History*, 154. See also his *Early India.*

[11] Thapar, *Early India*, 15.

[12] The German Indologist Max Muller maintained that the 'Aryans' invaded in large numbers and subordinated the indigenous population of Northern India in the second millennium BCE. Since a mechanism for maintaining racial segregation was needed, this took the form of dividing society into socially self-contained and separate castes. Though the equation of language and race was seen to be a fallacy by Muller, there was yet a tendency to use it as a convenient distinction (Thapar, *Early India*, 13). In colonial India, H.H. Risley the late nineteenth-century British Census Commissioner and ethnologist, maintained that the dominant factor in the formation of caste was the conquest of one race by another. His scientific ambition was to trace the correlation between marriage customs, physical types and the racial origins of caste (Dirks, *Castes of Mind*).

[13] I would like to thank Dr Mandakranta Bose for bringing this history to my notice.

[14] Ratna Bhushan, 'Fairness Cream Ads Acquire Darker Hue', *The Hindu Business Line*, 4 March 2003, available online at http://www.blonnet.com/catalyst/2003/03/04/stories, accessed 15 October 2005.

[15] Baudrillard, *Selected Writings.*

[16] However, there have been a few protests against fairness cream TV commercials in India. Following a petitioning by THE All India Democratic Women's Association in September 2002, the government of India recently wrote to several television channels to stop them airing advertisements promoting fairness creams on the premise that these are demeaning to women and promote skin colour prejudices.

References

Baudrillard, Jean. *Jean Baudrillard: Selected Writings*, edited by Mark Poster. Stanford, CA: Stanford University Press, 2001.

Dirks, Nicholas B. *Castes of Mind*. Princeton, NJ: Princeton University Press, 2001.

Guha, Ramachandra. *A Corner of a Foreign Field*. Delhi: Picador, 2002.

Majumdar, Boria. 'Politics of Leisure in Colonial India'. *Economic and Political Weekly* 36 (1 Sept. 2001): 1–21.

Thapar, Romila. *Ancient Indian Social History*. New Delhi: Orient Longman, 1978.

——. *Early India*. London: Allen Lane, Penguin Press, 2002.

The Great Indian Willow Trick: Cricket, Nationalism and India's TV News Revolution, 1998–2005

Nalin Mehta

The emergence of India as the financial and spiritual heart of world cricket in the 1990s is intrinsically linked to India's satellite TV revolution in the same period. The 1990s began with just one Indian television channel – the state owned Doordarshan – but by 2006, Indian viewers were remote-controlling their way through more than 300 private satellite television channels. While the reasons for this phenomenal growth of the television industry are varied and complex, cricket has played a central role in the story. This paper will outline Indian satellite television's linkages with cricket and what they mean for notions of identity and expressions of Indian nationhood. In particular, it focuses on India's 24-hour television news networks – there are more than 50 in 14 languages. Unlike any other country in the world, the Indian television news industry has consciously ridden on cricket's shoulders to such an extent that by 2006, cricket-oriented programming accounted for the greatest expenditure in news gathering and the greatest visibility across most news channels. Television producers looked towards cricket because of its indelible link with what might be called Indian-ness, but their focus on the game, in turn, substantially redefined and reinforced these linkages.

Introduction: Kargil and Cricket Nationalism

On 9 June 1999, with the mountain war in the icy peaks of Kargil at its height and the Indian Army still struggling to evict the Pakistani intruders, a group of senior army officers in Srinagar's Badami Bagh cantonment sat glued to a TV set. These were officers of the 15 Corps which was responsible for the Kargil operations, but for them only one thing mattered on that day: the World Cup cricket match between India and Pakistan in Manchester, which they were monitoring as keenly as the progress of the battle in Drass, Kargil and Batalik. Their passion that day was not entirely due to love

Nalin Mehta, La Trobe University.

for the game. The army's top brass believed that the World Cup clash with Pakistan was crucial for the morale of Indian troops and a defeat on the cricket field would leave the soldiers, already with their backs against the wall on the battlefield, in a terrible state of mind. [1] The issue was so pertinent that after meeting injured soldiers in Kargil, former captain Kapil Dev publicly called for all scheduled India–Pakistan matches to be cancelled because all of the injured had pleaded 'please do not lose a match to Pakistan'. [2] And so the generals crossed their fingers and prayed for victory. Press reports described the Badami Bagh cantonment, which was the centre point of troop and ammunition movement to Kargil, as deserted through the day as the match progressed, but as soon as India won 'a thunderous chorus followed by a bursting of crackers ruptured it as officers and jawans...celebrated India's morale-boosting victory over Pakistan'. 'We will throw them out of LOC [the line of control in Kashmir] using the same precision with which our bowlers bowled to the Pakistani batsmen', exulted a senior officer in relief. Soldiers were seen chanting '*Bharat Mata ki Jai*' along the streets of the cantonment in the dead of the night and one soldier, on his way to the battle front, told reporters: 'We have won the battle of nerves [on the cricket field] and will surely win the battle of bullets also.' [3]

The game with Pakistan had turned into a marker of Indian patriotism and it was a day that captured in its entirety the centrality of cricket to notions of modern Indian nationalism and identity. While the ongoing military conflict certainly gave a bitter edge to the Manchester game, the passions it aroused reinforced the link between cricket and Indian nationalism. There has been a substantial literature in recent years focusing on cricket's journey from colonial mortar during the British Raj to national cement in independent India. [4] Over the past decade, India's huge numbers and economic dynamism have transformed it into the spiritual and financial heart of global cricket, but the satellite television boom unleashed after the economic reforms of the 1990s has been intrinsic to this story. From just one television channel in 1991 – the state-owned Doordarshan – Indian viewers in 2007 have access to more than 300 different television channels: 55 of these are 24-hour news channels (33 in Hindi and English alone), while news is broadcast in 14 different languages across 108 different television networks. [5] No other country in the world has such a concentration of news television; this is a TV revolution by any standards. While the reasons for this phenomenal growth of the television industry are varied and complex, cricket has played a central role in the story – transforming television and, in turn, being transformed by it. This paper will outline the process through which the burgeoning television industry rode on the shoulders of cricket to expand at an unprecedented rate and, in particular, focus on television news networks and how they have consciously adopted cricket as a vehicle for attracting greater viewer interest by constantly increasing cricket-related programming. The news channels have been chosen in preference to regular sports channels because their emphasis on cricket indicates how central the game has become to changing ideas of India, which directly feed in to the commercial considerations at the heart of the television industry. Cricket, along with Bollywood, has come to be seen by TV executives as the pan-Indian pastime and the political economy of television is a useful entry-point to examining changing ideas of Indianness.

News Television: Setting the Framework

The first Indian news channels started only in 1998 and, out of the many that have mushroomed since, this paper will focus on the four major round-the-clock national news broadcasters – Star News, Aaj Tak [Till Today], Zee News and NDTV. It will also look at three newer networks still striving to carve out a niche for themselves – Channel 7, [6] India TV and Sahara Samay – to provide a comprehensive overview of the industry and how it approaches cricket.

An exploration of the role of cricket in these channels' evolution must be located within the overall framework of India's satellite television industry and its place within the country's political economy. While television broadcasting began in India in 1959, the state maintained a monopoly on the airwaves on the premise that this would ensure judicious use of the media in developmental tasks. [7] However, this monopoly began to break after 1990 when Hutchison Whampoa, a Hong Kong-based company, bought and repackaged the only geostationary satellite over the Indian Ocean, AsiaSat-1. [8] This was the first private satellite for commercial broadcasting over the south Asian region and Indian viewers were suddenly exposed to international news channels such as CNN, which became very popular during the first Gulf War. The availability of new technology happened to coincide with India's economic liberalization programme in 1991 and ignited the television revolution.

Star TV, launched in 1991 with five channels including the 24-hour Prime Sports, was the first major international network to directly target the Indian market. With its English programming, Star initially focussed only on the Pacific-rim economies but changed its plans after India became its biggest market within six months of its entry. Rupert Murdoch's News Corporation bought a controlling stake in Star in 1993 and it is now a wholly-owned subsidiary of News Corp. [9] In 1996, Star started a daily India-specific news bulletin through a content-sharing agreement with television production company New Delhi Television (NDTV). NDTV, which had produced state broadcaster Doordarshan's first live election coverage in 1984, produced this 30-minute daily bulletin for Star's flagship channel in India, Star Plus. This alliance was upgraded in 1998 when Star launched India's first 24-hour news channel. [10] Under the terms of the agreement, NDTV produced the content and retained editorial control for a fee, while Star provided the brand name, the cost of production and took care of the distribution. The Star News channel was a bilingual carrier, with half its programming in Hindi and half in English. In 2003, when the agreement expired, NDTV launched its independent news channels, NDTV 24 × 7 in English and NDTV India in Hindi, while Star News restarted with an entirely new team of its own.

Long before this, however, Star's first big challenge came from Zee TV, the first satellite channel created exclusively for India's roughly 400 million Hindi speakers. It was launched by Indian entrepreneur Subhash Chandra in partnership with Star in October 1992 and completely re-invented television for the mass Indian market. Its spectacular success meant that the channel owners broke even on their initial investment within nine months of its launch and it had captured 65 per cent of the satellite market by 1994. [11] Zee soon capitalized on its advantage by launching a series of entertainment channels to rival Star TV's collection and in 1998 started India's first totally Hindi 24-hour news channel to counter Star News. It also launched a 24-hour sports channel, Zee Sports, in 2005. [12]

Zee's dominance in the news market was challenged in December 2000 by the new Aaj Tak channel, which was launched by the India Today Group, owner of the prestigious *India Today* magazine. The company had made its first foray into television as far back as 1988 with a highly popular video news programme, *Newstrack*, which was initially distributed on videocassettes. It then started the influential daily news bulletin called *Aaj Tak* on state broadcaster Doordarshan in 1995 and used the same brand name to launch its own 24-hour news channel in December 2000. With an emphasis on colloquial Hindi, better technology and focus on '*sab se tez*' (faster than everybody) journalism, Aaj Tak re-invented the Zee experience and quickly became the most popular news channel in the ratings, a position it has managed to hold on to until mid-2007.

Once the potential for news television became clear, newer players such as India TV, Channel 7 and Sahara Samay entered the market to partake of the advertising pie. India today is the third largest television market in the world and this sector is by far the biggest revenue-generating sector in the Indian entertainment industry. [13] The 2006 National Readership Survey (samples size of 284,373 households) claims that television now reaches 112 million Indian homes, more than half of all Indian households. Of these, 68 million homes have access to cable and satellite channels and an average of 230 million individuals watch satellite TV per week. An average urban adult now spends more time with TV than any other media – 11.8 hours a week or 1 hour and 42 minutes daily. [14] It is little wonder, then, that television accounts for nearly 50 per cent of the overall advertising pie in India and, of this, news television accounts for 11 per cent of the revenues. [15]

The Discovery of Cricket

Who Will Become World Champion?

It was Star News that launched the first cricket-specific programme on news television, *Turning Point*, during the 1999 World Cup. With former Indian captain Bishen Singh Bedi as a resident expert and guest appearances by English batting legend Sir Geoffrey Boycott, *Turning Point* was an important innovation, but it only ran for the duration of the World Cup and was not part of regular programming. News television was essentially concentrated on politics – in fact, Star News had initially been launched only as an election channel in 1998 – and cricket was covered as part of sports news, which itself was relegated to a small section towards the end of every news bulletin. [16]

All this changed in 2001 when the newly-launched Aaj Tak, in a bid to establish itself, decided to aggressively tap into cricketing passions and build a news agenda based on the game. Steve Waugh's all-conquering Australian team was coming to India and the Australian captain had publicly declared that India was the 'final frontier' in his team's quest for total domination of the game. The Australians were coming two months after Aaj Tak's launch and the channel deliberately decided to use cricket as a means of gaining a foothold in the television news market. It launched a programme series titled *Kaun Banega World Champion?* ('Who Will Become World Champion?') which included a daily half-hour show in the evening for the entire duration of the month-long series and saturation coverage on match days. This meant that on match days the news channel interrupted its regular morning news bulletins with a specially designed programme looking ahead at the game's prospects. Its news programming would also halt at every break in the game thereafter – lunch, tea and drinks – when specially hired cricket experts in the studio would discuss the day's play threadbare. In addition, during the regular news programme, Aaj Tak introduced the then novel concept of a text graphic on the top right hand side of the television screen displaying the cricket score live. This was meant as a device for inducing news viewers who might be tempted to watch cricket instead to stay on and watch the news while keeping abreast with the score.

The whole strategy was to convert a cricket series that would otherwise have been covered as part of the regular sports news into a mega-news event like the general election or the annual union budget. According to Uday Shankar, then Aaj Tak editor:

> We started hyping it up. Our agenda was very simple. We knew cricket was important. We wanted to plug in.... We knew that it was going to be a high viewership activity but until then news channels hadn't found a way of plugging into the cricket activity and creating a news agenda based on cricket. We had serious limitations with pictures [Aaj Tak did not have broadcast rights for the series and could only use a few minutes of match footage daily] so we decided to hire Bishen Singh Bedi [former India captain] as our resident expert. And our promotional campaign was: watch the match on your sports channel and understand the match on our channel. [17]

Aaj Tak's 'Who Will Become World Champion?' tag to the series is particularly instructive. Portraying what was only a bilateral Test series between two countries as a boxing-style knockout match for the world championship, it was hoping to channel the national passion for cricket to its advantage by positioning itself in the centre of the Indian cricket fan's aspirations. As Shankar says:

> The sports logic of it was a little suspect, because you do not become world champion by just beating one team, and India was nowhere in that league at that time.... Our

logic was that if somebody was to go and beat Mike Tyson, the guy would be considered world heavyweight champion, so why should we not apply the same rule to cricket, regardless of the fact that whether it had been applied so far or not, whether the format of ICC allowed that or not. So if Australia are the world's best team then the team that beats Australia becomes the world's best team...at least definitely has a claim to that....We invited a lot of flak in the media...but...we were looking at it in a different light. Because Aaj Tak's whole pitch was that it was not a channel which looked at news or any event the way the experts look at it. We looked at an event the way people looked at it and in popular mind there was no confusion that if India were to beat Australia, India was the world champion. [18]

Aaj Tak's strategy paid rich dividends and its rise as the pre-eminent Hindi news channel can, at least, partly be attributed to the manner it piggybacked on cricket's tremendous popularity. By the next series, every news channel began to replicate the same model and this strategy – special programming with resident cricket experts and saturation coverage – became the standard way of covering Indian cricket.

Navjyot Singh Sidhu, Ratings and the Economy of Television

Before the 2001 Australian tour, not a single news channel had a separate sport show. By mid-2007, by contrast, every news channel has at least one programme dedicated exclusively to cricket, as Table 1 details. The two NDTV channels – 24 × 7 and India – have weekly one-hour programmes, *Cricket Controversies* and *Kissa Cricket Ka* [A Story of Cricket], devoted exclusively to cricket the whole year around, irrespective of whether cricket is being played or not. [19] As Rahul Bhattacharya points out:

> Perhaps we have on our hands a unique combination of a nascent and exploding media and a single pan-national sport, but it is worth pointing out that none of the major general news channels in the USA, Australia or England – where Sky have a dedicated sports-news channel – feature extensive single-sport programming. [20]

Two features stand out in this programming: the high frequency of the coverage on match days and the fact that every channel has resident experts. The high priority attached to cricket means that 'in terms of costs of events in India, cricket has already emerged as one of the most expensive news gathering activities, if not the most expensive activity'. [21] Between 2005–06 NDTV, for instance, reportedly paid its resident expert Navjyot Singh Sidhu between Rs14–16 million a year for appearing on its weekly cricket programmes as well as on match days. [22] This is more than the Rs8 million that Greg Chappell is said to have earned for coaching the Indian cricket team and more than what India's international cricketers earned in the same period as yearly match fees, not counting endorsements. [23] Sidhu, more than anybody else symbolizes the emergence of the well-paid cricket pundit on television. His peculiar style of aggression and humour – *Kya thook mei pakode tal sakte hai? Kya moot meii*

Table 1 Programmes Dedicated to Cricket on Indian News Channels

Channel name	Programme name	Format/frequency
1. NDTV 24 × 7	*Turning Point*	Interactive caller-based show with celebrity expert (Navjyot Singh Sidhu) on match days
	Cricket Controversies	Weekly one-hour audience-based show with Navjyot Singh Sidhu as celebrity guest.
2. NDTV India	*Googly*	Interactive caller-based show on match days with celebrity expert (Navjyot Singh Sidhu)
	Kissa Cricket Ka (A Story of Cricket)	Weekly one-hour audience-based show with Navjyot Singh Sidhu as celebrity guest.
3. Aaj Tak	*The Wisden Show*	Interactive caller-based show with celebrity experts (Madan Lal and Saba Karim) on Indian match days, before/after play and during each break.
4. Star News	*Match ke Mujrim* (Criminals of the Match)	Interactive kangaroo court with celebrity expert Bishen Singh Bedi acting as public prosecutor against poor-performing players on match days. Another former player acts as defence lawyer. The case is judged by viewer polling.
5. Channel 7	*Showdown*	Interactive caller-based show with celebrity expert (Ajay Jadeja) on every match and pre-match day.
	Speedster Challenge	Weekly game show to select India's fastest bowler
6. Zee News	*Ghamasaan* (Intense)	Interactive caller-based show with celebrity expert (Chetan Chauhan) on every morning and evening of match day.
7. India TV	*Cricket Xtra*	Ten-minute commentary every hour on match days by Chetan Sharma
8. Sahara Samay	*Silly Point*	Hourly show on match-days with former cricketers Maninder Singh, Kirti Azad, Ashok Malhotra and Javagal Srinath.

Sources: Anisa Khan, personal interview; Rahul Bhattacharya.

machliyaan ho sakti hai? ('Can pakodas be fried in spit? Can fish swim in urine?') – makes him the most sought-after cricket expert on television: 'He is able to always shout…and never doubt the strength of his point no matter how uninformed or irrelevant. He is so outrageous that it's hard not to stop and gawk.' [24] His high popularity since he started television commentary has made him a BJP Lok Sabha MP from the Punjab and a roving artist for hire on various comedy shows such as *The Great Indian Laughter Challenge* (Star One), which he judges.

Most news channels also pay current Indian players for exclusive coverage during big Indian tours. For Pakistan's tour of India in 2005, Aaj Tak contracted then captain Saurav Ganguly (reportedly for $500,000) as resident expert, while NDTV hired Rahul Dravid, Harbhajan Singh and Pakistan coach Bob Woolmer. In addition, from the 2003 World Cup onwards, news channels started sending teams to cover overseas tours for live reportage, and this has meant huge satellite costs. An average international satellite feed from Australia, West Indies or South Africa costs about $1,500–2,000 for ten minutes and between $900 and $1000 from London or Dubai (which are better connected to India on the satellite loop). On match days most channels go live from location several times a day, at huge cost. To put the expenses on cricket in perspective, Indian news channels send camera teams abroad for news coverage only at times of international crises. In order to save satellite costs, news channels largely depend on international wire services for most international news coverage. The Indian cricket team, in contrast, plays for at least 10 months of the year, mostly overseas. The focus on cricket means that cricket absorbs a great deal of news budgets.

The fact that cricket is the one sport that India does well at also means that it features prominently in regular news updates and daily sports bulletins. It's a tactic that registers well in television ratings and helps channels connect to younger audiences. According to Anisa Khan, who anchors NDTV India's daily sport show *Khel India* ('Sport India'), 'On all channels, sports coverage is primarily cricket coverage. Except for Sania Mirza, everything else is ritualistic, with the sole exception of World Cup football or Olympic Games. The bulk of programming is cricket.' [25]

Within general news programming as well, cricket competes with political and social news and, almost always, wins. To quote the head of Star India:

> Almost on a regular basis, we open the news bulletin with cricket. Today if you were to ask me to gauge the mind of a newsroom producer, a run-down producer in the news room of all channels, I think it will require a big national, natural disaster for a person to relegate a cricket match involving India to a second- or third-headline status. [26]

Apart from the popularity of the game, the reasons for this concentrated focus on cricket lie within the economic structure of Indian television. TV has to be understood by looking at the industry's business model, because revenue flows effectively define the parameters of programming. The key feature of the Indian satellite market is its origin as an illegal medium, which has led to the most unique distribution system in the world. Because the state had a complete monopoly over broadcasting until the mid-1990s under the colonial Indian Telegraph Act of 1885, satellite channels had to broadcast from outside India and could not organize their own distribution. This is why cable operators who set up their own satellite dishes and distributed the satellite signals for a fee emerged as crucial middlemen between the broadcasters and viewers. A significant proportion of television signals is distributed through local cable operators who do not share correct information on the number of households serviced by them. This means that most broadcasters today cannot really pinpoint how many viewers are actually viewing their channels. Once a cable operator has decoded the broadcaster's signal, it can be supplied to as many people as it wants and the broadcaster has no way of knowing the numbers. 'It is estimated that local cable operators declare only about 5–20% of the households on their network to broadcasters who receive only 10% of total subscription fees as against globally accepted distribution standards between 30–40%.' [27] The only country that comes close to India in this regard is Taiwan, and it is this factor that makes Indian television completely different. While there are 68 million satellite connections in India, according to one senior TV executive, 'no media company is being paid for more than eight to ten million homes... only about 15 per cent of homes are reported and that is the money that comes back to the broadcaster'. [28]

This has huge implications for the business models of Indian broadcasters. They have to depend far more on advertising than their counterparts in most other television markets. All Indian channels, therefore, work on business models where they earn 70 to 80 per cent of their earnings from advertising and only 20 to 30 per cent from subscriptions. This is the reverse of what happens in most developed television markets and it means that broadcasters are even more dependent on daily ratings to get the advertising rupee.

In the absence of control over distribution, television ratings become the only means of determining which programmes are being watched and which should, therefore, receive advertising. The importance of ratings is further accentuated by the fact that most news channels are free-to-air and do not charge any subscription to begin with. Their dependence on advertising, and by extension on the ratings, is total. Indian TV ratings are measured by TAM (Television Audience Measurement) Media Research India Ltd. Between 1998 and 2003, TAM represented only 1,500 households in 27 cities. The panel was expanded in 2003 to 4,800 households (73 cities) and 6,917 samples by January 2007. [29] The TAM sample is minuscule for a market of 68 million TV households and it only represents urban markets; the rural market is not represented at all. Yet in a world where more than 50 news channels compete with each other, the only way to stay in the game is to remain high on the TAM meters. Given the narrow base of these ratings, cricket has emerged as an easy option to register on them.

Cricket, along with Bollywood, has a pan-Indian appeal cutting across socio-economic and regional categories. News of a small-town crime in Mathura may not interest anybody in Kerala, but news of the Indian cricket team interests people in every region of India. This is why when news editors want to lift the ratings of any show they look towards cricket. According to Rajdeep Sardesai, former managing editor of NDTV and CEO of CNN-IBN, 'Cricket does sell. I once did an interview with Virender Sehwag for the Hindi show *Takkar* and the ratings on that were much higher than for politicians and even film stars.' [30]

Another TV editor draws the deep connection between cricket and national identity to explain its emergence as a prime attraction on television, even more so than Bollywood:

> I think as far as Indian identity is concerned, cricket overtakes even Bollywood. While Bollywood is a big source of entertainment, its conscious articulation as an Indian medium by the common people is not so pronounced. But cricket is

perhaps consciously the most nationalistic activity that Indians indulge in. So to that extent, there is no cricket minus India. Every time you watch cricket you are subconsciously and consciously reminded of the Indian identity.... Now in terms of importance, cricket has left Bollywood far behind. It is next only to big political stories and really big economic stories.... And very often it overtakes political and economic stories as well. [31]

This is why cricket sells and is big on news television. Newer networks such as Channel 7, launched by the Dainik Jagran group in early 2005, have positioned their entire programming on the twin planks of cricket and crime – two things the channel's managers believe will yield high ratings. In October 2005, on the day that Sachin Tendulkar made his comeback after a six-month injury lay-off, Channel 7 hosted a special programme with astrologer Bejan Daruwala to predict the outcome. Channel 7 has also coopted a show that earlier ran on ESPN, *The Speedster Challenge*, to select India's fastest bowler. The show travels around the country with a select team of former and current Indian bowlers to select a winner who will be awarded Rs100,000 and sent to the MRF Pace Academy, Chennai, at the BCCI's expense. [32] Current Indian bowler V.R.V. Singh is a product of the show's earlier version on ESPN, a sports channel, but it is now the most promoted show on a news network. On 29 October, the day of the Delhi blasts that claimed nearly 60 lives, Channel 7's coverage of the blasts was superimposed on the left side of the screen with an animation advertisement for the show.

Conclusion: Cricket and Treason

During Pakistan's tour to India in early 2005, the Star News channel started a programme called *Match ke Mujrim* ('Criminals of the Match'). Set up like a court trial, the show was telecast on the evening of every match and featured a 'trial' of four Indian players who did not perform well on the day. It would be performed with a live audience and featured a prosecution attorney, former Indian captain Bishen Singh Bedi, and another former cricketer as defence lawyer. The two would present their cases and ask viewers to vote on which Indian player was the villain of the day through SMS. Despite vehement criticism in the media, the show generated a tremendous response for Star News. On the day India lost the Bangalore Test against Pakistan, it was staged live out of a public park in the city and more than 10,000 people turned up at the venue. This is in addition to the 20 million or so viewers Star News claims to have access to. During its one-hour duration, when its phone lines were open for voting, Star News received 35,000 phone messages. This means that nearly 600 people were calling in every minute. The average SMS count for a typical episode, though, hovers around 5,000–10,000.

For the Star News CEO who initiated this programme, the justification was simple:

For an average Indian cricket lover, *a player doing something that costs India the match is the closest thing that comes to treason on a daily basis....* When people are let down then, unlike in the case of politicians, who still people feel they can fix when some day the guy comes to seek their votes.... With cricketers they have no such comforts... because cricketers in this country make so much money... people feel the guy can still get out to a very casual shot and there is nothing I can do about it.... We have channelized that popular anger in a very democratic forum... we felt it would be a good idea to give people a forum to vent their anger and their point of view. ...

The kind of interventions we make in other activities like politics, civic and municipal administration, economics... we have started doing that in cricket. In the same way that I would look at who's responsible for misery during Bombay floods... who is responsible for this goof-up in administration.... Here we look at who is the culprit in the match. [33]

Match ke Mujrim perfectly encapsulates why cricket is so big on Indian news television, which is constantly searching for a national 'public' while attempting to create a national 'market'.

I have argued that in the quest for television ratings in a cluttered market, news TV channels find an attractive option in cricket's pan-Indian appeal. Television producers believe nothing is more 'Indian' than cricket and their quest for the elusive viewer has turned cricket into a winner. The dynamics of the 'market' and perceived demands of the 'public' have turned cricket into a dominant driver of India's news television boom. This is a two-way process and world cricket itself has been transformed by the massive infusion of capital from Indian television that has changed the entrenched power structure of the global game, though the details of that transformation are beyond the scope of this paper.

In conclusion, cricket's pre-eminence in news television is a crucial pointer towards its intrinsic equation with modern Indian identity, a relationship that television channels have not only recognized but consciously tried to augment. The commercial battle for the Indian news viewer must be seen in this context because the dependence on cricket showcases the often forgotten centrality of cricket as a binding force in a land divided on various linguistic, regional, religious, caste and cultural lines. Satellite television programming is an arena where the idea of India is debated over and fought for every day, and judging by the evidence we have the verdict is clear: cricket sells because it matters deeply to India.

Notes

[1] Harinder Baweja and Ramesh Vinayak, 'Postcards From the Ridge', *India Today*, 21 June 1999, available online at http://www.india-today.com/itoday/21061999/cover3.html, accessed 30 Oct. 2005.
[2] Onkar Singh, 'Country First, Cricket Next, Says Kapil', 1 July 1999, available online at http://www.rediff.com/news/1999/jul/01kapil.htm, accessed 10 Aug. 2006.
[3] 'Jawans Rejoice', *The Indian Express*, 10 June 1999.
[4] See Guha, *Corner of a Foreign Field*; Majumdar, *22 Yards to Freedom*.

[5] The numbers are based on Ministry of Information and Broadcasting data and are update up to 30 June 2007, available online at http://mib.nic.in/informationb/CODES/frames.htm, accessed 7 May 2007. And Ministry of Information and Broadcasting, *Answer to Lok Sabha Unstarred Question No. 2056*, 9 March 2006, http://164.100.24.208/lsq14/quest.asp?qref= 26637, accessed 29 May 2006. These figures do not include a slew of additional news channels in various languages that were slated to be launched in 2007.

[6] Channel 7 was renamed IBN-7 on 15 August 2006 after its owners, Jagran TV Limited, entered into a new shareholding arrangement with Global Broadcast News. *Global Broadcast News Limited Draft Red Herring Prospectus*, p. iii. All references in text refer to its programming before the changeover and it will be referred to as Channel 7.

[7] Rajagopal, *Politics After Television*.

[8] Kohli, *The Indian Media Business*.

[9] By 1993, Star claimed access to 7 million homes through cable: Star TV Homes Penetration Study 1993, cited by Page and Crawley, *Satellites Over South Asia*, 245.

[10] NDTV IPO Presentation (Internet edition), April 2004, available online at www.ndtv.com/ investors/ndtvipopresentation.pdf, accessed 21 Sep. 2004.

[11] Page and Crawley, *Satellites Over South Asia*, 78.

[12] Subhash Chandra bought back the bulk of News Corp's shares in Zee in 1999.

[13] Television accounts for 65 per cent of the entertainment industry, with estimated earnings of Rs12,870 crore in 2004: PriceWaterhouse Coopers, *The Indian Entertainment Industry*, 12.

[14] National Readership Survey 2006, *NRS 2006 Press Release – Key Findings*, 29 Aug. 2006; *NRS 2005 – Key Findings Press Release*, 8 June 2005.

[15] Figures from Atul Phadnis, Vice-President and S-Group Director, TAM Media Research, 2001–2005, personal interview, Mumbai, 14 Jan. 2005.

[16] The Star News channel was initially launched only to cover the 1998 general election campaign for three months, but its success convinced its managers of the potential for a round-the-clock national news channel and they signed a five-year deal with NDTV. The Zee TV network launched its 24-hour channel, Zee News, soon thereafter. Prannoy Roy, President, NDTV, personal interview, New Delhi, 28 Oct. 2005.

[17] Uday Shankar, CEO Star India and editor Star News (2004–07); and editor, Aaj Tak (2000–3), personal interview, Shanghai, 22 Aug. 2005.

[18] Ibid.

[19] Anisa Khan, sports correspondent and presenter, *Khel India*, NDTV India, personal interview, Melbourne, 9 Oct. 2005.

[20] Rahul Bhattacharya, 'Zoo TV', Cricinfo, Jan. 2006, 90.

[21] Uday Shankar, personal interview.

[22] The salary figures for Sidhu's annual contract are from NDTV sources who wish to remain unnamed.

[23] I am grateful to Rahul Bhattacharya for information on salaries. Until the 2007 World Cup, Indian top-tier cricketers were paid Rs250,000 for a test match and Rs160,000 for a one-day game. On an average the team plays about 30 one-day games and 10–12 test matches a year so match fees accounted to a yearly average of Rs7,300,000. Under this system, apart from match fees, players were contracted by the BCCI in brackets of Rs5,000,000, Rs2,000,000 and Rs1,500,000 as a yearly retainer. A player in the highest contracted category, therefore, could expect to earn about Rs12.3 million a year. In addition, the team sponsor paid the players for logo money. This system was changed after the Indian debacle at the 2007 World Cup. For the pre-2007 salary structures of Indian players see Sharda Ugra, 'Perform or Pay Up', *India Today*, 20 Nov. 2006, 70–72.

[24] Bhattacharya, 'Zoo TV', 91.

[25] Anisa Khan, personal interview.

[26] Uday Shankar, personal interview.

[27] Ernst and Young, *The Indian Entertainment Industry*, 37.

[28] Avinash Kaul, vice-president, NDTV Media, personal interview, Mumbai, 14 Jan. 2005.

[29] TAM data is from Mehta, *Indianising Television*.

[30] Quoted in Bhattacharya, unpublished article.

[31] Uday Shankar, personal interview.

[32] Shantanu Guha Roy, sports and business editor, Channel 7 (2005), personal interview, New Delhi, 27 Oct. 2005.

[33] Uday Shankar, personal interview.

References

Ernst and Young. *The Indian Entertainment Industry: Emerging Trends and Opportunities.* New Delhi: Federation of Chambers of Indian Commerce and Industry, March 2004.

Guha, Ramachandra. *Corner of a Foreign Field.* New Delhi: Pan Macmillan, 2002.

Kohli, Vanita. *The Indian Media Business.* New Delhi: Response Books, 2003.

Majumdar, Boria. *22 Yards to Freedom.* New Delhi: Penguin, 2004.

Mehta, Nalin. *Indianising Television: News, Politics and Globalisation.* Melbourne: La Trobe University, unpublished PhD thesis, 2007.

Page, David and William Crawley. *Satellites Over South Asia.* New Delhi: Sage Publications, 2001.

PriceWaterhouse Coopers. *The Indian Entertainment Industry: An Unfolding Opportunity.* New Delhi: Federation of Indian Chambers of Commerce and Industry, 2005.

Rajagopal, Arvind. *Politics After Television.* Cambridge: Cambridge University Press, 2001.

Reading Cricket Fiction in the Times of Hindu Nationalism and Farmer Suicides: Fallacies of Textual Interpretation

Nissim Mannathukkaren

This paper will critique postcolonial theory's attempt to read the cricket nationalism portrayed in the Oscar-nominated Bollywood film Lagaan *as one that subverts the civilizing mission of British colonialism and also restores the agency of the subaltern classes. Instead, it will argue that this cricket nationalism replicates Indian bourgeois nationalism, which has no place for the subaltern in its imaginary. It will also argue that the postcolonial thesis of decolonization and indigenization of cricket supposedly achieved by* Lagaan *is marked by a culturalism that does not take into account structural factors such as capital, class and caste that dominate the institution of cricket in India. Finally, against postcolonial theory's tendency to read a text in isolation from the context, it will be contended that the cricket nationalism of the film can only be understood by locating it in relation to the present socio-historic conjuncture wherein forces of capital and nationalism are hegemonic.*

> Fascism sees its salvation in giving these masses not their right, but instead a chance to express themselves. The masses have a right to change property relations; fascism seeks to give them an expression while preserving property. The logical result of fascism is the introduction of aesthetics into political life. [1]

Since the emergence of postcolonial theory, there has been a veritable explosion of interest in phenomena such as 'colonialism' and 'decolonization'. It is therefore natural that the game of cricket, being one of the lasting legacies of the British Empire, should be the subject of scrutiny among theorists in the former British colonies. How 'vernacularized' and 'indigenized' the game has become, or the extent to which it has transformed itself from a medium to carry forward the colonial

Nissim Mannathukkaren, Dalhousie University.

enterprise to one that disseminates nationalism are some of the questions that have animated theorists. [2] Recently, similar debates have emerged about the nature of cricket portrayed in the famous Bollywood film *Lagaan* ('Tax', 2001), which was not only a box-office success in India but also attracted international attention through its Oscar nomination. One of the attempts to understand the cricket nationalism in *Lagaan* has been through the lens of postcolonial theory (more specifically, the subaltern studies project in India, one of the most influential proponents of postcolonial theory). [3] By critically engaging with this essay, I will propose an alternative reading of the cricket nationalism in *Lagaan* which, in turn, will look into the question of the efficacy of postcolonial theory in understanding decolonization (especially with regard to cricket).

With the rise of postcolonial theory (under the influence of postmodernism and post-structuralism), there has been an extensive focus on concepts such as 'culture', 'language', 'texts' and 'discourse'. While this in itself was not an unwelcome trend, problematically, the predominant tendency in postcolonial theory has been to reduce historical, social practices and processes to merely texts and discourse. There is a total 'disanalogy between texts and institutions ... [and] the consequent inability to give an appropriate account of the latter'. [4] This evasion of the non-textual reality leads to a position similar to the famous Derridean dictum *'il n'y a pas de hors-texte'* – there is nothing outside the text. Since signifiers do not signify anything outside of the text, we are forced to construct 'meanings' (if you can call them that) from the endless chain of signifiers themselves. This is the terrain where material problems are converted into metaphorical ones. [5]

As Rosalind O'Hanlon and David Washbrook note about postcolonialism's solutions, 'methodological individualism, the depoliticizing insulation of social from material domains, a view of social relations that is in practice extremely voluntaristic, the refusal of any kind of programmatic politics – do not seem to us radical, subversive or emancipatory. They are, on the contrary, conservative and implicitly authoritarian.' [6]

Chakroborty makes two important claims with regard to *Lagaan*: firstly, in *Lagaan* there is a recuperation of the 'agency of the subaltern classes and the subversion of the civilizing mission of the British imperial enterprise through [its] representation of cricket in the colony'. [7] This is achieved through devices such as 'mimicry' and through the 'vernacularization' and 'indigenization' of colonial cricket. Secondly, 'Indian popular cinema [especially *Lagaan*] extends the subaltern studies project in the visual medium' and it not only *'can* effectively decolonize the imagination of the Indian masses' but also 'through films like *Lagaan*' can reveal 'its potential to *empower* the masses that are otherwise silenced, forgotten or marginalized in dominant discourses'. [8]

This essay will question all these claims. In the first section I will try to demonstrate that the attempt to understand *Lagaan* through the subaltern studies project is flawed. I will also posit that, rather than recuperate the agency of the subaltern classes, the cricket nationalism that emerges in *Lagaan* is starkly similar to Indian bourgeois nationalism (in its different forms, from the Gandhian to the Hindu nationalism of the present) which has no place for the subaltern in it. In the second section I will look at the hierarchies that dominate the institution of cricket in India to highlight the flaws of Chakraborty's postcolonial theory, which harps on decolonization (only in cultural terms) and vernacularization without addressing the question of democratization of the game. In the final section, against Chakraborty's tendency to read the *text* in isolation from the *context*, I will explicate the socio-historic and linguistic context in which a film such as *Lagaan* is situated. It will be obvious by the end of the discussion that the *empowerment* of the masses claimed through the film is a vacuous notion which has no connection to material reality.

Erasing the Subaltern

Chakraborty argues that 'the film's appeal to the peasant-spectators is enhanced by *Lagaan*'s plot construction around a drought-affected peasantry and portrayal of parched lands'. This is because the film was released at a time when severe drought plagued the western regions of India. [9] The condition of the peasantry in the film is akin to the real-life conditions of the peasantry, leading the latter to empathize with the film's content of a marginalized people overcoming all odds. [10] Moreover, by portraying the peasant subalterns as not only playing cricket, an elite game, but also winning a match against their colonial masters, the film defies 'history, writes the dispossessed of the colonial margins... into the history of a popular sport'. [11] This is where supposedly the similarities between the film and the subaltern studies project emerge in trying to write a history from the point of view of the subaltern and recover his/her marginalized voice. As Ranajit Guha, the founding father of the subaltern studies project theorized, a new form of history writing was an absolute imperative as the historiography of Indian nationalism until then was dominated by 'elitism – colonialist elitism and bourgeois-nationalist elitism'. If colonialist historiography reduced the history of Indian nationalism to the efforts of the 'British colonial rulers, administrators, policies, institutions and culture', in the nationalist version, it was 'written up as a sort of spiritual biography of the Indian elite'. On the other hand, what the subaltern studies project was seeking to achieve was to write a history that brought to the fore 'the contribution made by the people *on their own*, that is *independently of the elite* to the making and development of [Indian] nationalism'. [12] Marxist historiography too came under scathing critique from the subalternists for its alleged class reductionism, which failed to understand the unique modes of subaltern resistance under colonialism. [13]

Chakraborty's defence of the subaltern studies project and its extension to understand *Lagaan* is highly problematic for the reason that it does not map the complex turns and twists that the project has undergone. In assuming that the project's central problematic has remained the same in the two decades and more of its existence, the author has ignored the drastic shift in the theoretical and epistemological frameworks of the project. In doing so, her essay too participates in the evasions, erasures and contradictions that mark the writings of the subaltern historians. The theoretical framework that Chakraborty uses is that of later subaltern studies which are markedly culturalist and which have totally abandoned their initial critical Gramscian thrust. She either ignores the earlier writings or when she does refer to them totally misrepresents them.

Nothing demonstrates better the shift in emphasis of the subalternists from Gramsci, Hobsbawm and E.P. Thompson to Foucault, Derrida and Said than Partha Chatterjee's (one of the most prominent figures of subaltern studies) writings on nationalism. From a position similar to that of Guha's – which we saw above – that spoke of the deep complicity of the nationalist elite in silencing the voice of the subaltern and the *'failure of the Indian bourgeoisie to speak for the nation'*, [14] Chatterjee moves to one that, at least partially, redeems the nationalist elite of the colonial era. [15] The argument now is that nationalism cannot be viewed as a political movement alone and that what is significant in anti-colonial nationalisms is its cultural and spiritual component. The elite nationalism of the colonial era, in Chatterjee's view, already establishes its sovereignty in the spiritual domain before it even begins the battle for political sovereignty. If in the material domain anti-colonial nationalisms have no option but to imitate the various Western models of nationalism, it is in the spiritual and cultural domain that the latter launch their

> most powerful, creative, and historically significant project: to fashion a 'modern' national culture that is nevertheless not Western. If the nation is an imagined community, then this is where it is brought into being. In this its true and essential domain, the nation is already sovereign, even when the state is in the hands of the colonial power. [16]

Language, art and aesthetic, education and family constitute, for Chatterjee, the 'inner domain of national culture'. The split between the material and cultural domains that Chatterjee posits is highly problematic, for it artificially divides the two. He does not take into account the complex and dialectical ways in which the two domains interact and constitute each other. This position believes that decolonization can be achieved in the cultural domain without a corresponding decolonization in the political and economic spheres. The dominant tropes and motifs of postcolonial theory are now slowly being erected: 'culture', 'difference', 'the spiritual' etc. It is relevant here to note that Chatterjee chooses to term the cultural domain as the *true* and *essential* domain. Sumit Sarkar argues with regard to the theoretical shifts of subaltern studies:

> What had started as an understandable dissatisfaction with the economistic reductionism of much 'official' Marxism is now contributing to another kind of narrowing of horizons, one that conflates colonial exploitation with western cultural domination. Colonial discourse analysis abstracts itself, except in the most general terms, from histories of production and social relationships. A 'culturalism' now further attenuated into readings of isolable texts has become, after the

presumed demise of Marxism, extremely nervous of all 'material' histories: the spectre of economic reductionism looms everywhere. [17]

I will argue, as we will see shortly, this regressive rupture of the cultural from material processes that characterizes later subaltern studies is also present in Chakraborty's essay. Decolonization is something that is primarily conceived in discursive and cultural terms. Also, the crucial question of internal decolonization is not addressed at all.

The other major and related shift in subaltern studies, increasingly coming under the influence of post-structuralism, is to shun modernity itself. Western Enlightenment and Eurocentrism become the new objects of critique. Thus state, civil society, individual rights etc. are products of Western Enlightenment and imposed by colonialism, which are deeply at odds with non-Western societies. What can resist the modern disciplinary regime, bourgeois civil-social institutions and the narrative of capital is the narrative of community. This is where the figure of Gandhi and his 'anti-modernist, anti-individualist' rhetoric of 'love, kinship, austerity, sacrifice' becomes the symbol of the struggle for the sovereignty of the inner domain. [18] The redemption of Gandhi in the later subaltern writings goes against their earlier trenchant critique of the elite and bourgeois nature of Gandhian nationalism. Chakraborty glosses over this and also the subalternists' move from a rejection of all kinds of nationalisms to 'a certain kind of [cultural] nationalism that shuns modernity'. [19]

Finally, one more significant shift that characterizes subaltern studies is a shocking abandonment of the focus on the subaltern itself. Instead, the focus begins to be on subjects such as the Bengali middle class, colonial prisons, the nation, the community, Indian religion and language. [20] As Ramachandra Guha notes in a review of volume 8 of *Subaltern Studies*: 'Over the years, most members of its editorial collective have moved from documenting subaltern dissent to dissecting elite discourse, from writing with (Socialist) passion to following the (postmodernist) fashion.' [21] Without acknowledging these momentous shifts, it is difficult to claim that *Lagaan* is extending the subaltern studies project as Chakraborty does.

Chakraborty argues that characterization of the peasants in the film goes against the stereotypical assumptions of the colonialist and nationalist historiographies that peasants were ignorant and naive and needed leadership from outside to organize them. This is because the peasants themselves identify the 'English officer as the "real enemy"', rather than their king'. [22] Contrary to this, I have argued earlier that here lay the defining moment of the film, where it appropriates the peasant to the cause of an elite nationalism. By identifying the English officer as the 'real enemy', the film omits the role of the native princes and feudal lords, the collaborators of the British Raj in the oppression of the peasants. This is the classic move of bourgeois nationalism by which all exploitative relations within the nation are erased to posit an enemy outside the nation, in this case the White colonizer/racial other. [23] Cricket nationalism in the film merely replicates this bourgeois nationalism. I have also argued that this moment of the identification of the real enemy in the film was very similar to the Gandhian advice to the peasants of Awadh in 1921 to absolve the feudal lords of any crimes towards them for the former were slaves of the British (this was reflective of his united-front strategy of seriously downplaying caste and class oppression until independence of the nation was achieved). [24] What Chakraborty fails to recognize is that this nationalist united-front strategy has acquired a stronger currency among the ruling elites in the present, who use it to shore up their eroding legitimacy by harping on the threat that the nation state faces from trans-national and sub-national entities.

It is really incomprehensible that Chakraborty could posit the moment when the peasants reduce their multi-faceted oppression to a single oppressor – the British state – as a sign of their agency and subjecthood. The gargantuan scale of exploitation by the feudal lords which led to Jawaharlal Nehru describing them as 'complete parasites on land and people' [25] is not even hinted at in the film. Chakraborty takes solace in the argument that the local ruler is portrayed as 'an effete and ineffective ruler' who does not take on the British and also that 'in the scheme of the film he is also oppressed by the colonial state [!]'. [26]

Forgetting the fundamental principle of writing critical history, she buys the assumptions of the film rather than interrogates them. Critiquing my position that the 'other' in the film becomes defined as belonging outside the nation, she argues that there are 'layers of otherness in the film'. [27] But it is never convincingly demonstrated as to how these layers question the dominant social order (either of the period portrayed in the film or of the present times) considering that the film has been touted as extending the subaltern studies project. The only minor and superficial aberrations in the synthetic unity of the village space are when the villagers question the inclusion of Kachra, who belongs to an 'untouchable' caste, in the village cricket team formed to play the British. The other dissonance arises when Lakha, a Hindu villager, tries to prevent Ismail, a Muslim, from joining the team by suggesting that the Hindus may not accept him (Lakha does this out of personal animosity between himself and the hero Bhuvan over winning the affections of a woman they both love). The misgivings among the villagers about the inclusion of the 'untouchable' are easily resolved when the hero convinces them by pointing out that the Hindu god Rama had condemned untouchability. Chakraborty does not at all note the implications of this crucial moment in the film. She casually comments on it: 'The articulate hero conveniently and temporarily resolves the resistance [of the villagers] by referring to Hindu mythology.' That this particular version of the mythology which the hero expounds is an upper-caste Brahminical one escapes the attention of the author. The *dalit* (the formerly untouchable castes) movement in India is strongly opposed to such versions which erase the oppressive nature of Brahminical Hinduism and portray it as benign and benevolent. By again uncritically following the assumptions of the film as common sense, Chakraborty effaces the counter-hegemonic history of *dalits*. Here it should be noted that Kancha Ilaiah, scholar and prominent *dalit* activist, writes that even the subaltern studies collective was impervious to incorporating a *dalit* perspective in the writing of Indian history. [28]

Even though the untouchable is incorporated into the team and also contributes to the victory, he does not utter a single word of significance in the film. As Siriyavan Anand notes in a trenchant *dalit* critique of the film:

> The subaltern cannot speak. Totally stripped of agency, Kachra (in Hindustani, it also means waste or garbage) has to simply follow caste-Hindu Bhuvan's words. He never exercises a choice. Kachra – someone excluded from every other social-cultural-religious aspect of village life – is never asked whether he would like to be included in such a game. It is not clear whether this Dalit, portrayed so pathetically, is even aware of why the game is being played. [29]

Chakraborty is forced to concede that the portrayal of the *dalit* is marked by 'servility and muteness' and his inclusion in the cricket team does not alter the wider caste-ridden social system. Still she does not find anything amiss in the portrayal, for it 'points to the improvisational modes of peasant political agency, as the untouchable youth is *allowed* to be part of the cricket team because of his exceptional spinning ability, which could potentially facilitate a victory for Champaner'. [30] So the incorporation of the untouchable is an instrumental tactic with the only goal of winning the match. After that, the normal state of affairs will return in which the untouchables will continue with their routine of subhuman existence. [31] Is this any different from the post-independence Congress Party's manipulation of the *dalit*s through corporatist vote-bank politics or the recent desperate attempts by the BJP to wean them back them into the Hindu fold? In Ilaih's view, what tokenism and 'co-optation' do is to appropriate *dalit*s as 'fallen Hindus' and in the process eliminate their non-Hindu identity and their separate culture, language and philosophy. [32] The film's caste politics can be seen as a continuation of the Brahminic appropriation of counter-hegemonic resistances through centuries. [33] Chakraborty, by endorsing the film's premises, participates in it.

The author claims that the hierarchy of social relations is evident from the 'depiction of the economic disparity between peasant landowners with varying amounts of farming land' and from the doubts that exist about the inclusion of the untouchable and the Muslim and the total exclusion of women from the cricket team. [34] The first example is a figment of imagination of the author: there is no scene in the film which categorically depicts peasants with varying amounts of farming land. [35] In a fallacious argument, the author believes that showing different social and class positions itself is a revolutionary move. By that criterion every Bollywood film will fit the bill: in each one, the hero belongs to an upper caste, the women are always in a subordinate position and there are, of course, servants and members of the working class. [36]

The social order in *Lagaan* is portrayed as a 'natural' one. No hierarchy is questioned except vis-à-vis the English officer. The women are perfectly happy: they sing, dance and cook for the men. Their exclusion from the cricket team is not something that bothers them; it is accepted as the 'natural' state of affairs. Even the doubts about the untouchable are expressed by the upper-caste villagers; the untouchable, as we have seen, does not speak. Also, there are no other untouchables in the film. The caste identity of any of the other villagers is also not known.

Academic studies have shown that rural India in the colonial era was characterized by the 'tridentine oppression' of the '*sarkar, zamindar, sahukar*' (state, landlord, moneylender). [37] *Lagaan* does not seem to acknowledge any oppression that exists beyond the colonial state. And again, Chakraborty does not find anything lacking in this portrayal where 'dismantling structures of indigenous oppression is presented beyond the scope of the subalterns' for 'the limit of the peasants' identity is fixed by the very conditions of the subordination under which they live and work'. [38] She again relies on Guha's argument that peasant resistances were characterized by 'negative consciousness' which was not powerful enough for them to develop a struggle for national liberation on their own. It is no one's argument that the film should have portrayed such a struggle (but one would have expected the supposedly radical 'subaltern' film to dream up a counter-factual history). Instead, what can be demanded is that it show some affinity to history as it happened. But what it does is mutilate history beyond recognition. Take for example, the 1921 peasant rebellion of Awadh. As subaltern historian Pandey documents, it was 'when the *landlord* decided to levy new and oppressive imposts in a period of considerable hardship for substantial sections of the peasantry that resistance was taken up in Awadh as morally right and necessary' (my emphasis). So it was the landlords' decision to levy new taxes that had no sanction in tradition and which were over and above what the British state had imposed that led the peasants to revolt. Most importantly, the rebellion showed the ability of peasants to identify their 'enemies'. The small tenants and the agricultural labourers attacked the 'taluqdars...small zamindars, large cultivators and [even] the high castes in general'. They also targeted merchants, goldsmiths and weavers who they thought had exploited the situation to make huge profits: 'There was also a growing feeling of antagonism towards Europeans and the abuse of policemen for deserting their countrymen and serving an alien race.' [39]

This rebellion is, of course, not the first one to have taken place in colonial India. As Guha's study shows, from the year 1783 (even before the British had established their real hegemony) to 1900, there were nearly '110 agrarian disturbances in many forms and on scales ranging from local riots to war-like campaigns spread over many districts'. [40] Of course, these were not infused with any nationalist consciousness, but they definitely were not confined to an attack on the British alone but extended to their native collaborators as well. This is what *Lagaan*, a film supposedly extending the subaltern studies project, occludes in favour a simple binary of the natives versus the British. This binarizing and racializing strategy reifies and essentializes the two categories and, in the process, eliminates all markers of difference such as class, culture, gender, internal to both. As a result, even without any explicit references to nation and nationalism (the usual rhetoric of recent commercial cinema), *Lagaan*'s cricket politics get invested with a nationalism that is starkly reminiscent of Indian bourgeois nationalism from the 1920s onwards. I have argued earlier that this was anachronistic and a deliberate attempt at nationalizing the past, for in the 1890s (in which *Lagaan* is set) there was no 'Indian nationalism' as we know today. [41] Chakraborty erroneously believes that since there is no 'overt reference to the nation or motherland', [42] there is no nationalism in the film. According to her,

> Cricket nationalism is depicted as temporary and provisional and thus different from nationalist politics, which sees itself as linear and evolutionary. It would be, therefore, anachronistic to read the specificity (local and contextual) of the fictional past depicted in *Lagaan* in terms of the present, where cricket has become an 'instrument for mobilizing national sentiments'. [43]

Chakraborty fails to note that the film is attempting to do precisely this, to transpose the massive popularity of the game and its associations with (mainly jingoistic) cultural nationalism in the present [44] to another period in history. It is strange that Chakraborty's subaltern reading wants to deny this anachronism even when Dipesh Chakrabarty, prominent subaltern historian, also identifies a 'deliberate anachronism' in *Lagaan* for it transposes the 'aggressive', 'mass mediatized nationalism' of the present to the 1890s. According to him, the film 'deliberately mixes up historical chronology and uses the mediatized mass-spectacular nature of limited-over cricket – now set back into the 1890s – as a visual metaphor for Indian anti-colonial nationalism.... The whole accent of the game in the film, as in one-day cricket, is on winning.' [45]

Chakraborty, who had earlier argued for the restoration of the agency of the peasant and the need to recognize that the 'villagers are intelligent enough to recognize their oppressor of the moment', now abandons this agency by arguing that 'dismantling structures of indigenous oppression' is 'beyond the scope of the subalterns' for the insurgent consciousness is always a 'negative consciousness'. This is a selective rendering of Guha's work. Guha's point is that peasant consciousness was fragmented and not powerful enough to develop a *national liberation movement*. But *negative consciousness was not a hindrance in identifying the native and foreign oppressors and mounting violent resistance against them*, as Guha and Pandey have shown. A more discerning reading of Guha would have found him arguing that despite the negativity, peasant consciousness was developed enough to identify 'some of the basic elements of economic exploitation and the political superstructure which legitimised them'. [46]

Since the historical evidence is overwhelming, now Chakraborty has no other option but to justify the film's story as a specific case and not as representative of the general tendency. But this begs a most important question. From a vast archive of peasant rebellions and resistances to choose from, why does the filmmaker choose an exceptional case, in which all the indigenous groups are benign and positive figures and the local raja a closet nationalist? This question cannot be answered by Chakraborty's textual hermeneutics. For that one has to step outside the text to understand the material, ideological and institutional structures to which it is dialectically related. The author argues that the peasants' questioning of only the British and not the other indigenous dominant groups is a sign of their 'dynamic and improvisational modes of peasant political agency'! The unity of all the indigenous groups in the film is only 'contingent, provisional and contextual' and it would be 'ingenious to regard anti-colonial alliances such as these permanent or immutable'. [47] But where are the examples of such anti-colonial alliances in history when, in most rebellions and resistances, the peasants targeted the native oppressors and collaborators of the Raj? In the 1921 rebellion, for example, Gyanendra Pandey points out that the higher-caste tenants openly worked against the rebellion and also welcomed police action against the (lower caste) peasants. [48] Even when such anti-colonial alliances have come about, they have proved highly advantageous to the dominant groups. In any case, the native princes and the feudal landed classes were thoroughly opposed to the national movement; their position of power had a higher chance of survival in British India than in a republican India. [49] Chakraborty's enthusiasm for the anti-colonial alliance portrayed in the film ignores the conclusions of subaltern historians in their early works: 'A united front of the whole Indian people – landlords and peasants, millowners and manual labourers, feudal princes and the rural poor – in the anti-colonial campaign was scarcely feasible: no major struggle for change anywhere has ever achieved such unity.' [50] An anti-colonial alliance of all classes will only be fruitful if it is under the hegemony (in the Gramscian sense) of the labouring majority. [51] And it would naturally involve substantial sacrifices from the hitherto oppressor classes and castes. Otherwise it will degenerate into a machine for perpetuating the existing social order sans the colonizer. Pandey is absolutely right that the 'nature of the Swaraj [self-rule] that eventuated from [the anti-colonial struggle] would very much depend on the "unity" that was forged'. Therefore,

> the Congress's insistence... on a united front of landlords as well as peasants and others, was a statement in favour of the *status quo* and against any radical change in the social set-up when the British finally handed over the reins of power.... [It was also] a statement against mass participatory democracy and in favour of the idea of 'trusteeship' – the landlords and princes acting as trustees in the economic sphere, Gandhi and company in the political. [52]

In *Lagaan*, the debate about the nature of the alliance does not arise at all; for that to happen, the parasitic and exploitative role of the indigenous oppressors has to be acknowledged, which it does not. Chakraborty can only defend this bourgeois nationalism by conjuring up another interpretation for which there is no basis in the film itself: the peasant hero 'gestures to the possibility of fighting against the local ruler, if need be, at an undetermined future'. [53]

Caste, Class and Capital in Indian Cricket

According to Chakraborty, '*Lagaan*'s most significant contribution to popular culture lies in its ability to convincingly portray how cultural improvisations by subaltern groups can co-opt and critique the master forms and tropes of the West'. [54] This happens because the hero of the film asserts that cricket is only a poor copy of their own age-old children's game of *gilli-danda*. So this mockery inverts the colonizing mission of civilizing the childlike natives on its head and also 'desecrates the "purity" of cricket roots' asserted by the British. By 'mimicry', through assertion of the similarity between *gilli-danda* and the natives' own excellence in the game, the 'British subject, the assumed original . . . [becomes] merely a sophisticated copy'. [55] All the Victorian ideals of sportsmanship, fair play, the downplaying of individual interests, loyalty et cetera and the British policy of inculcating them in the natives through games such as cricket become an object of critique in the film through the mismatched cricket game between the poor villagers and the British led by an arrogant officer. The goodness and strength of character of the peasants shown in the film is a paean to the qualities of the peasants and not the Victorian gentleman. Through 'mimicry' and repetition, the peasant does not merely copy, but subverts and 'de-Victorianizes the national sport of the United Kingdom'. [56]

All that Chakraborty asserts about the Bakhtinian inversions that supposedly riddle the film is seriously handicapped by the absence of any reference to the material context. Therefore it becomes a mere symbolic act. But as Marx reminds us, 'the arm of criticism can certainly not supplant the criticism of arms. Material force must be overthrown by material force.' [57] There is no real decolonization unless both symbolic and material foundations of colonialism are uprooted. In the present, a 'reversal of the terms and tropes of colonialist discourse', as Chakraborty asserts, is a luxury that few of the privileged minority can afford in 'postcolonial' nations. To ask a relevant question: what are the chances of a *dalit* from a landless agricultural family playing for the national cricket team in India? Since his whole life would most likely revolve around the question of survival, the question itself would be spurious. One million *dalits* work as scavengers in India. It is not uncommon to read reports about *dalits* being lynched, paraded naked or forced to eat faeces. In a land where bonded labour is illegal, there are 40 million bonded workers, a vast majority of whom are *dalits*. In the year 2000, the number of crimes (only recorded ones) against *dalits* was 25,455. [58] *Lagaan* and commercial cinema (with miniscule exceptions) do not portray such stark and gruesome realities. Therefore to posit, as Chakraborty does, that popular cinema has the 'potential to empower the masses' is to, as Walter Benjamin would famously argue, aestheticize politics and by implication, the concepts of emancipation and liberation. The mute untouchable does not 'point to the repressive strategies and practices within the subaltern tale of victory' [59] as Chakraborty asserts; rather his muteness is a reflection of the reality of the *dalits* and his unquestioning servility merely reinforces it as a 'natural' state of affairs.

Merely asserting that cricket is a poor copy of *gilli-danda* does not take us anywhere. It has to be read along with the drastic decline of *gilli-danda* and a whole lot of other indigenous games, especially in the last two decades when capital (both Indian and multinational) has really flooded the game of cricket. Now, in the rural areas people are forced to play games such as cricket in which they have few chances of succeeding because of its elite nature. [60]

If we were to delve further into the sociology of cricket, what emerges is its strong casteist nature. The game in India has been shockingly dominated by Brahmins. From the 1960s to the 1990s, Indian Test teams have fielded an average of six Brahmins, sometimes even nine! [61] This is despite the fact that Brahmins do not constitute more than four per cent of the Indian population. It is not shocking considering that eight of the 14 prime ministers India have had belonged to the Brahmin caste and virtually every single institution of the Indian state has been dominated by it. What is shocking is that the 'success' that Brahmins have had in cricket has come despite their traditional ritualistic injunctions against pollution by touch, physical labour and activity. Being a 'knowledge-producing' priestly class, they obviously left the hard manual tasks to castes below them. But the Brahmin dominance in the most popular and lucrative game in India shows how 'cultural capital' accrued over centuries has been productively converted. It is another example of the successful mutation of the Brahmins in the transition from the traditional-sacred realm to the secular-modern realm. [62] As anthropologist and cricket historian Ramachandra Guha comments, 'Cricket being a non-body contact sport was certainly one attraction for the Brahmin. Besides, to play this game you did not have to be physically very strong.' [63] Ashis Nandy has also theorized about the close relationship between the mythical structures of Hindu (read Brahmin) philosophy and cricket. [64]

As market forces lead to the plebeianization of elite games, cricket still holds its Brahmin fort, despite some changes. [65] It is highly instructive that while in the United States Blacks have not only defined games such as boxing and basketball and art forms such as jazz (and even penetrating hitherto white-dominated games such as tennis and golf), not a single *dalit* cricketer has played for the Indian national team in six decades after independence. [66] 'Cricket and the values it promoted fitted well with the hierarchies that our feudal and caste society engendered. It did not break them.' [67] Therefore what is urgently needed is democratization of the sport in which all sections of the Indian population have an equal chance of playing the game at the highest level. What this implies is that in the Indian context the issue that needs urgent attention is not what *Lagaan* is trying to achieve in Chakraborty's interpretation – the 'vernacularization and indigenization of colonial cricket [and the hijacking of] cricket from the monolithic structures of Englishness'. [68] Rather, it seems, what is required is the extrication of cricket from the monolithic structures of Brahminism.

There is another colonization that characterizes Indian cricket. That is the colonization of it by the forces of capital and also by a private body masquerading in the guise of a public one. Since the entry of trans-national (and Indian big) capital into cricket, the game has been increasingly forced to adapt to its needs. This is a phenomenon that is obviously not confined to India. The emergence of the now hugely popular one-day version of the game, with coloured clothing, white ball and day-night matches, was a direct impact of this and had already shaken the game out of its Victorian and traditional English moorings. Commercialization is further pushing cricket to new shorter formats such as 20/20. India, being the biggest market for cricket, has borne the brunt of its commodification. Therefore the number of one-day games the country has played (at the expense of traditional five-day Test matches) far exceeds other countries. [69] The liberalization of the Indian economy since 1991 has aided the process of the sway of capital in cricket. Now cricket works in a symbiotic relationship with other industries. Television takes the game to the most far-flung regions of India. [70] Cricket's popularity is used to sell consumer goods (by players endorsing them) produced by multinational and Indian companies. [71] The relentless incursion of luxury goods into rural areas is simultaneously creating new wants and desires.

The thesis of vernacularization or indigenization of cricket that Chakraborty propounds conceives the process of the spread of cricket in India in a one-sided manner: (Western colonial) modernity in the form of cricket being appropriated and consumed by a 'traditional' society. But this ignores the fact that India, through its structures of commercial sponsorship and state support and its spectator base, is the driving force in the modernization of cricket in the world. [72] Therefore it 'is possible to speak of another dynamic starting from a tightly controlled game dominated by England and associated with a certain set of Victorian values, one could speak of processes of modernization . . . through which a part of "unchanging" English tradition was appropriated for modernity'. [73] What Chakraborty ignores is the fact that cricket is a rare exception in the international sporting arena, for it is one game in which the non-West (mainly South Asia) is dominant in terms of decision-making, generation of revenues, spectatorship etc. This reverses the core-periphery relations that exist in other sports. [74] One of the main reasons for this is the decline of the game in the country of its origin, England. [75] As Arjun Appadurai points out, the present period is one in 'which the impact of media, commercialization, and national passion have almost completely eroded the old Victorian civilities associated with cricket. Cricket is now aggressive, spectacular, and frequently unsporting, with audiences thirsting for national victory and players and promoters out for the buck.' [76]

In the West Indies, where cricket once upon a time constituted not just a game but also a way of assertion against the colonizers, the game is in terminal decline. Not because the 'monolithic structures of Englishness' have been reasserted once again, but because in the era of commodification of cricket, the tiny Caribbean nations cannot generate their own domestic capital to sustain the game. While the youth increasingly take up American-dominated games such as basketball, whatever is left of cricket in the Caribbean is appropriated by trans-national capital, with serious consequences for its domestic structure. [77] India, as one of the emerging economic powerhouses, will avoid this calamity in cricket. This is a conjuncture in which 'subcontinental cricket [is] an ideal vehicle for multinational corporations seeking to penetrate "emerging markets"' and is 'used to sell goods in Europe, North America, the Middle East, and South-East Asia'. Mega-events such as the World Cup thus become a 'kind of carnival of globalization – sponsored by tobacco, soft drink and credit card giants'. [78] Chakraborty's undue emphasis on the indigenization and (cultural) decolonization of cricket ignores this reality, in which the game has been irretrievably enmeshed in the international circuits of capital, and the postcolonial problematic of colonialism (sans capitalism) can hardly provide us the clues to understanding it. [79]

The apex organization for cricket in India is the Board of Control for Cricket in India (BCCI). Unlike other games in India, cricket escaped the clutches of the gigantic arm of the state: The BCCI is a private body with its own constitution, and the government does not interfere in its functioning. But this also has meant that the public exercises no control over the richest cricket body in the world. [80] This has led to the most popular sport in the country being hijacked by a clique of businessmen and politicians who have had no experience at playing the game at a serious level. The BCCI has always faced allegation of misdemeanours and malpractices, the latest being the TV rights scandal. [81] A more serious controversy has arisen about the 'private' status of the BCCI. [82] It is most likely that the highest court in India will insist on instituting a mechanism to ensure some degree of public accountability. The absolute opposition by the BCCI to any form of government control shows mainly not the concern for maintaining autonomy and efficiency but the eagerness to avoid public scrutiny at any cost despite its decisions affecting a vast section of the cricket-loving public.

The biggest irony is the fact that despite the immense wealth it generates, the BCCI gives a fraction of it back to the game and the paying spectators. Domestic cricket in India is grossly neglected in favour of international cricket. In the worst manifestation of class division, the subalterns who throng the stadiums are subject to unimaginable physical discomfort. The majority of the cricket stadiums in the country are a 'living hell' for the spectators and many of them do not even have toilet facilities. [83] I.S. Bindra, former BCCI president, says, people are 'packed like sardines' in stadiums. They cannot even leave their seats to get a bottle of water for fear of losing them. And this is after waiting for almost six hours to get into the stadiums. [84] Chakraborty notes that 'violence has become a common phenomenon in cricket stadiums all over the country' but seems to reduce it to 'patriotic fervour and frenzy' [85] without looking into factors like the physical trauma and bodily violence that the masses undergo in the course of a match that act as catalyst in unruly behaviour.

All the factors above point to the fact that cricket cannot be discussed in terms of (cultural) decolonization alone, as postcolonial theory does; the relations of domination of caste and class that structure the game in the present have to be read along with it. [86] Cricket in India has been inextricably linked with global circuits of capital. It is now an instrument for mobilizing 'national sentiment in the service of trans-national spectacles and commoditization'. [87] The way caste and class shape the game is more detrimental to the democratization of the game in India than some 'monolithic structures of Englishness', which have been dismantled sometime ago. Indian cricket shows all the characteristics of the Trotskyite law of 'uneven and combined development of capitalism', in which a minority in the form of international cricket players, administrators and businessmen prosper by exploiting a majority of cricket followers. The latter are reduced to literally being 'spectators' with absolutely no control over the game.

The Text in its Context

An understanding of the film *Lagaan* cannot be undertaken in isolation from the broader socio-historical context in which it is produced and received. And this context is one in which the forces of global capital and cultural nationalism are hegemonic – a period I would characterize as late capitalism and high nationalism. Chakraborty's 'textual hermeneutic' has no place for the socio-historic context and the way in which the filmic text is constituted by and at the same time constitutes it. [88] Since the liberalization of the Indian economy in 1991, the pace of the process called the 'bourgeoisification of India's propertied classes' has strengthened, 'in effect an expansion of the bourgeoisie, and its political assertion'. [89] While this has contributed to the emergence of a significantly large middle class, it has also led to the immiseration of a large section of the working class and peasantry, mainly affecting those in the rural areas. The economist Utsa Patnaik argues that there has been 'unprecedented decline in purchasing power in rural areas' brought about by declining state support through rural development expenditures and the falling of agricultural growth rates. Therefore, in a shocking statistic, the foodgrain absorption for the year 2000–1 was less than the early years of the Second World War, which included the Bengal famine. [90] Needless to say, this decline affected the rural areas more, for foodgrains constitute the staple diet there. The effects of the neoliberal policies influenced by the Bretton Woods institutions have been catastrophic for the lower peasantry: the opening up of the Indian seed sector to corporations such as Monsanto, Cargill and Syngenta and rigged agricultural prices at the global level have led to Indian peasants losing \$26 billion annually. Unable to pay their debts back, more than 25, 000 farmers have committed suicide since 1997. [91]

Such a conjuncture should have led ideally led to a massive mobilization of the lower classes of Indian society across the urban and rural sectors. Unfortunately, the discontent of the masses has been channelled into causes and movements that offer no chances for the alleviation of their condition. Thus the farmers' movement which has arisen in India is characterized by a 'romantic celebration of the authentic rusticity of a harmonious pristine "Bharat" [the native name for India] pitted against the menacing might of urban and industrial "India"'. [92] The positing of the rural-urban divide obscures the more fundamental divide that exists between classes and castes. The multi-class coalitions of farmers in India drawing upon notions of 'moral community' are inevitably driven by the interests of the rich commercialized farmers.

[93] Unfortunately, peasant politics in *Lagaan,* rather than question this pattern of class obfuscation, replicate it.

A similar kind of papering-over of class contradictions as in farmers' movements occurs in the construction of the 'master community' – the nation. If third-world nationalisms (even the bourgeois variety) of yore were characterized by the most important element, that of anti-imperialism, the present ones are defined by their total subordination to imperialism. [94] Desai argues that this has seen the rise of cultural nationalisms, especially in Asia. While all nationalisms have a cultural component, cultural nationalisms are differentiated from the earlier developmental nationalisms that arose out of popular anti-colonial struggles and thus had a semblance of egalitarian content. But as they give way to cultural nationalisms, 'the popular cultural elements tended to be appropriated, contained, or, in the most radical cases, excluded or destroyed by the dominant elements. Shorn also of its forward-looking developmentalist project, what reasserted itself was the largely backward-looking hierarchical ordering of the national culture.' [95] Hindu nationalism in India is a typical example of this: it has aligned with global capital completely while at the same time pursuing an atavistic majoritarian nationalist project. Since the Indian government's decision to go nuclear and the war with Pakistan, there was an unprecedented rise in jingoism parading as patriotism. And commercial culture was awash with products espousing such content. [96] While *Lagaan* does not portray such jingoism (and also the enemy becomes the English rather than Pakistan), it is definitely imbued with a racialized aggressive nationalism with the sole accent on winning. The rise of aggressive nationalism in the late 1990s has to be squarely located in the context of the Hindu nationalist government's emphasis on the agenda of securing 'great power' status on the world stage, restoring the glory of Hindu civilization and so on. *Lagaan*'s nationalist resolution of the peasant question is very similar to the cultural nationalist attempt to provide a cultural solution to increasing economic segmentation under globalization. [97] As Aijaz Ahmad argues, 'any kind of nationalism which is solely constituted by "the experience of colonialism and imperialism" [is ultimately] suspended outside the modern systems of production (capitalism and socialism)'. [98]

Chakraborty argues that *Lagaan* makes the spectators aware (through 'village unity and the incorporation of normative outsiders') of the 'past unity of the freedom struggle'. [99] We would have thought that a 'subaltern' film should obviously be questioning this unity considering that it was achieved by suppressing the legitimate demands of caste, class and gender, and this very same unity was consummated in the bourgeois 'land reforms' of 1950s which completely ignored the rights of the low peasantry and the landless agricultural labourers (a predominant majority of whom are *dalits*). Chakraborty does not find anything odd in the fact that the unity of the freedom struggle is being invoked by a 'peasant film' even after six decades of rule by what Pranab Bardhan has characterized as the alliance of dominant proprietary classes consisting of the industrial capitalist class and the agrarian rich. [100] She does not question the fact that the film should be invoking this unity at a time when peasant communities are being wiped out due to the incursion of international capital acting in collaboration with the native propertied classes. The nationalism that emerges in the film parallels actually existing nationalism in India and (the majority of) 'postcolonial' nations. This national consciousness, in Frantz Fanon's prophetic words, 'instead of being the all embracing crystallization of the innermost hopes of the whole people, instead of being the immediate and most obvious result of the mobilization of the people, will be…only an empty shell, a crude and fragile travesty of what it might have been'. [101] Postcolonial theory, by solely focusing on Western cultural domination at the expense of all other forms of exploitation, ends up being complicit in the transmission of this hegemonic elite nationalism.

The film has to be understood not only in relation to the socio-historic context but also the linguistic context, which here would mean the language of popular commercial cinema in India. Of course, commercial cinema (or entertainment) does not 'simply reproduce unproblematically patriarchal capitalist ideology' [102] or nationalism or any other dominant ideology. But how much does a commercial film resist them depends on the film's ability to 'contradict the premises of its production through oppositional signs, which could radically interrogate the content of the overall construction'. [103] *Lagaan*, as I have argued, does not provide such oppositional signs. In arguing that popular commercial cinema is a 'reflection of the audiences' "concerns" and "wishes"', [104] Chakraborty (other than indulging in reductionism) very problematically ignores the ideological aspects inherent in mass entertainment. [105] Surely, utopia – the power to imagine and visualize a better reality – is a central component of entertainment. But she occludes the fact that 'while entertainment is responding to needs that are real, at the same time it is also defining and delimiting what constitutes the legitimate needs of people in this society'. Usually such needs are those related to class, race and gender. [106] In the Indian context, one should add caste to this list. The fact that a xenophobic film such as *Gadar* was the biggest grosser in the last decade [107] shows the extent to which the ideology of regressive nationalism has become an important part of entertainment (it does not mean that its success can be reduced to this one factor). Here, there is collusion between state and the market in the 'manufacture of consent' [108] for a reactionary nationalism.

In the context of Chakraborty's argument on popular cinema, it would be instructive to spend some time on the role of popular cinema in the Indian state of Tamil Nadu. As is widely known, no society elsewhere has probably seen such an impact by popular cinema on its politics and culture. The state has had many chief ministers who were demi-gods of the film industry, none more famous than M.G. Ramachandran (popularly known as MGR). Analysing the 'MGR phenomenon', subaltern historian M.S.S. Pandian gives a brilliant account of the processes through which the ruling elites produce consent from the subaltern classes. [109] Contrary to the portrayal in *Lagaan*, MGR films show a universe of unequal power relations. The exploiters are the landlords, moneylenders, rural rich, industrialists, casteists and so on. The victims naturally are the landless poor, the lower castes, exploited workers, illiterates and helpless women: 'Power is seen as all pervasive, omnipotent and undifferentiated while its victims are always already meek, beaten and homogeneous in their suffering.' But the subalterns have hope; they have the invincible MGR as one among them. In a challenge to the semi-feudal social system of the villages that the films portray, MGR as hero is constantly appropriating and subverting its three important signs of authority: '(a) the authority to dispense justice and exercise violence, (b) access to education and (c) access to women'. [110] MGR's heroics were closely modelled on the heroes of the folksongs and ballads popular among the poor and lower castes. But there is a crucial distinction between the ballads and the films, which is that the latter lack the former's progressive content. Ultimately, in MGR films the subaltern protagonist establishes justice, but justice within the system thus reaffirming the system itself: 'It is a world of transformed exploiters with untransformed property and power relations.' [111] Needless to say, in the 11-year rule of MGR as chief minister, Tamil Nadu did not see any structural changes in the system that would benefit the subaltern classes. [112] This is a good example of the way in which the critical potential of popular culture is appropriated by the elites and middle classes who are (primarily) the creators of mass entertainment.

Without a dialectical understanding of ideology and critique as the two elements of mass culture, Chakraborty's one-sided celebration of Bollywood degenerates into a cultural populism that views it as a 'critique of modernity'. [113] This obscures the fact that commercial culture has had a significant role in the rightward shift in politics all over the world, including India. As Simon During argues, 'cultural populism requires a very nuanced account of the relations between cultural markets and cultural products, and between culture and politics, in order convincingly to celebrate (some) popular culture as "progressive"'. [114] Chakraborty's exclusion of politics (and the economy) does not allow us to do this.

Conclusion

I have argued that the subaltern reading of the film is riddled with the same problems and contradictions that characterize the subaltern studies project itself. Ultimately, it follows the thoroughly culturalist framework of later subaltern studies. From a commitment to recovering and documenting subaltern voices, slowly the project began to focus on the critique of Western 'Enlightenment' and Eurocentrism. Postcolonial theory's all-pervasive tendency to focus only on decolonization (that too only in cultural terms) is visible in Chakraborty's essay (*Lagaan* raises the 'issue of postcolonial nations trying to resist western hegemonizing gaze' [115]). It does not ask the question as to where should (cultural) decolonization figure in a list of priorities for a programmatic politics in the so-called 'post-colonial' countries. As Vinay Bahl asks, 'one wonders if non-European countries, by simply being less Eurocentric, could enjoy a happier state of affairs despite economic globalization and increased global communication'. [116] The focus on culture without material relationships leads to the consequent focus on Eurocentrism sans capitalism. This obsession with Eurocentrism and colonialism leads to an evasion of the present. As Dhareshwar points out, 'politically relevant, and intellectually challenging questions about even Eurocentricity are to be encountered in our relationship to the post-colonial present. Without the thematization of that relationship, the attempt to provincialize Europe may, paradoxically, simply trap us in that province.' [117] While Chakraborty gets caught in this trap of the 'phantasmatic west', [118] the reality is constituted by the hegemony of what Vandana Shiva evocatively calls 'corporate feudalism, the most inhumane, brutal and exploitative convergence of global corporate capitalism and local feudalism, in the face of which the farmer as an individual victim feels helpless'. [119] When 40 per cent of the rural population in India has a food intake that matches Sub-Saharan Africa, [120] it is difficult to imagine that films like *Lagaan* can 'empower the masses'.

The voluntarism that characterizes postcolonial theory is marked here. In true cultural studies fashion, the emphasis is on the agency of the ordinary folk, who indulge in Bakhtinian resistance through 'ironical mimicry, symbolic inversion, orgiastic letting go, even day-dreaming'. [121] But as Kumkum Sangari points out, '[c]onceptions of individual or collective transformative agency and struggle are vacuous without an accompanying understanding of their dialectical relation with determining material, epistemic, institutional, and ideological structures which they both reproduce and transform'. [122]

Of course, it is no one's case that such everyday forms of resistance are not an inevitable part of subaltern social life. But to valorize them at the expense of any larger project of social change is to participate in the channelling of such resistances to the sustenance of hegemonic power relations. The valorization of quotidian resistance emerges in Chakraborty's statement that the vision that emerges from the film is 'not of equity but of self-sustenance and survival'. [123] Why is it that, even in the twenty-first century, we are reduced to fighting for survival rather than dreaming about and working towards an egalitarian future?

The indigenization of cricket portrayed in *Lagaan* 'successfully draws the poor and subordinate classes into debates about modernity and history'. [124] But it is not asked as to why a film glorified as one that extends the subaltern studies project (which questions the 'master texts and master codes' and 'resists the closures of history and gestures to the possibility of other perspectives and histories' [125]) cannot even imagine having a *dalit* as a hero, after six decades of 'de-colonization'. After all, *dalit*s, the most oppressed of communities, are the real subalterns in the Indian context. Why is it that a film that supposedly re-maps 'a fictionalized past' in an 'effort to rewrite the present' [126] does not include class and gender oppression as part of the reality of the present? The answer can be found only outside the parameters of the textual hermeneutic, by stepping outside the text. In the current socio-historic context of late capitalism and high nationalism, *Lagaan* is another symbolic attempt to hegemonically appropriate the subaltern to the elite imaginary.

To adapt Walter Benjamin, nationalism gives the masses the right to express themselves, but not the right to change property (or power) relations.

Notes

[1] Benjamin, *Illuminations*, 241.
[2] For two famous statements with regard to India, see Appadurai, 'Playing with Modernity; Nandy, *The Tao of Cricket*.
[3] See Chakraborty, 'Bollywood Motifs'; also idem, 'Subaltern Studies'.
[4] Dews, *The Logic of Disintegration*, 35.
[5] See Dirlik, *The Postcolonial Aura*, 79.
[6] O'Hanlon and Washbrook, 'After Orientalism', 145.
[7] Chakraborty, 'Bollywood Motifs', 551.
[8] Ibid., 551–2 (my emphasis).
[9] The author discusses 'the disastrous consequences' of drought as if they were merely 'natural' phenomena. There is no mention of the (major) role of the exploitative class rule by the state and the propertied in causing them.
[10] There is an eagerness on the part of Chakraborty to establish the success of the film in the popular domain. She claims that it is a 'phenomenal success' in both 'elite and subaltern circles' (Chakraborty, 'Bollywood Motifs', 565) without substantiating it with any facts or figures. The film is only a 'superhit' by Bollywood industry standards – 'superhit' is below the categories of 'blockbuster' and 'all time trade hit'. It is only the seventh biggest hit in the last four years. It does not even feature in the top 200 grossers (inflation-adjusted figures) since 1950 (all the ticket collection data are from the *International Business Overview Standard Network*, available at http://www.ibosnetwork.com/default.asp, accessed 9 Nov. 2004).
[11] Chakraborty, 'Bollywood Motifs', 552–3.
[12] Guha, 'On Some Aspects', 1–3.
[13] See Chakrabarty, 'Radical Histories'.
[14] Guha, 'On Some Aspects', 5.
[15] Chatterjee, *The Nation and its Fragments*; also see Himani Bannerji, 'Projects of Hegemony', *Economic and Political Weekly*, 11 March, 2000, 904.
[16] Chatterjee, *The Nation and its Fragments*, 6.
[17] Bannerji, 'Projects of Hegemony', 903.
[18] Chatterjee, *The Nation and its Fragments*, 220–39.
[19] Bannerji, 'Projects of Hegemony', 904.
[20] Bahl, 'Situating and Rethinking', 91.
[21] Guha, 'Subaltern and *Bhadralok* Studies', 2057.
[22] Chakraborty, 'Bollywood Motifs', 555.
[23] It does not mean that bourgeois nationalisms cannot target an internal enemy, mainly ethnic and linguistic minorities – Nazi Germany being the worst example and Hindu nationalism in India a contemporary example.
[24] See Mannathukkaren, 'Subalterns, Cricket and the Nation'.
[25] Pandey, 'Peasant Revolt', 161.
[26] Chakraborty, 'Bollywood Motifs', 557–8.
[27] Ibid., 555.
[28] See Ilaiah, 'Productive Labour'.
[29] Anand, 'Eating With Our Fingers'. [Editors' note: To set the record straight, Nissim is wrong. Kachra had a few dialogues to deliver in the film. But as Anand rightly points out, this did not amount to any assertion of the self.]

[30] Chakraborty, 'Bollywood Motifs', 557.

[31] This is so similar to the attempts by the right-wing Hindu nationalist government under the Bharatiya Janata Party to appropriate successful Indian Muslim cricketers such as Irfan Pathan and Mohammad Kaif as 'good Muslims' and 'national icons' while at the same time perpetrating communal genocide in the state of Gujarat which killed more than 2,000 Muslims.

[32] Ilaiah, 'Productive Labour', 165–6.

[33] See Lele, *Hindutva*.

[34] Chakraborty, 'Bollywood Motifs', 556.

[35] [Editors' note: Nissim is partly wrong. Although no scene categorically indicates the disparities in land-ownership in the village, yet a few occasions in the file are certainly suggestive of such disparities.]

[36] As Rustom Bharucha points out, 'representative of the "working class" or the "destitute"... have almost always been inscribed in the master narratives of Hindi cinema' but 'their modes of representation have been contrived, melodramatic and exploitative' (Rustom Bharucha, 'Utopia in Bollywood', *Economic and Political Weekly*, 15 April 1994, 803).

[37] Sathyamurthy, 'Indian Peasant Historiography', 109.

[38] Chakraborty, 'Bollywood Motifs', 559.

[39] Pandey, 'Peasant Revolt', 171 and 179–80.

[40] Guha, *Elementary Aspects of Peasant Insurgency*, 2–3.

[41] See for details, Mannathukkaren, 'Subalterns, Cricket and the Nation'.

[42] Chakraborty, 'Subaltern Studies', 1881.

[43] Chakraborty, 'Bollywood Motifs', 558.

[44] Mannathukkaren, 'Subalterns, Cricket and the Nation'. Chakraborty's arguments are contradictory in many places. Towards the end of the essay, after all her strictures against reading the film in terms of the present, where cricket is deeply associated with nationalism, she argues that the 'victory of *Lagaan*'s fictional cricketers is a testament to the quality of the Champaner villagers, and perhaps by extension, as nationalist readings of the film would argue, to that of India's citizens'. Further, she says tha 'cricket match in the film entertains because it reflects the spectators' wishes that the Chamapaner village team, and by extension, their Indian team, will be victorious against other foreign [not just the British] teams'. In further confirmation of the racializing and binarizing strategy that I detected in *Lagaan*, Chakraborty argues that the film's phenomenal success in both elite and subaltern circles is because Indians (and other postcolonial nations) 'derive such pleasure from scoring against the West' which, in turn, is the result of them 'vesting their self-esteem in their cricketers, expecting them to be "ideal citizens"' ('Bollywood Motifs', 565–6). The ideological nature of nationalism and its role in securing consent of the ruled is not mentioned at all here by Chakraborty. This also goes totally against her argument in the earlier version of the essay: 'to read *Lagaan* as a mythology of nationalism... is to regard all forms of oppositional movements, including Indian nationalism(s), as a linear, evolutionary project ('Subaltern Studies', 1883).

[45] Chakrabarty, 'The Fall and Rise of Indian Sports History', 341–2. The reliance on the present-day televised spectacle of limited-over cricket emerges clearly from the words of the director of *Lagaan*, Ashutosh Gowarikar: 'We wanted to lend the climax [of the film] a stadium feel.' (*Rediff on the Net*, 17 July 2001, available at http://www.rediff.com/entertai/2001/jul/17ash.htm, accessed 11 Nov. 2004).

[46] Guha, *Elementary Aspects of Peasant Insurgency*, 28.

[47] Chakraborty, 'Subaltern Studies', 1883.

[48] Pandey, 'Peasant Revolt', 179.

[49] Appadurai, 'Playing with Modernity', 97. Of course, there may have been a minuscule number of nationalist-minded princes.

[50] Pandey, 'Peasant Revolt', 187.

[51] See Forgacs, 'National-Popular'.

[52] Pandey, 'Peasant Revolt', 187–8. Dipesh Chakrabarty argues that cricket nationalism portrayed in *Lagaan* is not Gandhian but mediatized mass nationalism of the present which has the sole purpose of winning. Gandhian nationalism always placed 'the question of being good above and beyond the issue of winning or losing.'(Chakrabarty, 'The Fall and Rise', 342). While I agree with Chakrabarty that Gandhian nationalism was not fixated with the end result, he crucially ignores the fact that both the nationalisms are bourgeois nationalisms (with only minor variations). By refusing to look at the class nature of nationalism, Chakrabarty's essay exemplifies the 'cultural turn' of later subaltern studies and its partial redemption of nationalist leaders such as Gandhi.

[53] Chakraborty, 'Bollywood Motifs', 558. She also states that 'with *Lagaan*'s success in the box office it will not be surprising to find ourselves viewing a sequel to the film with Bhuvan leading the villagers in a rebellion against the local ruler (Chakraborty, 'Subaltern Studies', 1884). But the director of *Lagaan* points out categorically: 'I have no intention of repeating myself. I will not make another historical film. That is for sure' (*Rediff on the Net*, 17 July 2001, available at http://www.rediff.com/entertai/2001/jul/17ash.htm, accessed 11 Nov. 2004).

[54] Chakraborty, 'Bollywood Motifs', 560.

[55] Ibid., 561.

[56] Ibid., 563–5.

[57] Marx, 'Contribution to the Critique', 60.

[58] Hillary Mayell, 'India's "Untouchables" Face Violence, Discrimination', *National Geographic News*, 2 June 2003, available at http://news.nationalgeographic.com/news/2003/06/0602_030602_untouchables.html, accessed 11 Nov. 2004.

[59] Chakraborty, 'Bollywood Motifs', 568.

[60] In states such as Kerala, where passion for football matched Latin American levels, cricket has emerged as the most important sport.

[61] Siriyavan Anand, 'The Retreat of the Brahmin', *Outlook*, 10 Feb. 2003, available at http://www.outlookindia.com/full.asp?fodname=20030210&fname=KBrahmin+%28F%29&sid='1, accessed 11 Nov. 2004.

[62] Aditya Nigam, 'Secularism, Modernity, Nation: Epistemology of the Dalit Critique', *Economic and Political Weekly*, 5 Nov. 2000.

[63] Quoted in Anand, 'Retreat of the Brahmin'.

[64] Nandy, *Tao of Cricket*. But the popularity of the game among the masses cannot be reduced to the cultural factors that Nandy bases his arguments on. It also does not explain the immense popularity of the game in non-Hindu countries such as Pakistan and Sri Lanka.

[65] Even as recently as in the year 2000, there were eight Brahmins in a team of 11 (Anand, 'Eating with our Fingers').

[66] Vinod Kambli, who played for India and is usually thought as being a *dalit*, does not technically belong to the scheduled caste – a category of the government denoting *dalit*s (see Anand, 'Eating with our Fingers').

[67] Rajdeep Sardesai, quoted in Anand, 'Retreat of the Brahmin'.

[68] Chakraborty, 'Bollywood Motifs', 564.

[69] The International Cricket Council (ICC) has sought to prevent the 'death' of Test cricket through the introduction of a mandatory number of Test matches to be played every year since 2001.

[70] The ever-burgeoning viewership market can be gauged from the fact that TV rights for telecasting cricket in India which sold for $2 million in 1998–9 are now being quoted at $75 million per year, a phenomenal increase of nearly 40 times in five years (see Manu Joseph,

'Sachin Doesn't Play for India', *Indiatimes*, 15 Oct. 2004, available at http://cricket.india-times.com/articleshow/msid-851406,curpg-2.cms, accessed 12 Nov. 2004.

[71] The Indian consumer durables market is worth nearly $5 billion (see ' Koreans Top of the Heap for Consumer Durables', *Economic Times*, 8 Oct. 2004, available at http://economic-times.indiatimes.com/articleshow/msid-877626,prtpage-1.cms, accessed 13 Nov. 2004.

[72] Madhava M. Prasad, 'Public Modernity: Some Issues', *Economic and Political Weekly*, 2 May 1998.

[73] Ibid., 1021.

[74] For details on the rise of the non-West in cricket, see Gupta, 'The Globalization of Cricket'. The dominance extends to the 'star value' of the players too. Indian cricketers earn more than their counterparts elsewhere.

[75] For a cogent analysis of this phenomenon, see Marqusee, *Anyone But England*.

[76] Appadurai, 'Playing with Modernity', 107.

[77] Gupta, 'The Globalization of Cricket', 258.

[78] Marqusee, quoted in ibid., 265.

[79] This does not mean that the race question which was an integral part of colonialism is not an issue in international cricket in the present. English cricket has seen its worst manifesta-tions with the white establishment's discrimination against British players of colour. There have also been many instances when white media and players have hurled racial abuses at players from non-white countries (see Marqusee, *Anyone But England*; also 'Cricket's Racial Conundrum', *East*, November 1996, available at http://usa.cricinfo.com/link_to_database/SOCIETIES/ENG/HR46/ARTICLES/RACIAL_CONUNDRUM.html, accessed 13 Nov. 2004.

[80] In the calendar year 2004–5, the BCCI was set to earn $96.5 million, whereas the ICC's earnings were expected to be only $76 million. BCCI's earnings exclude the ten percent share of profits from ICC-held events and also the 40 per cent share in the income generated by state cricket boards through ticket sales ('BCCI has the Highest Strike Rate', *Economic Times*, 8 Sept. 2004, available at http://economictimes.indiatimes.com/articleshow/msid-853736, curpg-1.cms, accessed 9 Nov. 2004).

[81] See Joseph, 'Sachin Doesn't Play for India'.

[82] The Delhi High Court has already ruled on a public-interest litigation (PIL) that since the BCCI performs public functions and also claims to represent India, it has a duty towards the public and therefore it will be subject to some judicial scrutiny. The PIL argues that since the BCCI gets tax concessions from the government and also land grants for building stadiums etc., the Comptroller and Auditor General of India should be the appropriate authority to audit the finances of BCCI.

[83] Kanpur's Test match venue, the Green Park, has been termed 'the worst Test stadium in the world, before and after the game'. An *Indian Express* report writes: 'Green Park's walls are dilapidated. A tin roof on the main pavilion creaks spookily. The 60-odd toilets in the 50,000-seater stadium are nauseatingly choked. The scoreboard and sightscreens are mere metal frames. Graffiti decorates, if that be the word, the stadium's deserted corners.' Sardar Patel stadium in Ahmedabad, a former Test match venue, has no toilet facilities (see 'India's Wicked Wicket Ways', *Indian Express*, 3 Aug. 2003, available at http://www.indianexpress.com/archive_full_story.php?content_id=28820, accessed 13 Nov. 2004.

[84] Bindra also admits that facilities for the public are much better in other countries of the subcontinent (Clayton Murzello, 'We Owe It to The public, Says Bindra', *Mid-Day*, 18 Sept. 2004, available at http://web.mid-day.com/sports/international/2004/september/92733.htm, accessed 13 Nov. 2004. In the last one-day match held at Mumbai's Wankhede Stadium, one of the premier venues, spectators waited for 12 hours before the ticket counter opened, which closed after 5,000 tickets were sold; 80 per cent of the 45,000 tickets

were reserved for politicians, sponsors and officials (see Joseph, 'Sachin Doesn't Play for India').

[85] Chakraborty, 'Bollywood Motifs', 550.

[86] Needless to say, gender hierarchies are so evident with women's cricket being hardly popular.

[87] Appadurai, 'Playing with Modernity', 109.

[88] In the beginning, Chakraborty mentions that subaltern classes' entry into history through 'modernizing devices' like cinema and cricket will depend on 'the historical and social context' ('Bollywood Motifs', 551). But after that, there is not a single attempt to link the film to the socio-historic context (the words capitalism, or capital, for instance, do not figure even once), reducing the initial statement to a platitude. Similarly, the author states that whether a film can decolonize the mind will 'depend on the viewer's affiliation, perception, experience, etc' (ibid., 570). But not only is there no explication of the latter conditions in the essay, it also betrays a form of elitism in which the theorist decides for the masses about their feelings. Without any kind of empirical evidence, Chakraborty is sure that 'what has enthralled the Indian masses is *Lagaan's* unique theme: the subalterns' destabilizing of the history of colonial cricket' (ibid., 551).

[89] Radhika Desai, 'Culturalism and Contemporary Right: Indian Bourgeoisie and Political Hindutva', *Economic and Political Weekly*, 20 March 1999, 703.

[90] Average per capita foodgrain absorption fell from 177 kg. per year in 1991–2 to 151.06 kg. in 2000–1 (Patnaik, 'Rural India in Ruins').

[91] Vandana Shiva, 'The Suicide Economy of Corporate Globalisation', *Znet*, 5 April 2004, available at http://www.countercurrents.org/glo-shiva050404.htm, accessed 14 Nov. 2004.

[92] Desai, 'Culturalism and Contemporary Right', 704.

[93] See Harriss, 'Between Economism and Post–Modernism'; also Brass, 'Moral Economies'.

[94] Desai, 'Nation Against Democracy'.

[95] Ibid., 97.

[96] There have been a slew of 'patriotic' films released in Bollywood in the last few years. *Gadar: Ek Prem Katha, Maa Tujhe Salaam, LOC, Bharat Bhagya Vidhata, Sarfarosh, Indian, Ek Hindustani, Hindustan ki Kasam, Mission Kashmir, Border* are some of the films that have broken a new path, for they explicitly name the enemy as Pakistan (Ziya us Salam, 'Peddling Patriotism', *The Hindu*, 15 March 2002).

[97] In the priority agenda drawn by the BJP government, poverty alleviation was placed fifth. During its tenure, the Human Development Index (HDI) ranking of India went down from 124 to 127 (Nissim Mannathukkaren, 'Riding the Secular *Rath*', *Outlook Web*, 6 May 2004, available at http://203.200.89.67/full.asp?fodname=20040506&fname=kerala&sid=1, accessed 10 Oct. 2004.

[98] Ahmad, *In Theory*, 107–8.

[99] Chakraborty, 'Bollywood Motifs', 568.

[100] Bardhan, 'Dominant Proprietary Classes'.

[101] Fanon, 'National Culture', 156.

[102] Richard Dyer, 'Entertainment and Utopia', 273.

[103] Bharucha, 'Utopia in Bollywood', 801–2.

[104] Chakraborty, 'Bollywood Motifs', 567.

[105] Chakraborty, as we have seen, believes that just the presence of lower castes and women (in a marginalized position) points to repressive strategies and practices in the film.

[106] Dyer, 'Entertainment and Utopia', 278.

[107] *Gadar* collected Rs65 crore (nearly $15 million) at the box office, more than twice the amount that *Lagaan* grossed. It is placed 11th in the all-time grossers list (see http://www.ibosnetwork.com/default.asp, accessed 9 Nov. 2004).

[108] Rustom Bharucha, 'On the Border of Fascism: The Manufacture of Consent in *Roja*', *Economic and Political Weekly*, 4 June 1994, 1390.

[109] M.S.S. Pandian, 'Culture and Subaltern Consciousness: An Aspect of MGR Phenomenon', *Economic and Political Weekly*, 29 July 1989, PE–62.

[110] Ibid., PE–63.

[111] Ibid., PE–64, 65.

[112] Ibid., PE–62.

[113] See Nandy, *The Savage Freud*, 235.

[114] During, 'Introduction', 18.

[115] Chakraborty, 'Subaltern Studies', 1882.

[116] Bahl, 'Situating and Rethinking Subaltern Studies', 94.

[117] Vivek Dhareshwar, '"Our Time": History, Sovereignty and Politics', *Economic and Political Weekly*, 11 Feb. 1995, 322.

[118] Ibid.

[119] Shiva, 'The Suicide Economy of Corporate Globalisation'.

[120] Patnaik, 'Rural India in Ruins'.

[121] During, 'Introduction', 11.

[122] Sangari 'Consent, Agency, and Rhetorics of Incitement', 464.

[123] Chakraborty, 'Bollywood Motifs', 558.

[124] Ibid., 568.

[125] Ibid., 569.

[126] Ibid.

References

Ahmad, Aijaz. *In Theory: Classes, Nations, Literatures.* London: Verso, 1992.

Anand, Siriyavan. 'Eating With Our Fingers, Watching Hindi Cinema and Consuming Cricket'. *Himal*, March 2002, available at http://www.himalmag.com/2002/march/essay.htm, accessed 10 Nov. 2004.

Appadurai, Arjun. 'Playing with Modernity: The Decolonization of Indian Cricket'. In *Modernity at Large*. Minneapolis, MN: University of Minnesota Press, 1995.

Bahl, Vinay. 'Situating and Rethinking Subaltern Studies for Writing Working-Class History'. In *History after the Three Worlds*, edited by Arif Dirlik, Vinay Bahl and Peter Gran. Lanham, MD: Rowman & Littlefield, 2000.

Bardhan, Pranab. 'Dominant Proprietary Classes and India's Democracy'. In *India's Democracy: An Analysis of Changing State-Society Relations*, edited by Atul Kohli. New Delhi: Orient Longman, 1991: 214–24.

Benjamin, Walter. *Illuminations,* translated by Harry Zohn. New York: Harcourt, 1955.

Brass, Tom. 'Moral Economies, Subalterns, New Social Movements and the (Re-)Emergence of a (Post-)Modernised Middle Peasant'. *Journal of Peasant Studies* 18 (1991).

Chakraborty, Chandrima. 'Bollywood Motifs'. *The International Journal of the History of Sport* 21 (3/4) (June–Sept. 2004): 549–72.

——. 'Subaltern Studies, Bollywood and *Lagaan*'. *Economic and Political Weekly*, 10 May 2003.

Chakrabarty, Dipesh. 'Radical Histories and Question of Enlightenment Rationalism'. *Economic and Political Weekly*, 8 April 1995.

——. 'The Fall and Rise of Indian Sports History'. *The International Journal of the History of Sport* 21 (3/4) (June–Sept. 2004).

Chatterjee, Partha. *The Nation and its Fragments: Colonial and Postcolonial Histories.* Princeton, NJ: Princeton University Press, 1993.

Desai, Radhika. 'Nation Against Democracy: The Rise of Cultural Nationalism in Asia'. In *Democracy and Civil Society in Asia*, vol. 1, edited by Fahimul Quadir and Jayant Lele. New York: Palgrave Macmillan, 2004.

Dews, Peter. *The Logic of Disintegration*. London: Verso, 1987.

Dirlik, Arif. *The Postcolonial Aura*. Boulder. CO: Westview Press, 1997.

During, Simon. 'Introduction'. In *The Cultural Studies Reader*, edited by Simon During. London and New York: Routledge, 1993.

Dyer, Richard. 'Entertainment and Utopia'. In *The Cultural Studies Reader*, edited by Simon During. London and New York: Routledge, 1993.

Fanon, Frantz. 'National Culture'. In *The Post-Colonial Studies Reader*, edited by Bill Ashcroft, Gareth Griffiths and Helen Tiffin. London: Routledge, 1995.

Forgacs, David. 'National-Popular: Genealogy of a Concept'. In *The Cultural Studies Reader*, edited by Simon During. London and New York: Routledge, 1993.

Guha, Ramachandra. 'Subaltern and *Bhadralok* Studies'. *Economic and Political Weekly*, 19 Aug. 1995: 20–57.

Guha, Ranajit. 'On Some Aspects of the Historiography of Colonial India'. In *Subaltern Studies I*, edited by Ranajit Guha. Delhi: Oxford University Press, 1982.

——. *Elementary Aspects of Peasant Insurgency in Colonial India*. Delhi: Oxford University Press, 1983.

Gupta, Amit. 'The Globalization of Cricket: The Rise of the Non-West'. *The International Journal of the History of Sport* 21 (2) (March 2004): 257–76.

Harriss, John. 'Between Economism and Post–Modernism'. In *Rethinking Social Development: Theory, Practice and Research*, edited by D. Booth. London: Longman, 1994.

Ilaiah, Kancha. 'Productive Labour, Consciousness and History'. In *Subaltern Studies IX*, edited by Shahid Amin and Dipesh Chakrabarty. Delhi: Oxford University Press, 1997.

Lele, Jayant. *Hindutva*. Madras: Earthworm Books, 1995.

Mannathukkaren, Nissim. 'Subalterns, Cricket and the Nation: The Silences of "Lagaan"', *Economic and Political Weekly*, 8 Dec. 2001.

Marqusee, Mike. *Anyone But England: Cricket and the National Malaise*. London: Verso, 1994.

Marx, Karl. 'Contribution to the Critique of Hegel's *Philosophy of Right*: Introduction'. In *The Marx-Engels Reader*. edited by Robert Tucker. New York: W.W. Norton & Co., 1978.

Nandy, Ashis. *The Tao of Cricket*. NewYork: Viking, 1989.

——. *The Savage Freud and Other Essays on Possible and Retrievable Selves*. Princeton, NJ: Princeton University Press, 1995.

O'Hanlon, Rosalind and David Washbrook. 'After Orientalism: Culture, Criticism, and Politics in the Third World'. *Comparative Studies in Society and History* 34 (1) (January 1992).

Pandey, Gyanendra. 'Peasant Revolt and Indian Nationalism'. In *Subaltern Studies 1*, edited by Ranajit Guha. Delhi: Oxford University Press, 1982.

Patnaik, Utsa. 'Rural India in Ruins'. *Frontline* 21 (5) (28 Feb.–12 March 2004).

Sangari, Kumkum. 'Consent, Agency, and Rhetorics of Incitement'. In *Social Change and Political Discourse in India: Structures of Power, Movements of Resistance*, vol. 3, edited by T.V. Sathyamurthy. Delhi: Oxford University Press, 1996.

Sathyamurthy, T.V. 'Indian Peasant Historiography'. *Journal of Peasant Studies* 18 (1) (1990).

Virtually There: Cricket, Community, and Commerce on the Internet

Sanjay Joshi

This essay records a recent history of how dedicated and public-spirited lovers of a sport created a virtual community of cricket fans using what was then a new medium called the internet. The website "Cricinfo" was initially a product of this community. The essay then shows how commercial concerns came to override those of the virtual community, as Cricinfo was transformed from a community-based enterprise to a commercial entity. All of this happened at a time when the sport and the internet itself was being transformed by new technologies, and entrepreneurs were taking advantage of these changes to create new economic opportunities. The recent acquisition of Cricinfo by the media giant ESPN (itself owned by The Walt Disney Company) merely continues the trajectory outlined in this essay.

> We are not a site that developed a community....We're a community that developed a site. [1]

This is a small history of people who follow cricket on the internet. It is therefore necessarily a narrative of very recent times. Whether or not it qualifies as 'history' I will leave to my readers and their definitions of a tricky word. However, I do hope, through this essay, to record the fanatical dedication and tremendous sense of public service that drove lovers of a game to create a virtual community on a new medium of communication – the internet. I aim also to reveal the ways in which commercial concerns came to override those of the virtual community as the internet itself was transformed with new technologies, new possibilities and new opportunities. This is also, necessarily, an essay in the autobiographical mode. My interest in this subject derives squarely from being a witness, and only a very occasional participant, in this virtual world of followers of cricket. It would hardly be fair, therefore, if I did not begin this essay with a clear statement of my own involvement with the subject.

Sanjay Joshi, Northern Arizona University.

I moved to the United States in 1988 and like most expatriates, missed many things about home. Cricket was high on that list. I quickly discovered that cricket was as comprehensible to my new American friends as a Japanese tea ceremony – and regarded about as much of a sport! The fact that any game could take five days to complete, was, of course unfathomable. But, for some reason, what really brought the incredulous hoots of laughter was the notion of a sport which had a break for *tea*! Comparisons favouring horticultural growth as a spectator sport were too often forthcoming. Of course I was hearing this from people who play rounders (only they call it baseball) as their national sport. [2] But if that made me feel any better, it got me no closer to following cricket. I had to find some way of getting my cricket fix. Fortunately, my acquisition of elementary computer skills came to coincide with the growth of a new phenomenon which came to be called the internet.

Cricket, it appears, was part of the internet almost from the time the latter was created. Given how much we take the technology around us for granted, and how quickly it has become ubiquitous, it is perhaps important to recall how recently it has evolved. The earliest recognizable ancestor of the now-omnipresent personal computer is less than three decades old. [3] Though we can trace the origins of the internet to the 1969 ARPANET, the World Wide Web dates only from 1989. Internet Relay Chat (IRC), which hosts a wonderful community of cricket lovers among its thousands of chat rooms today, was created in the summer of 1988, and averaged only 12 users on 38 servers worldwide as late as 1990. [4] Probably nothing brings home the very contemporary nature of this history as the fact that the term 'internet' itself was formally defined only a decade ago. [5] It is important to keep in mind that even up to the middle of the 1980s, only a handful of scientists and technologists across the world used computers connected to a network to communicate with each other. It was fortunate for cricket enthusiasts living in the cricket wasteland of the United States of America that when these technologies did start reaching a slightly larger audience in the early 1990s, this audience included similarly deprived cricket-crazy technology buffs.

In the early 1990s, online forums became oases in the deserts of a cricketless America for expatriate cricket fanatics. From a universe bereft of cricket, passionate followers of the game discovered – while the really committed ones helped to create – a virtual treasure trove on cricket. It began with Usenet, that early online forum where discussion and votes among users – and they were then still a fairly limited number – were usually enough to set up a new newsgroup. Virtually anyone with access to a computer, modem and a server could then read or post on these newsgroups. [6] The request for discussion (RFD) for creating a newsgroup dedicated to cricket, rec.sport.cricket (RSC) was posted in March 1990 to existing newsgroups dealing with sports, as well as those discussing British and Indian cultural topics, indicating perhaps the geographic origins of most of those who participated in starting what was to become the cyber-world of cricket. [7] Critically important contributions to cricket on the internet have come from passionate followers of the game in South Africa, Australia, New Zealand and even Holland and Hong Kong, among other unexpected locations. However, 'Brits' and 'Desis' (British and folks from the Indian subcontinent, including Sri Lanka) were among the most visible and voluble contributors to the emerging world of cricket on the internet.

The newsgroup RSC became the first focal point for cricket enthusiasts mired in the cricketing wastelands of the world. Discussions, debates and arguments about players and teams, but most importantly quick updates on matches going on across the world, attracted more and more participants to RSC. There were 181 different postings to the new newsgroup in April 1980, its first month of existence, and this more than doubled in the following month. The newsgroup averaged more than 300 posts for the first six months of 1991, and currently averages almost 10,000 posts a month. [8] Discussions on RSC opened up other horizons of the internet to folks from the humanities such as myself, in particular the joys of real-time conversations on IRC. It was but a short step from real-time conversations to real-time updates and then something close to running commentary on cricket games from across the world.

Constraints of space make it impossible to include the names of all the people who played a leading role in pioneering cricket coverage on the internet. Among those remembered fondly even today is Professor K.S. Rao, then at North Dakota State University, who set up an email mailing list for those starved of conversations and information on cricket in 1991. [9] During India's tour of South Africa in 1992–3, Professor Rao apparently used a 'bot' (short for robot) – a computer program that automatically updated scores of ongoing matches on his account at North Dakota. Cricket lovers with connections to the internet could (and apparently frequently did) 'finger' his account to access the latest updated scores. [10] From there it was a short step to actual running commentary on the internet. During a discussion about the history of the newsgroup RSC, a group of the people who were actively involved in making it happen, recalled how running commentary on matches began on IRC. Apparently, in January 1993, a couple of cricket enthusiasts in computer science departments in the US sent over a special set of cables to friends in England, who were thus able to relay to them over the internet, completely illegally of course, audio commentary from the BBC's *Test Match Special* radio broadcast. These US-based enthusiasts, in turn, typed up the audio commentary over IRC for the rest of us to enjoy. [11]

Today, when pornography and/or commerce appear to be the main engines of growth on the internet, it is difficult to even conceive of the internet world little more than a decade ago. As cricket came on the internet almost at the same time as the net itself was emerging, examining this history allows us a glimpse into that very different world of the internet which existed then, and how quickly and completely it has changed. The world of cricket aficionados, fanatics if you will, on the internet in the early and mid 1990s was an amazing one where dedicated volunteers typed in ball-by-ball accounts of matches. Most of these folk were getting to see a game on the TV or were listening to radio commentary. Inspired by nothing more than altruism and sympathy for their deprived brethren, they manually typed in 'running commentary' on these matches to their eagerly waiting audience, across virtual worlds, who egged them on while offering their own 'readings' of the game.

Most online cricket buffs agree that the quality of the early ball-by-ball commentary was usually of the highest quality in this volunteer era, as opposed to the more 'professional' commentary offered now. Sadiq Yusuf (who writes under the nickname of 'Amol Cricketwallah') has been a participant in the world of cricket on the internet from the time it began. Reminiscing about how ball-by-ball commentary was done in the early 1990s, 'Amol' recalls there being around six people with access to live audio on IRC, with 'One to say something like "ball 1, 2 runs". The next to say "that was clipped away to midwicket, where Gooch stupidly misfielded …". And the third to say "the crowd doing a Mexican wave, firecrackers going off". And the fourth to chime in "butterfly fluttering across the field between the bowler and mid-on" :-)' All this while, Amol recounts, there would be two others eagerly awaiting their turn to provide commentary! [12] It is important to recall that even as late as 1997, providing running commentary over the internet was a completely voluntary enterprise, with folks often running up high phone bills (not to speak of inviting carpal tunnel syndrome) only with the end of serving a community of like-minded lovers of the game. Providing commentary, moreover, one first-hand account by a commentator recounts, was 'surprisingly hard work', leaving him exhausted by the end of a day's play. [13]

The days of this sort of volunteerism are now over. To be sure, professionalism comes with its advantages, but also at a cost. There are now many websites which offer some version of running commentary on matches, but their commentary is bland and for most part generated by an automatic scoring program manned by paid professionals. These professionals, 'Amol Cricketwallah' says, are not motivated by the same love for cricket as the 'fanatical amateurs' of a decade ago. They provide few details, and often get things wrong when they try to do so, he says. [14] On the plus side, there is hardly any game of any significance anywhere in the world that is not covered by sites such as Cricinfo today. But before the formidable marriage of passion and commerce that produced sites such as Cricinfo, cricket lovers really had to depend on the generosity of spirit (as well as of more material resources) of their compatriots across the seas. There was many a time when there was no coverage of matches. Folks would enter IRC chatrooms such as #cricket and the few who could afford to do so made periodic phone calls to cricket-playing countries to convey the latest scores to an audience starved of cricket news. Or casual visitors to a cricket chatroom who had access to radio or television coverage of a match were inveigled into staying on to provide updates on the match.

A memorable episode during an India-Pakistan limited-overs game in Sharjah in 1995 epitomizes the best and the worst of community-based efforts at providing cricket coverage on the internet. No commentary was available on this match over the internet, when a 15-year old by the name of Prakash, then living in Hong Kong, happened to visit the #cricket chatroom on IRC. Prakash was induced to stay on to type in commentary while watching the game on television at home. Prakash's typing and spelling was not of the highest order, and certainly the commentary was not of the quality which folks on #cricket had been getting from the regulars on the channel. Prakash made errors in spelling names of leading players, as well as in indicating who was bowling or fielding at a particular time. An IRC log of that day's commentary read as follows:

> \<prakash\> Sachin Tundukar [the correct spelling is Tendulkar] is bolwing [*sic;* bowling]
> \<prakash\> out out out out!!!!!
> \<prakash\> Sachin Tundukar is bolwing
> \<prakash\> sorry, kumble is bowling

But then, troubled by derogatory remarks he was receiving, Prakash temporarily left the chatroom, which provoked this response in the chatroom:

> \<srinivas\> prakash is gone
> \<wenyen\> prakash please come back
> \<gt4667c\> please prakash come back

Prakash did return for a while, but then – whether out of thrift, opportunism or sheer exasperation – said he wanted to be paid for his work, which completely alienated the rest of the chatroom ('VKFan' here is an 'op', or one with power to throw people off the channel):

> \<prakash\> ARE YOU PAYING OR NOT???????
> \<VKFan\> stop it prakash
> \<azzie\> prakash: its too hard to arrange
> \<prakash\> ARE YOU PAYING?????
> \<prakash\> ARE YOU PAYING?
> \<azzie\> prakash: no
> \<azzie\> this is not a pay channel
> \<azzie\> nobody here is paid for whatever services they may offer
> \<azzie\> its all done on a voluntary basis
> \<prakash\> fuck you!!!

At which point VKFan expelled Prakash off the channel #cricket, leading to:

> \<travis\> yay! 3 cheers for VKfan
> \<travis\> \<g\>
> \<VKFan\> :-)
> \<rogan\> We do not pay for comm on #cricket
> \<rogan\> That is all there is to it

As the Prakash episode reveals, it was never all roses on the online cricket forums. The discussions on RSC and in chatrooms such as #cricket, cover the range from the utterly puerile to incisive, from arguments about relative techniques of players to trading the latest gossip. Regional rivalries, and of course national ones, also bring the worst bigots to these discussions. This is one of the reasons why there are separate 'rooms' these days for commentary and discussion on IRC. Even in the discussion rooms, certain games, for instance those between India and Pakistan, have to be strictly moderated, with jingoists from both sides repeatedly thrown out of the chats, or even banned, for their abusive conduct. Passion for a sport is as capable of engendering magnificent altruism as it is of abuse and hatred. Given the anonymous though interactive nature of the internet, people often express their dissatisfaction with services or with other individuals in ways that would never be tolerated in face-to-face interactions. This was certainly evident in the way Prakash was treated on #cricket in 1995. Within two years of its inception, patrons of #cricket had come to expect a certain degree of professionalism in the commentaries provided to them by volunteers. When their expectations were belied, as by Prakash's efforts, they were quick to voice their ridicule, ignoring both the youth of the volunteer and the pressures he undoubtedly underwent in providing the commentary. In fact, the reason we still have a log of this particular session of IRC is because some cricket lovers with better English-language skills found Prakash's efforts worthy of their scorn. Travis Basevi prefaced his posting of this log on RSC by saying: 'I know it seems cruel to publish the whole episode on rsc, but...he deserves it.' [15]

Why did he deserve it? Certainly not only on account of his orthographic limitations. To understand this episode, we need to put it in its context. First, at this time, there was no real organization for providing commentary on the internet, except on special occasions. People just 'showed up' on the chatroom, and through this virtual community hoped to exchange news and information about the game. Second, the notion of a community based on voluntary effort was almost universally acknowledged as the norm among regulars on this and other cricket-related forums on the internet. The reason why Prakash was pilloried, and why the event became memorable, is because Prakash's demands for compensation in money for his time and effort completely transgressed the norms on which this community was built. Despite the service he evidently provided, his demand for money was anathema to the cricket lovers on this forum. They even cheered his departure, though it meant they lost access to updates of the match. At the same time, it is important to keep in mind that Prakash's efforts on this day, despite his later demands, were for most part also very much in the spirit of service which characterized the efforts of most people in the cricket community on the internet at that time. As Prakash noted during the acrimonious exchange that led to his being thrown off the channel, he was spending a lot of money for his internet connection and had been providing a service which other members on #cricket obviously craved. He was merely asking the community to meet the costs of the service he was providing. Yet 'rogan' summarized the prevailing norm well when he stated, rather disdainfully: 'we do not pay for comm[entary] on #cricket....That is all there is to it.'

Ironically enough, though, the very same spirit of proud volunteerism and public service also produced one of the most astonishing commercial successes of the 1990s internet dot-com boom. I refer of course to the website Cricinfo, which is not only the largest and most popular website for cricket today, but with 'more than 250 million page views per month,...is by far the world's favourite web site dedicated to a single sport'. [16] Of all the internet activity on cricket that has taken place, Cricinfo has, deservedly no doubt, generated the most publicity. *The Hindu*, one of

India's premier newspapers, wrote about Cricinfo as early as 1995. [17] Alex Balfour wrote a piece for the UK magazine *Wired* in February 1996, shortly before joining the management team at Cricinfo. [18] Alistair McLellan published the most detailed (though still very incomplete) history of Cricinfo in volume six of the *New Ball* series on cricket writing in 2001, where he lauds its meteoric rise 'from a loose collection of volunteers to a £100 m business in just seven years'. [19]

With journalists' penchant for focusing on personalities and Cricinfo's evident financial successes, much of the published coverage has focused on its 'founder', Dr Simon King, and on Cricinfo as a commercial entity. But this focus on the individual and the commercial successes or misfortunes of the website obscures the very different history and milieu from which Cricinfo emerged. That history is one that reflects much of the history of the internet, and illustrates the processes that have transformed communities to commercial enterprises. The narrative in turn depends on the nature of the sources used by the narrators. Most of the existing accounts of Cricinfo have relied on interviews with one or two of the leading figures in the organization. I have, however, relied on trawling the posts on RSC, where most of the people who contributed to the making of Cricinfo have posted their own perceptions about it. This 'Cricinfo Story' then, reflecting these sources (as well as the somewhat 'subalternist' orientation of this historian), is as concerned with the community that created Cricinfo as its later and more commercial incarnations.

Cricinfo emerged out of the same sets of conversations and predicaments that produced the ball-by-ball commentaries on matches over IRC, and around the same time. Virtually all that has been written in print and online forums recalls that Cricinfo began life as 'bot' on IRC written by Simon King, which would store scorecards of current games. He did this, apparently, because of too many folks showing up on IRC interrupting commentary and asking for scorecards of games. [20] However, given cricket lovers' fascination with statistics, Cricinfo transformed itself into a cricket database. For the record, it should be mentioned that Cricinfo was hardly the first cricket-related 'bot' on the internet. As mentioned earlier, Professor Rao had used a 'bot' (called 'dougie') during a cricket series in 1992–3, prior to the creation of Cricinfo. Other 'bots' (for instance, one called Crickoot or Creakoot) had been used to update scorecards and topics during IRC commentary. Simon King, according to some of the people who were most involved with putting cricket on the internet in the early 1990s, picked up on the idea of using 'bots' to retrieve and organize scorecards and wrote the Cricinfo 'bot' and registered the bot and the name Cricinfo with the bot registration system. [21] Thus, on 2 March 1993, was born Cricinfo. [22] If Cricinfo was not the first cricket 'bot' on the internet, nor the first cricket database, [23] it certainly became the most popular one, largely on account of the unpaid labour of love contributed by hundreds of volunteers who typed, scanned and otherwise wrote scorecards, articles, match reports and the like from cricket games past and present into the Cricinfo database. [24]

The contributions of volunteers to Cricinfo were made in the true spirit of the early internet. It was this spirit of the early internet that disdained commerce and was appalled that a contributor such as Prakash (whatever his age!) could ask for money for his services. It was this spirit that created a virtual community of people, many of whom had never met or even spoken with each other and who had little else in common other than their love for the game. As most (though by no means all) of these folks were based in the United States, the marginal existence of their object of love (obsession?) may also have contributed to the sense of community fostered by the internet. In any case, it was this spirit that allowed Cricinfo to grow and thrive. As the Cricinfo database grew, it needed more dedicated space. Professor K.S. Rao provided the initial space for it on his own machine, and even donated an older 386 computer for its use. Later, some people bartered a used microwave oven for an old workstation, and this became the 'home' of Cricinfo, which was hosted at the Oregon Graduate Institute, where many of the key contributors to Cricinfo worked or studied. Cricinfo was still a 'bot' on irc at this stage. It was after the move to Oregon that Neeran Karnik installed a 'gopher' server on the machine which made the Cricinfo database available to a larger and less computer-savvy audience, including yours truly. But the contributions kept pouring in, as did now the traffic to the database. Murari Venkataraman worked hard to organize the data. Finally, to update the hardware required to keep Cricinfo functioning, a funding drive was initiated on RSC and cricket. About $2000 was collected in a short period of time, and a newer machine provided even better access to the Cricinfo database. [25]

My focus on the community that built Cricinfo is not to suggest that Simon King did not play a critical role in its making. There are too many instances of beginnings of great ideas on the internet which then fall apart because their founders lose interest. For the community of cricket lovers to thrive on the internet, there was a need for coordination, for someone to ensure there would be people willing to type up commentaries on games, someone to remind contributors to build up the database. Too many voluntary internet ventures folded up because of lack of leadership. Simon King provided Cricinfo with that leadership. Without his work it is very unlikely that we would have today one of the most amazing databases on cricket, nor would there be a website to which cricket lovers across the world (and no longer only from cricket wastelands) turn to for the most recent updates on current matches. King does not identify himself as a cricket maniac, a label many others on IRC or Cricinfo gladly apply to themselves. Rather than mania, McLellan reveals that King had persistence, organizational skills and, significantly, also an entrepreneurial vision.

The dream of commercial success was not what drove people (King included) to create or contribute to Cricinfo. But the sheer quality of the database contributed by cricket lovers across the world, and the sort of coverage of matches volunteers were able to provide, was driving more and more people to Cricinfo. This expanded even further with the coming of the web interface. The number of visitors to the Cricinfo website grew exponentially, from 127,000 in 1993, to 1.1 million in 1994 and 3.5 million by 1995. [26] It is impossible to pinpoint the exact moment in time when the management team of Cricinfo, and Simon King in particular, decided to go commercial. But it is not difficult to locate this decision sometime in the 1994–6 period – some time after the web interface and massive increase in traffic to the website, and in an environment where dot-coms were beginning to make unimaginably huge amounts of money. Simon King, who had returned to England after his postdoctoral work at Minnesota in 1993, registered Cricinfo as a privately-held company in the U.K. in 1996. [27]

The drift of McLellan's history of Cricinfo, based as it is on interviews with King, is of an inevitable (and for a while a very successful) move to commerce simply as a way to keep up with the boom in the website. 'We weren't thinking commercially,' says King, 'just about the good Cricinfo could do for the game.' [28] King-McLellan in fact point out that the move to make Cricinfo a commercial body occurred only after an unsuccessful attempt by King to give the site away to the International Cricket Conference (ICC) – the London-based organization (and renamed descendant of the erstwhile Imperial Cricket Conference) which governs international cricket. The reluctance of the founder to admit that Cricinfo was moving towards being a commercial enterprise is easy enough to understand given its beginnings. Though all contributors were told that their submissions became the property of Cricinfo, not many folks would have put in huge number of hours and days contributing to the content, and hence the attraction of the site, if they had known they were contributing to the future fortunes of a few. The tone and content of public communications from Cricinfo, too, never made this future apparent. This was perfectly understandable in the early years of the database, when it was very much a community enterprise and the role of Simon King and the 'Cricinfo management' was mainly coordinating, compiling and formatting the inputs from volunteers. RSC is full of requests from Cricinfo in its early years, pointing out the various gaps in the database and asking volunteers to contribute scorecards or statistics. What is less understandable is the continuation of this rhetoric even at a time when the registration of the website as a private company must have been known to the management. A call as late as October 1995 for a 'West Indies representative' for Cricinfo, whose duties included liaison work, coordination and publicizing Cricinfo activities in the region, proudly declared that the position paid 'nothing whatsoever'. 'The CricInfo management,' the call went on to say, 'is a volunteer organisation dedicated to helping fellow enthusiasts follow their favourite sport wherever they are in the world. If you help out, others will too!' [29] This announcement was posted only months before Cricinfo was registered as a private company in 1996.

The first signs of unrest within the community of cricket-lovers on the internet came shortly before its 'privatization'. In 1995, Cricinfo made (free) registration a prerequisite for accessing the recent web version of their site, provoking some protest on RSC. In a long post to RSC, Badrinarayanan Seshadri, then a graduate student at Cornell, responded to the protests on behalf of the Cricinfo management. It is interesting to note, once again, that just months before the registration of Cricinfo as a private company, the language Seshadri chose to use in his defence of the management was that of community rather than commerce. He went to great lengths to explain that there was no deviation from the original principles of Cricinfo, as some people suggested on RSC. In fact registration was only being requested, he argued, so that Cricinfo would be able to make the strongest possible case before bodies such as the ICC for allocating better resources to Cricinfo for its users. He recounted the history of the community of cricket lovers on the internet to lament their current lack of trust. 'Hundreds of people trusted us and mailed us money for buying a computer. Haven't we acted exactly according to that trust? Haven't we served the user community to your satisfaction?' he asked. Switching registers somewhat, Seshadri moved from history and reason to a much more emotional tone. The Cricinfo management, Seshadri said, was 'deeply pained that not only have we [not] received enough registration but in fact people have rewarded us for our hard work by not even trusting us with innocuous information like email-address[es]'. The management, he argued, was trying to take decisions only with the best interests of the community in mind. 'Is it unjustified to ask for registration information just to serve you better?' he asked. The management itself, he pointed out, was 'not some impersonal entity.... We are also people like you, and we do this work in our spare time. Please show a bit of understanding for our efforts. A word of appreciation from you will make us happy.' Indeed, embedded in this long defence of Cricinfo policies was an invitation for anyone to join the management, as long as they were willing to contribute at least ten hours a week to Cricinfo 'without expecting any monetary compensation'. [30]

A majority of the respondents on RSC supported the management, and were very highly critical of the protesters whom they perceived as troublemakers undermining the ethos of trust upon which their community rested. The critics, however, were probably more prescient than the supporters of the Cricinfo management realized. An important thrust of the criticism was that Cricinfo was a community effort, and therefore its management had no right to restrict access to the database without a full discussion with the community of users. There were also serious concerns about corporate fundraising or even the involvement of the ICC, and what these changes may do to the autonomy of a website most still believed was the property of a loosely defined cricket-loving community. [31] The responses to such criticism tended to be dismissive of their concerns. Neeran Karnik, then part of Cricinfo management, insisted that registration was not creating any significant change in the way in which Cricinfo was being run. Karnik accused the protestors of reading too much into a small administrative change and said: 'You make it sound like we're setting out to sell CI [Cricinfo] to a money-grubbing corporation!' [32] Of course, this is exactly what happened soon after.

Some people in the Cricinfo management, however, evidently recognized the implications of some of the criticism. Thus Badrinarayanan Seshadri (who is currently described as the managing director of Cricinfo India Private Limited) [33] was careful in crafting another intervention in this debate, this time clarifying that he was speaking in his personal capacity rather than as a member of the management of Cricinfo. Seshadri insisted that he would be the first to 'oppose CI if it decides to charge money' but that such a scenario would never be on the cards. However, if 'a few paranoid people think that sky is going to fall on their heads, I can not help them'. Seshadri explained how *he* understood the 'ownership' of Cricinfo. Saying Cricinfo began as the property of one man (Simon King), Seshadri did acknowledge here that '[l]ater, because public money was involved in buying the equipment for CI, and because the data available in that machine was contributed by the public, it has become a public property'. He reiterated a call to respect the communitarian history of Cricinfo, but agreed that there was now a need for a more formal charter for Cricinfo, as well as a clear definition of the goals, and an explicit definition of distribution of power in the organization. [34] RSC would have been the logical place to post such a charter, but to the best of my knowledge, no such document was ever forthcoming. Presumably, once Cricinfo was registered as a private company the next year, the purpose of any such charter became redundant.

In his interview with Alex Balfour, Simon King points out that though he ran Cricinfo as a collective, with all members of the management having a voice in decisions, 'I usually get my way if I feel strongly about something'. [35] From his interviews with McLellan it appears that for a number of reasons, King was determined that Cricinfo should expand and grow in the mid-1990s. When registering the company in 1996, King also took out a bank loan of £10,000 and began travelling to draw in more revenue for Cricinfo. From the other side of the table, from the point of view of the venture capitalists who were funding the dot-com boom in the late 1990s, Cricinfo was a great investment. It had paltry running costs on account of volunteer contributions and a huge audience and name recognition. Andrew Hall, a marketing manager, called Cricinfo a 'no risk start-up'. Alex Balfour, later to be chairman of Cricinfo, was more explicit in an essay he published in a leading media magazine in the UK in 1998 and is worth quoting at length:

> A web entrepreneur starts with a solid idea…and publishes a basic site. Internet users come to the site…recommend changes. The entrepreneur listens to the users…or, better still, encourages the user to help make those changes. Delighted to see the site incorporate their ideas the users return, and continue to help. …
>
> In time the entrepreneur has a large pool of volunteer labour and advisers to draw on.…As long as the entrepreneur is sufficiently charming and well organised to keep the volunteers happy…the site will continue to develop rapidly.
>
> If volunteers believe that their work is helping to build something which they will find useful, if they can see that their work and ideas making an immediate difference…they will work hard. [36]

Evidently the new management (Balfour's CV says he joined 'Cricinfo Limited' in 1995 as co-founder and director) shared nothing of the communitarian ethos that had created Cricinfo. Contributors were no longer part of a community but only a pool of abstract volunteer labour who needed to be charmed into contributing to the profits of the web entrepreneur.

Cricinfo Limited went from strength to strength. In 1999 Indigo Holdings offered Cricinfo $5 million for growth. The next year, Satyam Infoway, one of the India's two

top software technology firms, bought out Indigo for $21 million and offered
Cricinfo another $16 million in exchange for a quarter of the firm's stock. From
proudly working for nothing, members of the Cricinfo board, which included King,
Seshadri, Balfour and two others, now owned a half-share in a $150 million firm. [37]
Cricinfo became the world's single largest dedicated cricket enterprise and board
members' personal worth was now in millions of dollars. Less than a decade had
passed since the time when Prakash's demands for ten dollars an hour for
commentary had led to his expulsion from an internet cricket channel, and less than
five years had passed since a member of management had debunked any idea of a
corporate sell-out.

That there would be some resentment from former volunteers is perfectly natural.
In fact what is surprising is how little of it there is on RSC. Very few appear to resent
the fact that some people became millionaires effectively on the back of the labour of
others. [38] It is either because many see nothing wrong with this, or perhaps it is
because they all understand and philosophically accept the workings of capitalism
better than historians do. Yet the issue of betrayal does reappear frequently in the
course of other discussions on RSC. Thus on a discussion of the history of Cricinfo,
Vicky Vigneswaran, who was at one time top of the list of contributors of data to
Cricinfo, said he was 'disappointed and angry' on hearing of the registration of
Cricinfo Limited and to see how 'the hard work of hundreds of volunteers' came to
be used 'by some smart operators to make money'. Vicky claims he was 'sidelined' in
Cricinfo for his views on going commercial. He appears more disappointed at how
the management at Cricinfo treated even people such as Professor Rao – whose
contributions of computer and server space had allowed Cricinfo to come into being
in the first place. [39] Evidently there is a great deal more that happened in the move
to going commercial than is discussed on RSC. Nor would some of these details be
entirely appropriate for this forum. But even RSC postings reveal the transformation
of Cricinfo, and not just in economic terms. As a commercial entity, Cricinfo was
now beholden to its financiers and profit margins rather than its volunteers. While
'management' had been quick to come to RSC and post a defence of its position in
1995, it has apparently seen no reason to do so when much more serious charges were
being levelled in 2000 and 2003.

Mismanagement and the lack of a sound business plan meant that Cricinfo
Limited faced serious financial difficulties again in 2001. Finally in 2003 Cricinfo
'merged' with the Wisden group, which also brings out the 'Bible of Cricket', the
annual *Wisden Almanack*. [40] The transformation to a corporate site is complete.
Today, Cricinfo.com proudly announces itself to corporate advertisers as 'the perfect
environment for fully-accountable advertising, sponsorship and promotions' on the
basis of the 250 million page views per month the site generates. [41] The very large
list of clients who have used Cricinfo to promote their products include such
multinational giants as Coca-Cola, McDonalds, Shell and IBM. [42]

Probably on account of its history, Cricinfo continues to provide completely free
access to its vast database. Ball-by-ball commentary on matches, now presumably

typed by Wisden Cricinfo employees, is also regularly piped in free to IRC cricket, which Cricinfo also controls via professional moderators. But it is quite interesting that the current website has actually blocked access to some of the files from the older Cricinfo site, including one where Simon King provided a history of Cricinfo. [43] An email request for that file to Wisden has not yet elicited a response.

Of course this essay has been written in a spirit of nostalgia. Nostalgia about the good old days – of the early 1990s! Yes, I do miss the somewhat arbitrary though passionate commentary provided by volunteers. I even miss the puritanism of the community spirit which refused to consider the possibility of paying for commentary or service. But then I also miss radio commentaries. The effort of having to imagine the events on the field, I would like to believe, actually made us more involved in the game, and less passive consumers of the images we now get off the television screen. But my love for the past does not stop me from enjoying the obvious advantages of multiple camera angles, slow-motion replays and the like provided by contemporary television coverage of the game. For the same reasons, nostalgia does not prevent me from making Cricinfo one of the first sites I open on my web browser each day.

Notes

All websites cited below were last accessed either 23 or 24 December 2004.

[1] Simon King, founder of Cricinfo, quoted in the Asian edition of *Time* magazine, 23 Nov. 1998, available at http://www.time.com/time/asia/asia/magazine/1998/981123/cricket3.html. I am grateful to a posting by Vicky B. Vigneswaran on the newsgroup rec.sport.cricket (hereafter RSC) for directing me to this quotation and website.

[2] The United States was not always a cricket wasteland, of course. For a brief history of how rounders, a.k.a. baseball, replaced cricket in the United States, see Steven Wells, 'What Goes Around, Comes A-rounders', *The Guardian*, 27 July 2004, available at http://sport.guardian. co.uk/cricket/comment/0,10070,1269611,00.html. For a more detailed history of cricket in the USA, see Melville, *The Tented Field*.

[3] The very earliest personal computer, according to the Blinkenlights Archeological Institute, was the 'Simon', described by Edmund Berkeley in his 1949 book, *Giant Brains, or Machines That Think*. Purists are, however, willing to accept that it is only back to 1977 that we can trace the earliest commercially marketable personal computer, the Apple II. The first IBM personal computer, the IBM 5150 PC, dates from 1981. See http://www.blinkenlights.com/pc.shtml

[4] Daniel Stenberg, 'History of IRC (Internet Relay Chat)', available at http://daniel.haxx.se/irchistory.html

[5] The Federal Networking Council passed a resolution to this effect on 24 Oct. 1995: 'A Brief History of the Internet' by the Internet Society, available at http://www.isoc.org/internet/history/brief.shtml

[6] See Wikipedia, the free encyclopedia on 'Usenet' at http://en.wikipedia.org/wiki/Usenet; also 'History of the Internet, 1970s' at 'Computer History Museum', available at http://www.computerhistory.org/exhibits/Internet_history/Internet_history_70s.shtml

[7] RSC, Badrinarayanan Seshadri, 14 Sept. 1996, 12.00 am, on 'The history of rec.sport.cricket', available at http://groups-beta.google.com/group/rec.sport.cricket/msg/16096beabf08efab. Seshadri notes that the RFD was posted on 6 March 1990 to the relevant newsgroups. [NB: The

Google archive of this newsgroup gives 12.00 am as the time for most of the messages. This is obviously an error.]

[8] Based on figures for the first six months of 2004. All data on RSC postings taken from http://groups-beta.google.com/group/rec.sport.cricket/about

[9] RSC, Badrinarayanan Seshadri, 14 Sept. 1996.

[10] RSC, Amol Cricketwallah, 24 April 2002, on 'Official Historian for RSC', available at http://groups-beta.google.com/group/rec.sport.cricket/msg/e4dc1f5c226cce15

[11] RSC, Manas Mandal, 28 April 2002, on 'Official Historian for RSC', available at http://groups-beta.google.com/group/rec.sport.cricket/msg/a021bf6b8ad74219. The dates for the first IRC commentary were provided by Uday Rajan, 5 Feb. 2003, 2.37 pm, on 'Wisden and Cricinfo to Merge!', available at http://groups-beta.google.com/group/rec.sport.cricket/msg/6ee8366753b fdbaf

[12] RSC, Amol Cricketwallah, 29 April 2002, 4.01 am, on 'Official Historian for RSC', available at http://groups-beta.google.com/group/rec.sport.cricket/msg/25009f3ef26de5c4

[13] For a first-person account of the typing up of ball-by-ball commentary, see Bob Dubery's long account of the voluntary work which went into providing commentary on IRC: RSC, Bob Dubery, 18 May 1997, 12.00 am, on 'Who are the Cricinfo commentators'. He provides this account in response to some unfair carping at the quality of the commentary by another poster on RSC. Most responses, however, lauded the spirit and effort of the voluntary commentators. See http://groups-beta.google.com/group/rec.sport.cricket/msg/6795e4cb400 d677c

[14] See Amol Cricketwallah on RSC, 29 April 2002, on 'Official Historian for RSC'.

[15] RSC, Travis Basevi, 7 April 1995, 12.00 am, on '#cricket Comm goes completely nuts', available at http://groups-beta.google.com/group/rec.sport.cricket/msg/b27f992ed34a42bb. Basevi posted virtually the entire log of that commentary session (with all the original typographical errors) and most others in this discussion agreed with his evaluation of Prakash's moral and orthographical infirmities. The only vote of sympathy for Prakash came much later from Vicky Vigneswaran, who expressed his disappointment that some of the 'respected #cricketers' ridiculed the young man because he was struggling with his typing. RSC, Vicky B. Vigneswaran, 6 Feb. 2003, 2.16 am, on 'Wisden and Cricinfo to Merge!', available at http://groups-beta.google.com/group/rec.sport.cricket/msg/d0ef1e2a8ae73872. For other instances of ingratitude towards volunteers, see the context to Bob Dubery's post, 18 May 1997.

[16] Cricinfo Wisden Media Kit, available online at http://usa.cricinfo.com/link_to_database/NATIONAL/ENG/MEDIAPACK/index.html

[17] R. Mohan wrote a column in the weekly internet edition of *The Hindu* in late 1995, which was reposted on RSC. RSC, Raghavan Suresh, 8 Nov. 1995, 12.00 am, 'About Cricinfo by R. Mohan in The Hindu', available at http://groups-beta.google.com/group/rec.sport.cricket/msg/0535f488f7f2b7ea

[18] Alex Balfour, 'Global Village Green,' *Wired UK*, Feb. 1996, available at the archives of the short-lived magazine, *Wired UK*, http://www.yoz.com/wired/2.02/es/cricinfo.html. Also see http://www.users.dircon.co.uk/ ~ mysore/html/archive6.html. Balfour's online resume shows him to be the current chairman of Cricinfo Limited, though the document may not have been updated since 2002. See http://www.users.dircon.co.uk/ ~ mysore/html/cv2.htm

[19] McLellan, 'From Minnesota With Love', 149.

[20] See ibid.; Balfour, 'Global Village Green'. Many postings on RSC tell of the beginnings of Cricinfo; perhaps the most authoritative is RSC, Badrinarayanan Seshadri, 21 May 1995, 12.00 am, on 'Letter to management of Cricinfo', available at http://groups-beta.google.com/group/rec.sport.cricket/msg/1da72c8c0194a512. Seshadri here is writing not just as poster to RSC but in his official capacity as member of the Cricinfo management, responding to certain criticisms of Cricinfo. He begins his post with a very official preface which reads: 'In the following document, "we", "our", "us" etc. describe the CricInfo Management.'

[21] RSC, Manas Mandal, 28 April 2002, on 'Official Historian for RSC', available at http://groups-beta.google.com/group/rec.sport.cricket/msg/a021bf6b8ad74219

[22] McLellan, 'From Minnesota With Love', 153.

[23] Manas Mandal, in another post argues that the newsgroup rec.sport.cricket.scores was in fact, 'the first "Internet Cricket Database" of any kind, and that the charter of the group reveals Professor Rao's dream 'of archiving the scorecard of *every* test match ever played': RSC, Manas Mandal, 17 Sept. 1996, on 'The history of rec.sport.cricket', available at http://groups-beta.google.com/group/rec.sport.cricket/msg/ea41e4309fca47c4

[24] A list of contributors on Cricinfo in August 1995 counted about 400 separate contributors, with at least 20 people having made more than a hundred separate contributions to the Cricinfo database by that date: RSC, Gautham N, 23 Aug. 1995, 12.00 am, on 'Top Contributors to the CI database', available at http://groups-beta.google.com/group/rec.sport.cricket/msg/ef49867c971a7ece

[25] See RSC, Badrinarayanan Seshadri, 21 May 1995, on 'Letter to management of Cricinfo'; also Uday Rajan, 3 Feb. 2003, 8.27 pm, on 'Wisden and Cricinfo to Merge!', available at http://groups-beta.google.com/group/rec.sport.cricket/msg/4215c26e028ed120

[26] McLellan, 'From Minnesota With Love', 155.

[27] Ibid., 156.

[28] Ibid., 155.

[29] RSC, Badrinarayanan Seshadri, 16 Oct. 1995, 12.00 am, on 'CricInfo and the West Indies', available at http://groups-beta.google.com/group/rec.sport.cricket/msg/0c36e47492249caa

[30] See RSC, Badrinarayanan Seshadri, 21 May 1995, on 'Letter to management of Cricinfo'.

[31] RSC, Sanpan (Sandip Pandey), 22 May 1995, 12.00 am, on 'registration at cric.info', available at http://groups-beta.google.com/group/rec.sport.cricket/msg/1f500ae27f1d37a6, and Amitabha Lahiri, 1 June 1995, on 'registration at cric.info', available at http://groups-beta.google.com/group/rec.sport.cricket/msg/857965d9655d4ae8. Also RSC, Ravindra Rao, 19 May 1995, 12.00 am, on 'Letter to management of Cricinfo', available at http://groups-beta.google.com/group/rec.sport.cricket/msg/c861b9690ae687c0

[32] RSC, Neeran M. Karnik, 23 May 1995, 12.00 am, on 'registration at cric.info', available at http://groups-beta.google.com/group/rec.sport.cricket/msg/fdf8662ddfcbcac1

[33] See http://www.tamil-heritage.org/ec/ec.html#_badri.

[34] RSC, Badrinarayanan Seshadri, 24 May 1995, 12.00 am, on 'registration at cric.info', available at http://groups-beta.google.com/group/rec.sport.cricket/msg/4125e535a9df85f1

[35] Balfour, 'Global Village Green'.

[36] Alex Balfour, 'The Only Web Publishing Model That Works', *NMA Magazine*, March 1998, available at http://www.users.dircon.co.uk/ ~ mysore/html/archive19.html

[37] McLellan, 'From Minnesota With Love', 161, 164.

[38] 'Dougie' appears as one exception. 'Who can blame a supposedly not for profit .org who used the labour of 'volunteers' to become a .com for the benefit of the few? nobody at all :) Who can blame those who ran a .org for becoming rich on the back of volunteers? err, nobody :) Who can blame those who employ computer programmers at slave wages? Nobody :) Who can blame those who do deals with media moguls and use the labour of 'volunteers' to make a mint? NOBODY :)' The 'smileys' are not enough to deflect an evidently deeply felt sense of injustice. RSC, Dougie, 29 June 2000, 12.00 am, on 'What's Happening at Cricinfo', available at http://groups-beta.google.com/group/rec.sport.cricket/msg/b609e513540eec58

[39] RSC, Vicky B. Vigneswaran, 5 Feb 2003, 3.18 am, on 'History of Cricinfo? [Re: "Wisden and Cricinfo to Merge!"]', available at http://groups-beta.google.com/group/rec.sport.cricket/msg/6652bec0aa01d81e

[40] See http://www.cricinfo.com/wisden/about.html

[41] Cricinfo Wisden Media Kit, available at http://usa.cricinfo.com/link_to_database/NATIONAL/ENG/MEDIAPACK/index.html

[42] Customer list included in the Cricinfo Wisden Media Kit, available at http://usa.cricinfo.com/link_to_database/NATIONAL/ENG/MEDIAPACK/advertising-customer-list.html

[43] For instance, I was prevented from access to an older newsletter from the management using the 'wayback machine' from the archives.org site. For that, try the following link, http://web.archive.org/web/19990210110536/http://www-ind.cricket.org/link_to_database/MANAGEMENT/NEWSLETTER (exercise carried out 23 Dec. 2004).

References

Berkeley, Edmund. *Giant Brains or Machines That Think*. New York: Wiley, 1949.

Melville, Tom. *The Tented Field*. Bowling Green, OH: Bowling Green State University Popular Press, 1998.

McLellan, Alastair. 'From Minnesota With Love – The Cricinfo Story'. In *The New Ball*, vol. 6, edited by Rob Steen. London: Sports Books Direct, 2001: 147–75.

Index

www.ingramcontent.com/pod-product-compliance
Ingram Content Group UK Ltd.
Pitfield, Milton Keynes, MK11 3LW, UK
UKHW010021280225
455677UK00023B/738